Revised Edition

COMPLETE HOCKEY INSTRUCTION

Skills and Strategies for Coaches and Players

Dave Chambers

CONTEMPORARY BOOKS

Library of Congress Cataloging-in-Publication Data

Chambers, Dave, 1940–
    Complete hockey instruction : skills and strategies for coaches and players /
Dave Chambers.—rev. ed.
        p.   cm.
    Includes bibliographical references.
    ISBN 0-8092-9937-2
    1. Hockey—Coaching.   I. Title.
GV848.25.C43   2000
796.962'07'7—dc21   00-38429

Author's Acknowledgments
I wish to express my thanks to Noroc Sport Services, Inc., and *Hockey Coaching
Journal* for their guidance in the preparation and typing of this manuscript as well
as my special thanks to Robert Thom, production manager of *Hockey Coaching
Journal*, and to John Lightfoot for the preparation of the diagrams in the book.

Special appreciation is extended to the many coaches I have played for and been
associated with, who contributed greatly to my knowledge of ice hockey.

The publisher gratefully acknowledges the assistance of the Canada Council, the
Ontario Arts Council, and the Ontario Publishing Centre.

This book was originally published in 1999 by Key Porter Books Limited in
Toronto, Canada.

Cover design by Nick Panos
Cover photograph copyright © Elsa/Allsport
Interior illustrations by John Lightfoot

This edition first published in 2000 by Contemporary Books
A division of NTC/Contemporary Publishing Group, Inc.
4255 West Touhy Avenue, Lincolnwood (Chicago), Illinois 60712-1975 U.S.A.
Copyright © 1999, 1995 by Dave Chambers

Printed in the United States of America
International Standard Book Number: 0-8092-9937-2

00 01 02 03 04 05 DR 20 19 18 17 16 15 14 13 12 11 10 9 8 7 6 5 4 3 2 1

CONTENTS

PREFACE

Hockey is one of the most exciting and fast-moving sports in the world. The game is composed of many intricate skills that can be mastered only by a highly skilled athlete. The European influence has had an impact on the game in such areas as conditioning and offensive tactics. The game now is a blend of the best from both North America and Europe. Hockey in the United States has never been more popular, as evidenced by the ever increasing numbers of minor league hockey players and the popularity of the National Hockey League, which has expanded to parts of the country such as Florida, California, Texas, Ohio, and Georgia.

Coaching has changed greatly in the past two decades. Coaching training and coaching certification now include areas such as technical, tactical, physical conditioning, and psychological preparation. The physical training is now periodized, and almost all hockey players engage in a year-round training program.

This book is an accumulation of materials from my 35 years of coaching at the university, junior, international, and National Hockey League levels. I have accumulated this knowledge from observing other coaches, from my former coaches and coaches I have worked with, and through clinic attendance, reading, and my own innovations and experiences.

I have attempted to include all aspects of the technical areas of coaching hockey so this book will be useful for both coaches and players. In-line skating hockey is also becoming quite popular, and most of the skills, drills, and theory in this book apply, although that game is not played on ice but on the concrete floor of an ice arena.

Throughout this instruction book we have used male pronouns exclusively to refer to both coaches and players of hockey. The fact is, however, that women and girls are playing hockey in ever increasing numbers and women's hockey is also now an Olympic sport.

This is the second revision of *Complete Hockey Instruction*. Sections have been added with updated terminology along with new drills and systems. The chapter on designing practices has been completely rewritten and a new chapter on nutrition and another on mental training presents some important new material that every hockey player and coach should know.

With these revisions it is my hope that *Complete Hockey Instruction* now includes all the aspects of hockey for both the coach and the player.

LEGEND

PUCK(S)		TIGHT/180-DEGREE TURN		PASS	- - - - →
PYLON(S)		360-DEGREE TURN		DROP PASS	
FORWARD SKATING	→	PIVOT		SHOT	⇒
FORWARD STICKHANDLE		STOP	= OR ‖	KNEE DROP	— OR ¦
BACKWARD SKATING		KERIOAKAS		SCREEN/PIC	
BACKWARD STICKHANDLE		STEPOVERS	‖‖‖‖‖‖‖‖‖	BODY CHECK	
RIGHT WINGER	RW	OPPOSITION RW	RW	PLAYER	X
LEFT WINGER	LW	OPPOSITION LW	LW	OPPOSITION PLAYER	X
CENTER	C	OPPOSITION C	C	DEFENSEMAN	D
RIGHT DEFENSEMAN	RD	OPPOSITION RD	RD	OPPOSITION D	D
LEFT DEFENSEMAN	LD	OPPOSITION LD	LD	GOALTENDER	G

1. PHILOSOPHY OF COACHING

Coaching is a very complex and demanding profession. It requires many technical and personal skills and a very sound philosophy. Most good coaches discover early that their philosophy, beliefs, and principles serve as a guide for the many decisions that have to be made daily in the training and supervision of athletes. The best coaches realize that these basic philosophical concepts must be applied in a skillful way to develop the essence of team work in the pursuit of excellence and success.

The philosopher Will Durant once said, "Science gives us knowledge, but only philosophy can give us wisdom." It is therefore important for every coach to have a well-thought-out philosophy of coaching that will guide his or her decision making, determine the coaching aims and objectives, and define the direction the team will take. The coach must develop a philosophy of competition, winning and losing, the value of athletics, criticism, and interacting with and motivating athletes.

The coach has an undeniable effect on the athletes he or she is associated with:

It is impossible to underestimate the important of the coach in the development of an athlete. From the youngest peewee player to the elite athlete, the coach is a pivotal character in the moral as well as the physical development of his or her charges.

The more intensive the training, the greater the opportunity for molding the athlete's character and personal philosophy as it pertains to his or her athletic career. Elite athletes appear to cleave to their coaches as mentors, guardians, and, in some cases, almost as surrogate parents. They are fortunate indeed if their coach is concerned with their moral and intellectual development as well as their athletic training. (Dubin, 1990)

One of the most important philosophical decisions a coach must make is how he or she will treat the athletes. An approach that is firm but fair appears to be the most successful, but athletes must feel that the coach cares about them. The age of the athletes and the type of coaching situation are also important considerations. Young, developing, amateur athletes may be treated differently from older professional athletes, but, regardless of age, athletes benefit from a sound coaching philosophy.

Two letters from parents and one from a young athlete serve to illustrate the responsibility the coach has when handling young people:

Dear Coach:

Tomorrow morning my son starts hockey. He's going to step out on the ice and his great adventure, that will probably include joys and disappointments, begins.

So I wish you would take him by his young hand and teach him the things he will have to know. Teach him to respect the referee, and that his judgment is final. Teach him not to hate his competitors, but to admire their skill. Teach him it is just as important to be a playmaker and get an assist as it is to score a goal. Teach him to play as a team and never to be selfish. Teach him never to blame his goaltender when a goal is scored against him, because five mistakes were made before the puck got to the goalie. Teach him that winning is not everything, but trying to win is. Teach him to be a competitor. Teach him to close his ears to the howling mob and to stand up for himself if he thinks he is right. Teach him gently but don't coddle him, because only the test of fire makes fine steel.

This is a big order, Coach, and I place my son in your hands. See what you can do for him. He is such a nice little fellow.

His Dad (Argue, 1979)

An eleven-year-old boy, the grandson of a former National Hockey League player, expressed his hopes this way:

Well, here it is another hockey season,
So I am writing you for just one reason!
Please don't scream or curse and yell,
Remember I'm not in the NHL
I am only 11 years old
And can't be bought or traded or sold.
I just want to have fun and play the game
And am not looking for hockey fame!
Please don't make me feel I've committed a sin
Just because my team didn't win!
I don't want to be that great, you see
I'd rather play and just be me! (Cosentino, 1995)

As these letters illustrate, the coach must decide early in his or her career how athletes are to be treated. In many ways, these early decisions will determine whether a coach's career will be successful.

PHILOSOPHIES OF WELL-KNOWN COACHES

We can learn from the philosophy and thoughts of prominent coaches.

Vince Lombardi (Former professional football coach)

Winning isn't everything, but making the effort to win is.

Lombardi's success lay not only in his inspirational personality, but also his ability to teach. He could communicate an idea to his players, explain it so they understood it—not only how to execute it but why.

He never expected more from us than he was willing to give of himself.

The philosophical basis of the Lombardi legend was total dedication to the pursuit of excellence.

Success is not a sometimes thing. In other words, you don't do what is right once in a while, but all the time. Success is a habit. Winning is a habit. (Walton, 1992)

Woody Hayes (Former college football coach)

I never talked down to the players.

Even when I thundered at the players, I thundered that they could do better.

They may outsmart me, or be luckier, but they can't outwork me. (Walton, 1992)

John Wooden (Former college basketball coach)

He made them winners, winners with character, not characters with wins.

Wooden's greatest achievement was his gift to others, his teaching on how to find the best in oneself, and how to find peace of mind.

Success is peace of mind which is a direct result of self satisfaction in knowing you did your best to become the best you are capable of becoming. (Walton, 1992)

Bill Walsh (former professional and college football coach)

The stylish, graceful, accommodating, easy-going, affable coach will get 80% of the job done. The final 20% can be directly attributed to making tough decisions, demanding a high standard of performance, meeting expectations, paying attention to details, and grabbing and shaking when necessary. (Walsh, 1993)

Joe Paterno (College football coach)

I feel that certainty of winning only when I know that we've done all the preparation, when we've practiced intelligently and thoroughly.

Success is perishable and often outside our control. In contrast, excellence is something that's lasting, dependable, and largely within a person's control. (Paterno, 1989)

Phil Jackson (Professional basketball coach)

He makes you think about more than just basketball. He makes you look at the larger picture.

One of his strengths is that he likes a debate. He wants us to express our ideas on things, even to the point of an argument. (Jackson, 1995)

Scott Bowman (Professional ice hockey coach)

The most important job as a coach is to get the right players on the ice at the right time.

His practices were in constant motion, shooting, passing everything done on the go, with speed, every drill rooted in high-pace skating. (Dryden, 1983)

Pat Burns (Professional ice hockey coach)

If you're not playing well you're not going to play. That is the bottom line. The players are responsible for themselves and the reward or punishment is going to be whether they play or not. It's just that simple. (McKenzie, 1993)

Coaching is a great challenge, and not for the faint of heart. It requires long hours and intense interaction with people who are in competition with themselves and others. It runs the gamut of emotions, involving success and failure, joy and despair. It involves wanting and trying to win, and learning how to accept defeat. It also involves the opportunity of participating, having fun, and learning to work with others toward a common goal.

Walter Gillet (1972) probably summarized the job of a coach best in "What Is a Coach?"

A coach is a politician, a judge, a public speaker, a teacher, a trainer, a financier, a laborer, a psychologist, a psychiatrist, and a chaplain. He must be an optimist and yet at times appear to be a pessimist, seem humble and yet be very proud, strong but at times weak, confident yet not overconfident, enthusiastic but not too enthusiastic.

He must have the hide of an elephant, the fierceness of a lion, the pep of a young pup, the guts of an ox, the stamina of an antelope, the wisdom of an owl, the cunning of a fox, and the heart of a kitten.

He must be willing to give freely of his time, his money, his energy, his youth, his family life, and his health. In return he must expect little if any financial reward, little comfort on earth, little praise but plenty of criticism.

However, a good coach is respected and is a leader in his community, is loved by his team, and makes lasting friends wherever he goes.

He has the satisfaction of seeing young people develop and improve in ability. He learns the thrill of victory and how to accept defeat with grace. His association with athletes help keep him young in mind and spirit, and he too must grow and improve in ability with his team.

In his heart he knows that, in spite of the inconvenience, the criticism, and the demands on his time, he loves his work, for he is the coach.

QUALITIES OF A GOOD COACH

Successful coaches do not seem to fit a specific personality type. They are as individual as members of the general population, but they do have specific leadership qualities. Many good coaches are outgoing and extroverted, while others are quiet and somewhat withdrawn. Some coaches are autocratic and hard-nosed, while others are democratic and accommodating. Here are some of the characteristics good coaches have in common:

Knowledge of the Sport
To be effective, the coach must have a sound knowledge of the sport. However, in most cases, participation alone is not sufficient to supply that knowledge. A good coach will continually read, observe, and use any other methods to further his or her knowledge of the sport. Most good coaches attend at least one coaching clinic per year and participate in any coaching certification program that is available.

Communication
A good coach is an effective communicator. Good communication with the athletes leads to mutual understanding. Problem areas between coach and player should be dealt with to avoid lasting misunderstanding, and an athlete should feel that the coach is approachable.

Ability to Understand and Handle the Athlete
The ability to communicate is related to the ability to handle and understand people. In order to be an effective communicator, a coach must understand the athlete and be able to relate to him or her. A lack of understanding of the athlete's motivation and/or problems is one of the major reasons for a breakdown in the coach–athlete relationship.

Organizational Skills
One common characteristic of all good coaches is that they are highly organized in all areas of team operation. A well-organized team gives the athletes confidence and pride in the team and the coach. A coach who spends the time to become highly organized will generally be respected by the athletes. Today's coach should have a yearly, monthly, weekly, and daily plan for the organization of his or her team. The physical, technical, tactical, and psychological preparation of the athletes should be part of a year-round training plan.

Knowledge of Training and Conditioning Methods
A coach should have an up-to-date knowledge of various training and condition methods. This knowledge can be applied in the day-to-day training of a team or individual athletes. The coach should have the ability to develop a plan for improving and/or maintaining his or her athletes' conditioning levels throughout the year, including off-season training programs.

Effectively Run Practices
One of the most important aspects of coaching is the ability to run effective practice sessions, which most coaches believe are the key to the success of teams and/or individual athletes. The coach should have the ability to run organized, active practices, stressing well-thought-out drills and the techniques used in competition.

Evaluation of Athletes
A good coach should be able to evaluate the ability of the athletes. This is an ongoing process for the coach, but it is most important in the initial selection of team members. Good coaches have an ability to evaluate an individual's performance based on previous observations of athletes and techniques in their sport. However, most good coaches also rely on other factors such as specific drills, reports by other observers, skill tests, potential, physical attributes, and personality traits to make their final selection. Character is a key factor in selection by most coaches.

Strategy
The ability to prepare a team for an opponent is an important attribute of a coach. The skill is developed through experience, learning, and the ability to analyze an opponent's strengths and weaknesses. As well as preparing a team for a contest, the coach should be able to improvise and adjust strategy during games.

Effective Use of Personnel
In team sports a good coach has the ability to make effective use of certain athletes at certain times. The coach must have a good understanding of what athletes can do in certain situations and must be able to react quickly and use good judgment during games to select the right players for critical situations.

Fairness
It is important that the coach give fair treatment to the athletes on a team. Athletes can quickly turn against a coach if they feel his or her treatment of the team is unfair or that he or she favors certain individuals over others.

Motivation

Good athletes should be self-motivated, but a coach should also be able to motivate in order to be effective. Not all coaches have this ability, but it appears to be a quality shared by those whose coaching is outstanding.

Dedication, Enthusiasm, Maturity, Ethics

Good coaches display dedication to the task, which has a positive effect on the athletes. A lack of dedication can seriously affect the athletes' view of the coach, and can be extremely detrimental; the coach may even be viewed as lazy and uncaring.

Enthusiasm is an important quality in a coach, and it is important that he or she maintain it throughout the year, especially at times when the athletes appear fatigued and/or unmotivated. As well, the coach should act in a mature manner. Immature behavior, such as harassing officials, can affect the athletes, leading them to imitate this behavior or to lose respect for the coach.

It is important for a coach to conduct him- or herself in an ethical manner both with and away from the athletes. The coach is a role model and should realize the importance of this position and be aware of the effect that he or she has, especially on the more impressionable, younger athletes.

Knowledge of How the Body Works (Exercise Physiology)

The coach should have a basic knowledge of exercise physiology in order to understand how the body works. This knowledge will allow the coach to understand the science behind various training techniques, such as work-to-rest ratios during training and games. A coach should also be able to interpret scientific articles on various training methods and conduct and interpret the outcomes of various types of fitness testing.

Knowledge of Growth and Development Principles

Many coaches are working with younger players who are still growing and developing. It is important that the coach have a knowledge of both the physical and the emotional stages that younger players go through. In some cases, growth spurts may affect a younger athlete's coordination and create certain emotional problems. This, in turn, may affect his or her athletic performance.

Ability to Teach

The coach is in many ways a teacher, and as such he or she must have an understanding of basic learning principles and teaching techniques. A good coach needs the ability to teach fundamental skills as well as team play. Factors such as voice, appearance, teaching formations, and planning are as important to the coach as they are to the classroom teacher.

Concern for the Athlete

Concern for each individual athlete is very important for a coach. Athletes must feel that the coach cares about them and that each individual is important to the team. The coach should also show concern for athletes after they have moved on. Some coaches receive a great deal of satisfaction by keeping in touch with their athletes after they have stopped participating for their team or organization.

Knowledge of the Rules

An effective coach should have a thorough knowledge of the playing rules. This knowledge should be passed on to the players and is important in both practice and game situations.

Discipline

Most good teams have a basic discipline code that sets down guidelines for behavior. Team rules are more likely to be followed when the athletes have input and agree with the coach on rules such as those related to punctuality for practices and games, and general conduct on and off the playing surface.

Media

A coach should have a good relationship with the media, as publicity can greatly affect the support the team receives. It is important for a coach to be available and cordial, no matter what the circumstances, when dealing with the media. Regular reporting of game results and of interesting team information can help the coach develop a good relationship with the media.

Humor

Not all situations in sports are serious. A good coach should have a sense of humor. Athletes will feel more relaxed if the coach is able to see humor in some situations. A coach who is always serious may put added pressure on the athletes and may not be able to relate to them. It is also important that the coach not take him- or herself too seriously and start to believe that he or she is the only reason for the success of an athlete or a team.

Ability to Recruit and Build a Program

Most good coaches have the ability to relate and sell both themselves and their program to a prospective athlete. When recruiting athletes, coaches should have a recruiting plan in which they are able to identify and relate information about themselves and the program to the potential team member.

Generally it is important to realize that each coach is an individual. Coaches should attempt to study and emulate the techniques of successful coaches rather than imitate their personalities. Be yourself, but do attempt to make yourself better by working hard at improving your coaching techniques.

COACHING RESPECT FACTORS

Halliwell (1994), a sport psychologist at the University of Montreal and a consultant for many professional and elite amateur athletes, developed twenty respect factors that make an excellent self-evaluation checklist for coaches:

1. Previous playing experience and success.
2. Previous coaching experience and success.
3. Good appearance—neatly dressed, fit.
4. Good living habits.
5. Good work habits—puts in the hours, is efficient.
6. Well-organized—practices, meetings, travel, and so on.
7. Good communicator—explains things clearly, good listener.
8. Availability—always has time for the athlete.
9. Knowledgeable—demonstrates knowledge of the game, both technical and tactical aspects.
10. Teaching ability—displays ability to correct technical and tactical errors.
11. Highly motivated—displays intensity, commitment, involvement.
12. Positive, upbeat, enthusiastic, optimistic—gives lots of praise and reinforcement.
13. Good bench coach—makes adjustments, reads and reacts, gets last change.
14. Good sense of humor—can keep things loose.
15. Good leadership skills—in the dressing room and during the games.
16. Good self-control skills—displays composure, emotional control.
17. Desire to improve—seeks new knowledge, attends coaching clinics, self-evaluates.
18. Honest and fair with players—doesn't show favoritism, is "tough but fair."
19. Open to suggestions—displays some flexibility, listens to players' and assistants' suggestions.
20. Shows a genuine interest in players as individuals—demonstrates knowledge and interest in their life away from the sport situation.

Knowledge of the sport, being a good communicator, being honest but fair with the players, and showing an interest in them, as well as being positive and upbeat, were deemed the most important of the 20 factors. These respect factors can serve as a useful checklist for periodical self-evaluation for coaches.

2. EVALUATION OF TALENT

Evaluating talent and selecting the team are two of the more difficult tasks in coaching. Who the better and poorer players are is usually quite evident, but selecting from the middle group of talent is where evaluation criteria are extremely important.

Evaluation of hockey players can be categorized in four areas: physical, technical, tactical, and mental.

PHYSICAL, TECHNICAL, AND TACTICAL ATTRIBUTES

The physical attributes include size, strength, cardiovascular endurance, quickness, and agility. Size is an important aspect in hockey, but quickness and agility are also extremely important. Don't rule out a small player if that player has strength and quickness.

The technical skills include skating, passing, puck handling, shooting, and checking. All these skills are important. The checking skill can be taught to all players, provided they have the basic skating skills.

The tactical skills lie in a player's ability to read the play and react, to understand team systems, and to adjust to different situations. Hockey sense and intelligence are important factors that some players seem to have more of than others. The great hockey players have hockey sense and that great ability to read and react to different situations.

MENTAL ATTRIBUTES

The mental attributes include work habits, general attitude and character, leadership, coachability, mental toughness, self-confidence, team orientation, motivation, and intensity. The mental attributes are sometimes more difficult to determine in a short period of time, and it is probably wise to get as much background information on a player as possible before the selection process begins.

Psychological profiling can be a useful tool in the coach's assessment of the mental attributes of athletes. Profiles with names such as TAIS (Test of Attentional and Interpersonal Style) and SportProFile are two such tests commonly used by a number of sports organizations. The TAIS measures factors such as leadership capabilities, impulsive behavior, extroversion, performance anxiety, desire to win, and ability to organize and plan. The SportProFile assesses competitiveness, motivation, self-confidence, effort, team organization, leadership, self management, the handling of pressure, and mental toughness. Information on the SportProFile can be obtained by writing to SportProFile, c/o Self Management Resources Corporation, 155 Rexdale Boulevard, Suite 304, Toronto, Ontario, Canada M9W 5Z8.

A brief description of these attributes is outlined as follows:

WORK HABITS
A player with good work habits works hard during practices and games.

GENERAL ATTITUDE AND CHARACTER
Does the player mix well with his teammates, and is he enthusiastic? Can he handle adversity with a positive attitude? Character signs to watch for are moodiness and negativity.

LEADERSHIP
Not every player can be a leader, but leadership skills are evident in successful players in varying degrees. Some players are quiet and lead by example, while other players are more vocal. Good teams have more than one leader, and the leaders cooperate with each other and the coach.

COACHABILITY
Does the player accept the coach's direction, and is he willing to learn and improve? Most top players are very coachable, as they wish to improve their skills and need the feedback and direction of the coach.

MENTAL TOUGHNESS
Does the player react well under pressure and adversity? Is the player able to be positive and under control when situations are not going well?

SELF-CONFIDENCE
Does the player have confidence in his own ability? Can the player keep his confidence when he is not playing, or does he lose confidence when things are not going well?

TEAM ORIENTATION

Does the player put the team first and himself second? Will he sacrifice for the team, or is he selfish? Can the player accept his role on a team, especially if he does not get as much ice time as other players?

MOTIVATION

A highly motivated player wants to make the team, to improve, and to be a success.

INTENSITY

A player with intensity plays hard on the ice and in practice.

SAMPLE FORMS

A Background Information Sheet like the one on page 15 may be used to record each player's experience and personal information.

During training camps it is important to have a standard evaluation form. The coach should meet with the evaluators before the training camp to discuss what he is looking for in players, and then the evaluators should meet after each practice or scrimmage to discuss and compare their observations. Evaluation at training camp usually comes from observing scrimmage games, regular practice drills, and special evaluation drills.

In the regular practice drills and scrimmage games the evaluators should be looking for a subjective evaluation of the physical, technical, tactical, and mental skills previously mentioned. Forms like Subjective Evaluation Form 1 on page 16 and Subjective Evaluation Form 2 on page 17 can aid in the evaluation process.

An overall ranking form like the Scrimmage Evaluation Form on page 18 may be helpful in evaluation when observing game scrimmages and practice drills.

EVALUATION DRILLS

Evaluation drills can be of assistance when the coaches have the final decisions to make. The following are some sample drills that can be used to assess defensemen, forwards, and goaltenders.

EVALUATION DRILLS FOR DEFENSEMEN
1. Agility

The front player in each line skates from the goal line to the blue line, chop-steps halfway across the blue line, skates backward to the middle of the circle, pivots to the outside, and skates to the corner. There, he makes a sharp turn and returns to the front of the net.

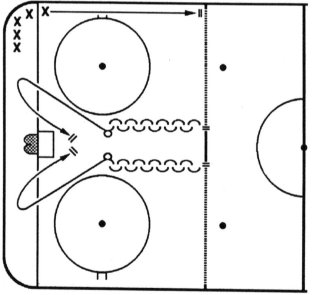

2. Backward Skating

F starts from the corner and skates behind the net, where he picks up the puck. He then skates down the boards outside the face-off marker. As soon as F touches the puck, D starts skating backward without turning until he reaches the centerline. He then turns and tries to ride F out to the boards; F attempts to cut in and score.

Note that D starts this drill halfway between the top of the goal crease and an imaginary line drawn between the face-off markers.

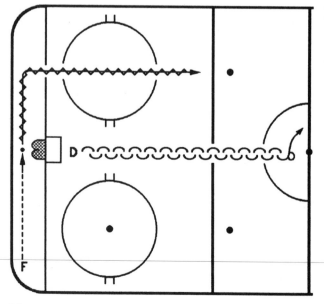

BACKGROUND INFORMATION SHEET

PERSONAL INFORMATION

Name: _____   Position: _____

Address: _____   Telephone: _____

_____   Doctor's Telephone No.: _____

_____   Grade: _____

_____   Date of Birth: _____

Next Year's School: _____   Skate Preference: _____

Age: _____   Height: _____   Weight: _____   Skate Size: _____

PLAYING EXPERIENCE

List teams and stats for last five years.

Year	Team	League	Goals	Assists	Points

List championship teams.

Year	Team	League	Championship

List academic (e.g., scholarship) or athletic (e.g., MVP) awards won in the past four years.

Year	Award

SUBJECTIVE EVALUATION FORM 1

Skating (agility, speed, acceleration, pivots) Can the player skate at this level? Does he have a definite liability in his skating?	
Puck Control Skills (passing, receiving, stickhandling) Can he handle the puck in a crowd? Can he handle the puck under pressure? Are his hands good or bad? Can he handle the puck at top speed?	
Defensive Play Does he show a desire to check? Is he active away from the puck? Does he show defensive anticipation, taking away options from the puck carrier? Would you use him as a penalty killer? Would you use him in critical situations (e.g., one-goal lead late in the game)?	
Offensive Play Does he display imagination and variation in moves? Can he beat the defender with speed and/or finesse? Would you consider him a "threat" man, one that you (as an opposition coach) would worry about? Would you give him special attention?	
Overall Comments Would you want him on your team? Do you rate him in the top 10 percent or top 1 percent? Do you consider him dependable? Does he have the skills and intelligence to play at a more competitive level in a few years?	

SUBJECTIVE EVALUATION FORM 2

The criteria below have been identified as parameters by which players may be evaluated at a camp. Each player is to be ranked on these criteria on a scale of 1 to 5.

1	2	3	4	5
Very Poor	Poor	Good	Very Good	Excellent

Name _____

	Rank
Hockey Sense Does he play with a sense of anticipation? Does he make the high-percentage play both offensively and defensively? Does he display an understanding of important concepts (e.g., headmanning, support, angling)? Does he understand the concept of picking or blocking out players? Does he play well away from the puck?	Rank
Positional Play Does he play with discipline in his own end? Is he capable of moving to open ice at the right time when attacking? Can he adjust his positioning to the movement of others?	Rank
Determination Does he show second effort when required, or does he quit? Does he work hard both offensively and defensively? (Is he "tough" on the puck and is he persistent when checking?)	Rank
Maturity Is he coachable? (Will he accept suggestions?) Does he have a good attitude toward referees? (Can he accept a bad call?) Does he have a good attitude toward opponents? (Does he retaliate or is he cool?)	Rank
Techniques Does he have any weak skill areas? Does he have skating agility? (Is speed a prime concern?) Are his strongest skill areas significant?	Rank

SCRIMMAGE EVALUATION FORM

To aid in the analysis and selection process, we are asking you as an evaluator to observe the ice sessions and assist us in the evaluation process.

These are the rosters for both the red and white teams for our scrimmages. Please indicate in the boxes your evaluation of each player using these ratings.

Rank all players from the best to the poorest.

> 2 for outstanding, exceptional performance
> 1 for good, average performance
> 0 for below average performance

Red Team		White Team	
1.		1.	
2.		2.	
3.		3.	
4.		4.	
5.		5.	
6.		6.	
7.		7.	
8.		8.	
9.		9.	
10.		10.	
11.		11.	
12.		12.	
13.		13.	
14.		14.	
15.		15.	
16.		16.	
17.		17.	
18.		18.	
19.		19.	
20.		20.	
21.		21.	
22.		22.	
23.		23.	
24.		24.	
25.		25.	

Goal
1.
2.
3.
4.

Defense
1.
2.
3.
4.
5.
6.
7.
8.
9.
10.

Center
1.
2.
3.
4.
5.

Left Wing
1.
2.
3.
4.
5.

Right Wing
1.
2.
3.
4.
5.

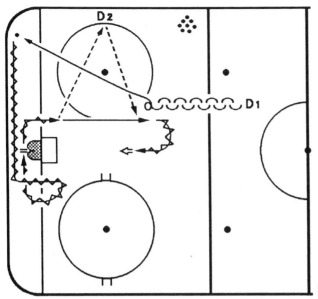

3. Agility, Skating, and Shooting

The coach shoots the puck into the corner. D1 skates backward, turns at the face-off marker, and skates to the corner to pick up the puck, executing a head-and-shoulders fake. He skates behind the net and toward the face-off circle, where he does a tight turn and returns behind the net. He stops, then starts again and passes to D2 near the boards. D1 skates out in front for the return pass from D2, does another tight turn, and shoots on goal. D1 then skates to D2's place on the boards, and D2 goes to the blue line to repeat the drill.

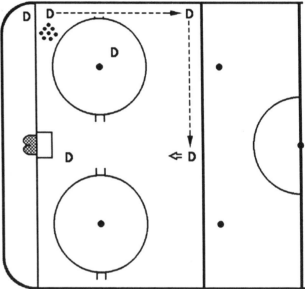

4. Shooting

The defenseman passes the puck from the corner to the near blue line to the middle of the ice for a low shot on goal. The defenseman in front deflects the puck at the goalie or acts as a screen. The defensemen rotate clockwise in this drill.

EVALUATION DRILLS FOR FORWARDS

1. Skating Speed

The players skate for speed at five distances: centerline and back, far blue line and back, far boards (one length), down and back (two lengths), and down and back twice (four lengths).

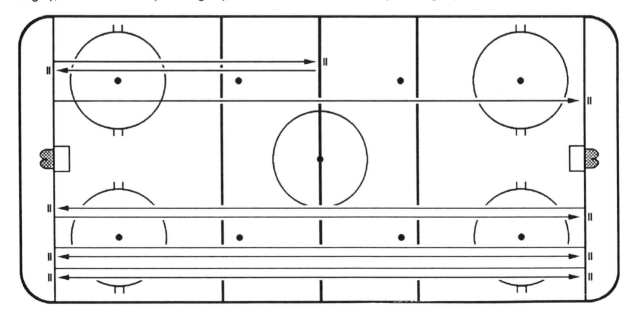

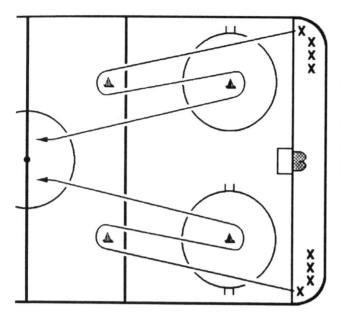

2. Race for the Puck

The forwards start in opposite corners, skate around the pylons, race for the puck, and shoot on the goaltender at the far end. The coach at the far blue line places a puck at the center of that blue line for which the players have to race.

3. One-on-One

The coach shoots the puck into the corner, and the two players race for the puck and attempt to score. The play continues until the coach blows the whistle, a goal is scored, or the goalie freezes the puck.

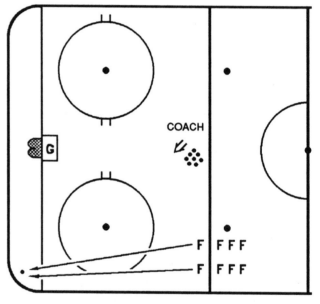

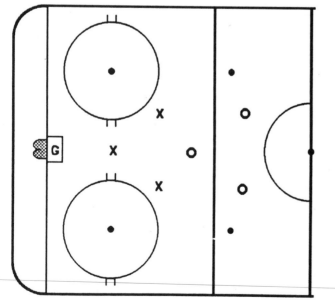

4. Three-on-Three

The forwards play three-on-three on the entire ice surface or in the two halves. Rotate the players and have them change every minute. The players change on the move with a whistle, and the team with the puck on the change passes back to its own goalie.

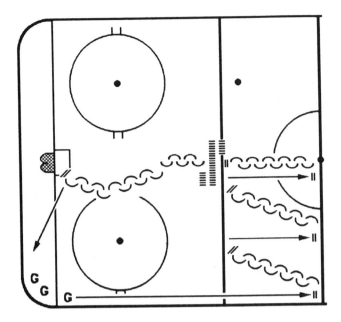

EVALUATION DRILLS FOR GOALIES
1. Agility Skating
Players start from the goal line, skate in the goal-tender's stance to the blue line, skate full stride to the red line and stop, skate sideways and backward to the blue line, skate forward in the goaltender's stance to the red line, skate sideways and backward to the blue line, skate full stride to the red line, and skate backward to the blue line; then they shuffle three steps left, six steps right, three steps back to the middle, backward to the top of the circles, backward and sideways to the right and then to the left, and end up in the crease.

2. Reaction, Agility and Stopping, Shots and Rebounds
The forward and rebounder start from the first line. The shooter shoots from the top of the far circle, and the rebounder drives for the net. The forward from the second line skates in and shoots from in close. The rebounder follows and drives for the net. The forward from the third line shoots from the near face-off dot, and the rebounder drives for the net

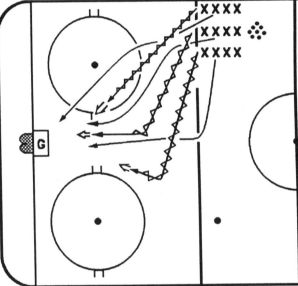

3. Side-to-Side Movement
The forward from one side skates in behind the goal line and passes the puck behind the net to the other forward coming from the other side of the ice. The pass is returned and passed out to the incoming third forward, who shoots a quick shot from the slot.

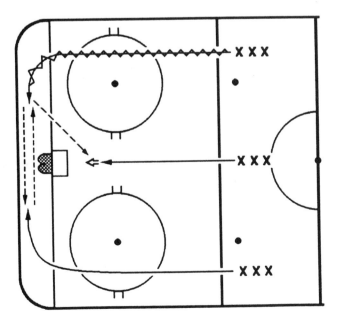

3. DESIGNING EFFICIENT PRACTICES

"Perfect practice makes perfect"
"How you practice is how you play."
"The game is an opportunity to see the results of your teaching."

These quotes have been around for many years in the sporting world, but they still say a great deal about the development of an athlete. The development of individual skills, tactics, strategy, mental preparation, and conditioning are all related to the practice situation. Running effective drills and practices is one of the most important aspects of coaching. Planning the season; the monthly, weekly, and daily practices; and the effective use and progression of drills are all intricate parts of the coaching responsibility. Game day, as many coaches comment, is only the result of all the hard work, preparation, and dedication of athletes and coaches.

Planning the Year

You should have a master plan for the entire year. The general areas of planning include the preparation, competitive, and transition periods used throughout the year.

The preparation period (off season) includes a general physical training period and a hockey-specific training period. Each period lasts approximately six to eight weeks.

The competition period is divided into pre-competition (training camp and exhibition), main competition (league schedule), tapering, and playoff competition period. The pre-competition period includes the training camp and exhibition schedules; the main competition period includes the regularly scheduled games. A tapering or unloading period lasts for a week to 10 days before the playoff competition period begins.

The transition period occurs after the season and playoffs are completed. It involves the athlete taking a break from specific hockey-related training but maintaining a good fitness level. The transition period can be part of a regular season of play if breaks are included, such as in high school, college, and university leagues.

During the various training periods, give consideration to the development of technical (skill), tactical (team play), physical (conditioning), and psychological (mental) training programs.

Include in your planning monthly, weekly, and daily programs of the different macrocycles (training periods) for these main training periods. Important factors to consider are practice-to-game ratio and the total amount of training time.

An example of periodization (planning) for hockey would be:

Apr	May Jun	Jul Aug	Sep Oct	Nov Dec Jan Feb	Mar
Transition	General Preparation	Specific Preparation	Pre-Competition	Competition Tapering[*]	Playoff

*Tapering to occur one week to 10 days at the end of February.

Planning the Practice

Scotty Bowman: *His practices were in constant motion, shooting, passing, everything done on the go, with speed, every drill rooted in high pace skating.* (Ken Dryden, *The Game*)

I feel that certainty of winning only when I know we've done all the preparation and when we've practiced intelligently and thoroughly. (Joe Paterno, Penn State Football Coach)

The individual practice is one part of the total plan. The development of individual skills (technical), team play with systems and strategy (tactical) and conditioning should be part of each practice. As well as having a set plan for each practice, consider weaknesses you have observed in previous practices and games. Also consider what mental training you are going to include and when.

Consider how much time is spent teaching and explaining and how much of the practice is to be of high intensity and flow. Also consider the skill and physical development level of the athletes and confirm that the equipment and facilities are in proper order to ensure the safety of the players.

Make skill or technical development a part of most practices. A skill progression drill and other suitable drills should be part of the plan; have a number of different drills to teach the same skill to prevent boredom and challenge the athletes. Systems and team play should be part of the tactical development of the practice. Make sure the systems such as breakouts and power plays fit the athletes' age and skill level, and progress from simple to the more complex.

Include physical preparation (conditioning) in each practice. Take into account the conditioning effect of each skill drill and team drill when you design the practice. Consider such factors as development of the energy systems, strength, and flexibility.

Don't forget the mental aspect of practice including tactics and strategy discussed and practiced during the training period. In your general plan also include the mental training skills of relaxation, positive self-talk, energizing, visualization, and concentration. This is an area that is not done particularly well by coaches.

Evaluate each practice after it has been completed and use this information to plan the next practice. Although you should plan the whole year, your daily and weekly planning must be flexible enough to take in day-to-day changes to adjust to the strengths and weaknesses of the athletes and the team.

Designing an Effective Practice

1. Set goals and objective of the practice first with the assistant coaches and then with the players to explain what you are trying to accomplish. A good idea is to meet with the team in the dressing room 10 minutes before the practice for discussions of the theme of the practice and specific drills.

2. Include stretching exercises before going on the ice 30 minutes before practice.

3. Have a general progression throughout the practice from individual skill to team play.

4. Teach new skills and drills early in the practice.

5. Keep all players active and include the goaltenders in all drills.

6. Give clear, concise instructions throughout the practice and be in command.

7. Use effective teaching formations and make sure you have the attention of all athletes when you are speaking to them. Explain and demonstrate skills and drills clearly.

8. Put the players into the drills quickly after an explanation.

9. Don't talk too long at one time. Be concise, keeping to one to one-and-a-half minutes of explanation.

10. Inform your assistant coaches and use them effectively. Keep them active in all drills and make them part of everything you do.

11. Keep the players active and use all the ice surface. You may wish to use all the ice surface for team drills and divide the team up for some individual skill drills using different parts of the ice.

12. Observe, evaluate, and give feedback throughout the practice. Assistant coaches should be involved in this process as well.

13. Keep drills effective, competitive, active, and challenging.

14. Be positive and upbeat. Greet the athletes using their first names before practice or at the start of practice. Use voice communication throughout the practice at the proper times. Early in the practice, use voice communication more frequently to get the players going and establish a good rapport.

15. Include a warm-up and cool-down in each practice. The warm-up should include stretching and skating, and the cool-down should follow the reverse order of the warm-up.

16. Use mass stretching and/or a fun skating warm-up drill to get the team together and ready for the main part of the practice.

17. Give water breaks every 10–15 minutes. Use numbered individual water bottles.

18. Include a fun drill in most practices.

19. Stop the drills when a general error or a lack of effort is apparent.

20. Choose drills for their conditioning features or have a conditioning drill or drills at the end of practice.

21. Speak to players as a group at the end of practice. Discuss the practice, upcoming games, general information, etc.

22. If time permits, have certain players work on specific skills with the assistant coaches after practice.

23. If possible, after practice have an off-ice conditioning area for strength, anaerobic, and aerobic conditioning.

24. Conduct individual meetings with players before or after practices if time permits.

25. Meet with assistant coaches and possibly the captains to discuss and evaluate the practice and plan for the next practice or game.

26. Keep a record of all practices to refer to during the season and in future games. Evaluate each session as to strengths and weaknesses.

27. Demand excellence. Repeat until players get it right.

Designing Effective Drills

The development, designing, and implementing of effective drills is a key ingredient in coaching. How the athletes relate to the coach is in many ways directly related to how the drills and practices are implemented. The coach's knowledge, planning, and communication skills are very evident in the training sessions. How you practice is how you play. Effective, well-run drills are the essence of training.

Some guidelines for coaches in developing drills:

1. The drill should have a specific purpose and meet the objectives you have set for the practice.

2. The drill should be suitable to the age, skill level, and physical maturity (i.e. strength, size) of the athletes.

3. The drills should be applicable to the skills used in the game. Running a drill that does not relate to the skills used in the game and does not serve any purpose is meaningless to both the athlete and the coach.

4. Drills should follow a progression, moving from the simple to the more complex. Build on previous drills, and develop a progression of drills for each skill taught.

5. Maximum participation of all the players should be an objective of every drill. All players should be involved in the drills and the number of trials or expectation of each skill should be at the maximum with only an adequate pause for recovery between trials or repetitions.

6. Drills should challenge the skill level of the athletes. If drills are too easy, the athletes will become bored quickly. Conversely, if the drills are too difficult, the athletes will become frustrated with lack of success.

7. Explain the drill clearly and demonstrate it before the athletes practice it. Your explanation should be clear, concise and, with the demonstration, should take less than three minutes.

8. Explain new drills in the dressing room using a rink diagram or on the ice using a rink board attached to the side glass. New drills may have to be demonstrated on the ice as well, especially if the drill is complex. In general, younger athletes need both an explanation and a demonstration while older, higher skilled athletes may need only a verbal explanation. Some coaches use the rink board on the ice before each drill while others do this in the dressing room before practice.

9. Drills should be varied and innovative. You should have a series of drills and a number of different ways of accomplishing the same purpose (e.g., one-on-one, two-on-one, etc.). Always be aware of new drills and be innovative in designing drills. With older mature athletes, you may wish to combine a number of skills and purposes in one drill.

10. Drills should be undertaken at a tempo that simulates the action in the game. Practices with a high intensity are more enjoyable for the athletes and provide a carry-over into the game situation. Teams that practice at high tempo play at high tempo. Exceptions would be a drill that introduces a complex skill and thus must be broken down into parts and practiced initially at a slower speed until the skill is perfected.

11. It might seem obvious, but the drills should be done correctly. After you give a clear explanation and demonstration, you have the responsibility to see that the drill is done correctly. If the execution is not correct, stop the drill and emphasize the correct method.

12. The athletes should work with intensity in every drill. Inform the players of the intensity and work ethic required and remind them that it is the responsibility of the players and the coach that this work intensity be evident in all drills.

13. It is your responsibility as coach to give effective constructive feedback during and after a drill is completed. The feedback can be general to all the players and/or specific to certain players. Athletes need to know how they are doing, and only with effective feedback can they correct the errors in their execution of a skill or drill. A complete understanding of the skills and the ability to observe and analyze are areas that all coaches must work on to become more proficient.

14. Assistant coaches should be actively involved in running the drills and give feedback. The head coach should outline the responsibility of the assistant coach during the drills. There may be some situations where the assistant coach runs a drill totally or at one end of the rink.

15. As much as possible, introduce competition into drills. Any time a race, battle, or a winner is involved in a drill, the participants' interest and intensity levels are raised. As much as possible, you should try to equalize the competition when there is a large discrepancy in the skill level, size, and strength of the players.

16. Remain flexible in the development and running of drills. Some drills may be too complicated and have to be changed; other drills may not work with certain age groups. Stop drills or improvise when drills are not working.

17. Drills should run for the ideal amount of time—generally, they should not last longer than eight to 10 minutes and should be no shorter than three minutes. Coaches should be alert during a drill and not allow the drill to drag on. On the other hand, too short a drill will not allow enough repetitions for each player. The timing of a drill is a skill that develops with your experience and close observation of the intensity of the athletes while they perform the drill.

18. Drills should flow from one to another with a minimum of time between drills. Drills built on a progressional flow make an effective practice when put together. A well-planned drill progression gives an overall flow to the practice.

19. The whole ice surface should be used for most drills. The ideal drill has all players involved using the complete ice surface. In some situations, the players may be split into groups executing different drills on different sections of the ice surface.

20. If drills are planned correctly and executed at high tempo, and a proper work-to-rest ratio is used, a conditioning effect should take place. Incorporate into each drill the number of repetitions along with the appropriate rest period for best results.

21. Drills should be enjoyable. Well-planned drills will allow the athletes to enjoy a practice. Make specific fun drills part of every practice.

22. At the more elite level combine a number of skills in one drill. (e.g. breakout drill moving back to defensive zone coverage)

23. Each drill should be evaluated after each practice. Did the drill accomplish its objective? Was the drill too difficult or too easy? Was the drill too long or too short? Was the drill executed properly? Did all the players understand the drill? Were there noticeable improvements in the skill level?

24. Use drills that will improve areas of weakness evident in a previous game or practice. A certain drill may be more effective after a weakness was shown in a game. For example, a defensive-zone drill may be necessary at the practice after a game in which there was poor defensive execution. Certain specific skill drills such as shooting or checking may be appropriate after a game in which these skills were performed poorly.

25. Overall effective drills should show improvement in individual skills and team play. Teams play as they practice. Individuals and teams should be evaluated on improvement, and effective, properly executed drills should make this improvement possible.

26. Keep a record of all drills on cards or in book form and categorize them (i.e. one-on-one, two-on-one, etc.).

TYPES OF PRACTICES

Before establishing the type of practice you want to run, you need to know the amount of ice time available to you. Ideally, you should have at least one-and-a-half hours of ice time, but in many cases you may find you have only one hour or only half the ice available. The effective use and planning of drills is even more important when ice time is limited.

Practices are generally of five different types:

- General skill
- Offensive
- Defensive
- Special Teams (Power Play and Penalty Killing)
- Simple (No Brainer), Fun

A general skill practice is a typical practice that includes skill development and some team play. This practice includes drills such as skill, offensive and defensive team play, and conditioning, and is the most common type of practice.

An offensive practice has a theme of passing, moving the puck quickly and scoring, and generally raising the players' level of offensive skills. The drills have a high tempo with little resistance.

A defensive practice has the theme of forechecking, backchecking, and defensive team play. Some teams have this type of practice once a week if a number of practices are available. If a team is suffering from poor defensive play, this practice can get the players focused on the defensive aspect of the game.

Special team practices in such aspects of the game as power plays and penalty killing are important and usually effective the day before a game because they tend not to be exhaustive. These special practices are very important in the game of hockey and should be held at least once a week. If practice time is limited, aspects of this practice have to be incorporated in general practice.

Fun and simple (no brainer) practices have their place and can be used when the players appear fatigued or need a change of routine. Fun drills in a practice or a whole practice devoted to fun definitely have their place in a long session. A simple (no brainer) practice is one where little thinking is involved; no strategy or tactics are included and drills with little or no resistance are used. These practices should be short and included for the same reasons as a fun practice.

When the number of practices per week is limited, some aspects of the different types of practices may be included in one practice. An example of this type of practice would be to include defensive and special teams work in a general skill practice.

TYPICAL PRACTICE

1. Dressing-room stretch—possible instruction 10 minutes before practice
2. On-ice warm-up—skating warm-up
3. Group fun—two pucks
4. Stretch together
5. Goalie warm-up
6. One-on-zero, two-on-zero
7. Individual skill drills—forwards, defense, goalies
8. One-on-one
9. Two-on-one
10. Three-on-one
11. Breakouts with re-groups
12. Short scrimmage—instructional
13. Conditioning drills
14. Cool-down
15. Final group discussions

Post-practice: aerobic exercises, strength training

Offensive Practice

1. Stretching and warm-up
2. Drive-for-the-net drill
3. Neutral zone lead-up drills
4. One-on-one and two-on-one flow drills
5. Neutral zone re-group breakouts—emphasize driving for the net
6. Resurface the ice (if possible)
7. Offensive scrimmage—this scrimmage should emphasize moving the puck, shooting, driving for the net
8. Three vs. three fun drill

9. Shooting drills

10. Conditioning drills

11. Cool-down

Defensive Practice

1. Cross-ice agility and cross-ice one-on-one

2. Bull in the ring (fun drill)

3. Give-and-go with a backchecker

4. Two groups—two groups perform drills emphasizing the defense taking the man in front of the net, taking the man coming from the corner, and forechecking

5. Backchecking drill—players perform breakouts, five-on-two, with one and two checkers, and then with one forechecker and one backchecker, then one forechecker and two backcheckers

6. Defensive zone coverage—players drill on five-on-none defensive zone coverage and then on five-on-five defensive zone coverage

7. Resurface the ice (if possible)

8. Defensive scrimmage—emphasis is on defensive zone coverage and preventing goals

9. Conditioning

10. Cool-down

Special Team Practice: Power Play/Penalty Killing

1. Warm-up and stretch

2. Circle—one touch (use power play units of five); Circle—man in the middle

3. Power play shooting; Forwards—one-timers, come off boards or pass across; Defense—move to the middle and shoot, one-timers, top of the circle and middle of the ice; One-timers from middle or top of the circle

4. Five-on-zero both ends, use various options, can use cones or chairs to pass around

5. Power play breakouts: Five-on-zero; five-on-one; five-on-two; five-on-three

6. Five vs. four; Five vs. three at both ends. Defensive team turn sticks or no sticks to begin with. Extra players play keep away or one touch in the neutral zone

7. Power play scrimmage—give each unit two minutes of continuous play. Keep record of goals scored and make it a competition, power play versus penalty killing. A suggestion: the defensive team shoots the puck down the ice when they get over the defensive blue line.

8. Shoot out (fun drill)

9. Cool-down

Simple (No Brainer) Fun Practices

1. Warm-up and stretch

2. Two and three pucks—everyone on the ice

3. Team stretch

4. One-on-zero, two-on-zero, three-on-zero, two-on-one, three-on-one, Czech flow drills

5. Breakout two re-groups, breakout two re-groups, second shot

6. Scrimmage four vs. four, three vs. three—can play with sticks in opposite hands

7. Cross ice—one-on-one, two-on-two

8. Cool-down

Remember: How you practice is how you play. Keep practices high tempo, intense, meaningful with skill instruction and feedback, and enjoyable for both the coach and the players.

One of the most important aspects of coaching is the organization and running of effective practices. Practices should be developed with the points outlined here in mind:

ORGANIZATION

Practices should be organized down to the last detail. Drills should show a natural progression through the practice from individual skills to team skills. The practice should have a smooth transition from drill to drill with constant movement and very little standing around.

WARM-UP AND COOL-DOWN

It is important that the athletes be fully stretched and warmed up before the intense part of the practice begins. Stretching exercises should be performed in the dressing room or in an exercise room in the arena if possible.

At the end of each practice the few remaining minutes should consist of stretching and slowing the intensity of work. The practice can end as it began, with basically the same stretching and flexing.

OTHER DETAILS

It is important that water be available to the athletes during practice. Individual plastic squirt bottles are best. The coach should schedule two or three water breaks during the practice.

The number of pucks available should be checked before each practice. The standard number for a team of 20 players is usually 40 pucks.

It is important that the practices are interesting and fun. There should be good discipline and order. The coach should talk to the players in a semicircle formation so that no player is behind the coach when he is speaking. Establish a signal, such as a short double whistle, at which the team assembles in front of the coach for practice directions.

It is sometimes a good idea to have a light, short skate between drills, especially if the drill was not of high intensity.

USE OF ASSISTANT COACHES

It is important that the assistant coaches are used effectively during practices. The assistant coaches should be active in giving feedback to the players and should have specific duties to support the coach. There are many occasions when the ice can be divided for specific defense and forward drills. A good practice has constant activity and high intensity with drills at both ends of the ice. The assistant coach should be constantly evaluating talent and should meet with the head coach after each practice to evaluate and plan the next practice.

Often assistant coaches direct the warm-up and conditioning part of the practices, and in some situations the head coach may have the assistant coach run certain drills.

It is important that the assistant coach feel like part of the practice's organization and implementation and that all coaches have agreed on systems of play and teaching techniques. The designing and implementation of conditioning programs is also another area in which assistant coaches play an active role.

On-ice Stretching Drill

If time permits, stretching drills, such as PNF, can be used for flexibility training (see chapter 20, "Conditioning").

The regular skating warm-up can consist of leg and groin stretches, leg slow kick to outstretched hands, knee to chest, trunk twisting with the stick on the shoulders, toe touching by raising the arms with the stick in both hands over the shoulders and then touching the toes, and wrist rotation holding the stick in one hand and then the other. This type of stretching is usually followed by fast and slow skating, either on the whistle or sprinting between the blue lines. Agility training can be added to this skating by having players turn backward between the blue lines, turn 360 degrees, or go down on one or both knees at the blue and red lines. Carrying a puck can be added to this warm-up, with the players starting by kicking the puck with the skates.

Warm-Up Skating Drill

This skating warm-up can be used with or without pucks. Players form two lines. Pairs of players skate together forward and backward down the ice. Turning at lines can be added. The players then skate down the ice and back, passing the puck.

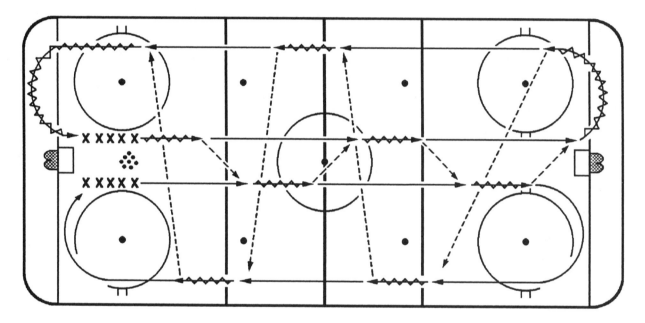

Warm-Up Shooting Drills
Three lines shoot one drill from the following.

(a) Wrist Shots
A player from each line skates in and shoots from the top of the circles starting at the right, then center, then left. Players should alternate lines and use wrist shots only.

(b) Shooting from Three Spots

One player from each line skates toward the goalie simultaneously. The player on one side shoots from just inside the blue line, the player in the middle shoots from the high slot, and the player on the far side pulls the goalie. The three players can start skating in on the goalie on the command of the coach. The players can change lines, and the order can be switched for shooting or pulling the goalie.

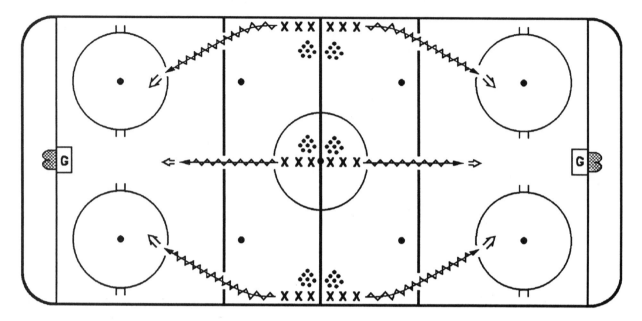

(c) Rapid Shoot

The players skate in one line coming in from the right, the center, and the left. The players are a few feet apart and shoot wrist shots in rapid succession.

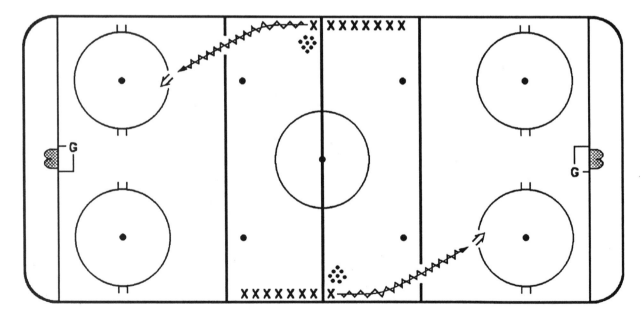

(d) One-on-None Drill Carousel and Variation

Players loop inside the blue line and receive a pass from the opposite line. The player passing the puck then goes over the far blue line, skates in, and shoots on the goalie from the end on which he started.

Variation: The player receives a pass, turns backward between the red and the blue lines, and then turns forward, skates, and shoots on the net.

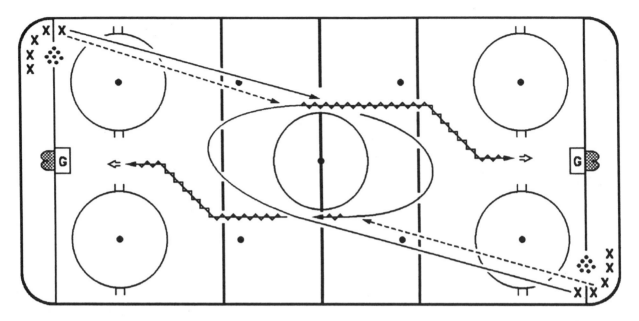

(e) Neutral Zone One-on-None

The player skates from the corner to the center red line and passes the puck to the near defenseman. The near defenseman passes the puck to his defense partner, who then passes the puck back to the forward, who has skated in front of the defenseman. The forward skates back to the end he came out of, shoots on the goalie, and then returns to the same line he started from.

Variation: The forward skates behind the defenseman, skates up the middle of the ice, and receives a pass from the other defense partner.

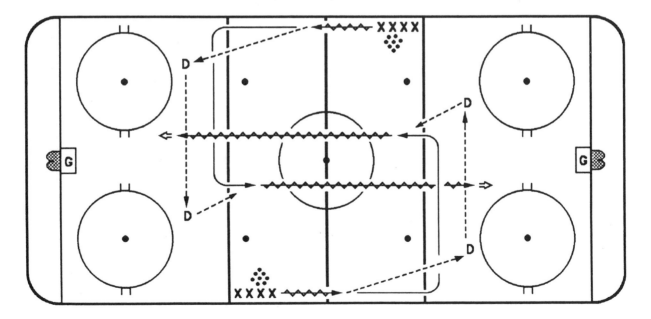

(f) Rebound Drill

Two players start the drill. The first player goes in on the net and shoots. The second player trails the first and goes for the rebound (if there is one), turns off, and receives a pass from the first player in the other line. He then skates the length of the ice and shoots. The player passing the puck then follows the shooter down the ice, goes to the net for a rebound, takes a pass from the other line, and returns and shoots at the same end he started at.

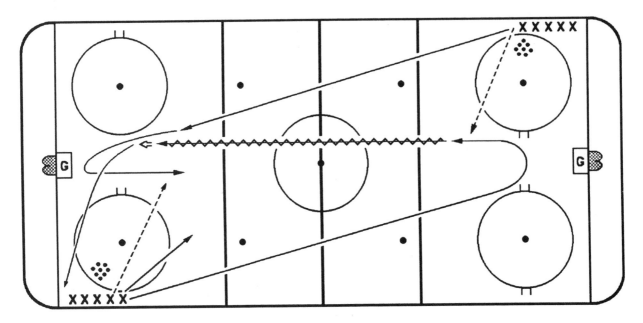

(g) Half-Ice Two-on-None

Two players skate down the ice passing the puck between them. Moving over the far blue line, the player on the board side shoots from just inside the blue line.

Moving in the opposite direction and after passing the far blue line, the player on the board side skates wide and passes the puck back to the trailing player in the high slot. The player who is shooting attempts to shoot the puck in one motion.

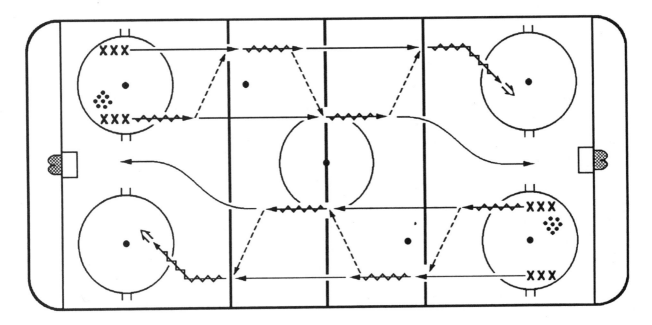

(h) One-on-None, Two-on-None, Pucks in the Middle Drill

The player skates to the middle of the ice, gets a puck, skates back to the same end, shoots, and returns to the same line he started in.

Variation: Two players skate from opposite corners of the same end, with one player picking up a puck at center and then returning to the same end two-on-none.

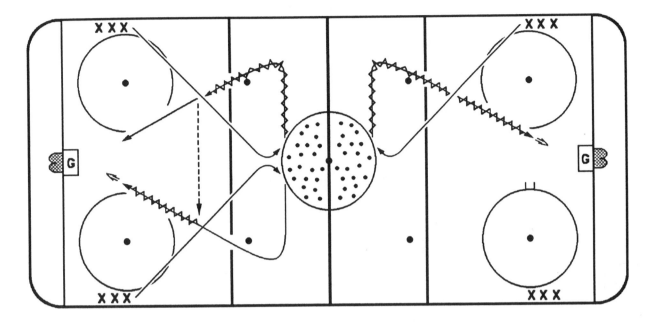

(i) Pucks in the Middle Variation

Add a defenseman on each blue line. The player, after picking the puck up at center ice, passes to the defenseman at the far blue line, receives a return pass, skates in, and shoots on the goalie at the end he started from.

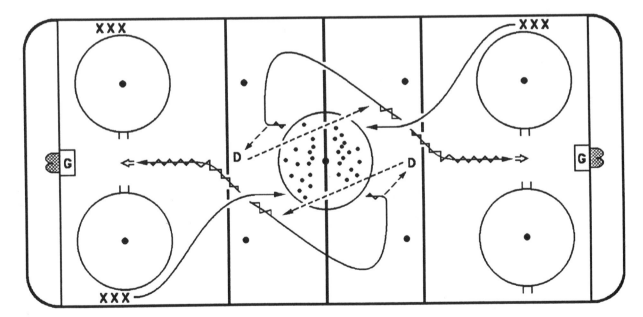

(j) Pucks in the Middle Variation

This drill can be done as a two-on-none as well, having two players skate from opposite corners, one picking up a puck at center and passing to the defenseman, and both returning two-on-none to the ends they started from.

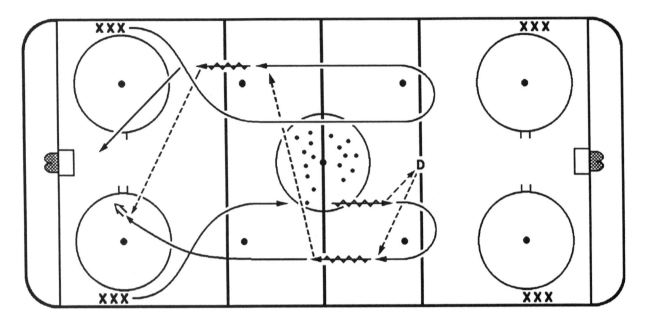

4. BASIC HOCKEY GUIDELINES

There are some basic rules that both the coach and the player must follow in order to become successful. The coach will teach his players these rules both on and off the ice so that they are clearly understood.

DEFENSIVE ZONE

- Think defense first and offense only when in full control of the puck.
- Keep your head up and take the man first and then the puck. Take the offensive man out after he has passed the puck to eliminate a return pass.
- Only one man moves to cover the point. If two men move to the point, the second man should drop back on the board side. Keep the head up when moving to the point and don't let the defenseman move around you.
- Cover the slot at all times. Move to a man coming from behind the net only when he is a direct threat to score.
- One defenseman should always be in front of the net and control any player in the low slot area. The defenseman should face up ice and be aware of players in front of the net. To watch the play in the corner, the defenseman should turn his head but keep his body squared up ice. The defenseman should not turn his back from the slot area unless a player is coming from behind the net and is a direct threat to score.
- When the defenseman has the puck just inside the blue line and is being pressured, he should dump the puck out over the blue line on the board side.
- When experiencing difficulty in moving the puck out under pressure, freeze or ice the puck to get a face-off.
- Never pass the puck rink-wide or through the center in your own end.
- Never pass the puck up the middle in your own zone unless you are absolutely sure. Pass to the winger on the boards or a defenseman in the corner if in doubt.
- Never pass the puck without looking in your own zone. The man must be there.
- Don't shoot the puck around the boards unless a man is in position or the puck has been shot in directly and the far side offensive defenseman is not in a position to pinch in.
- Never go backward in your own zone unless you're on a power play or there is no forechecking pressure.
- Never allow your team to be outnumbered in the defensive zone (e.g., forwards up too high).

NEUTRAL ZONE

OFFENSE
- If men are covered, dump the puck in or turn back and pass to the defense, and then regroup and attack again.
- Never try to stickhandle past the opposition when teammates are with you.
- The forwards without the puck should move to open ice with the stick on the ice, preparing to take a pass.
- Never go offside; straddle the blue line or cut in front of or behind the puck carrier.

DEFENSE
- Backcheck by picking up the offside forward. Take the man to the net if he stays outside the defenseman. If the player cuts to the middle in front of the defense, stay in the lane. The backchecker should be on the inside of the offensive man and should be slightly ahead of the man. Make contact with the man.
- If two forwards are back, pick up the lanes or one lane and the middle of the ice. The defense can force the play at the defensive blue line.
- If the backchecker is trailing the play, pick up the high slot area.
- Some teams have the first backchecker chase the puck carrier in the neutral zone.

OFFENSIVE ZONE

- One man always drives for the net.
- Drive for the rebounds. You must want to score. Release the puck quickly.
- One man should always be in the slot with the stick on the ice, ready to score or in a position to screen the goalie.
- Shoot the puck when in the scoring area (slot). Extra passes can end up in missed opportunities.
- The defenseman must shoot the puck quickly from the point. If the puck is mishandled or too much time is taken, the puck should be passed or shot back into the corner.
- Never pass the puck blindly from behind the net. If you do not see a man and have to release the puck, shoot the puck at the goaltender's skates.

PENALTY SITUATIONS

- Force the play in the opponent's zone but keep skating.
- Pick up the lane in the neutral zone whether an offensive player is there or not.
- Never go by the opponent's point man in the defensive zone.
- Cover the slot for cross passes.
- Force the play in the defensive zone until the offensive team sets up. Some teams continue to force the play.
- The man in the penalty box replaces the missing forward position, whether right winger, center, or left winger, no matter what position he usually plays.

POWER PLAY

- On a delayed penalty, the center on the next line replaces the goaltender. Some coaches designate a certain player to replace the goalie. If the puck is in your zone, the player goes to the center line; in the offensive zone the player goes to the front of the net.
- Have several methods of moving the puck out of your own end.
- Use four men in the neutral zone to move the puck over the offensive blue line.
- Move the puck to the point in the offensive zone.
- Move the puck quickly. If there is no man to pass to, the player should move. Don't stand still with the puck. Moving the puck quickly allows a man to move to the opening.

5. SKATING

It is very important for each of your players to have a good pair of well-fitting skates. Growing children should not wear a skate more than one half-size larger than necessary. Most hockey shops now have specialists who will fit skates properly.

When tying their skates, skaters should be sure the middle eyelets are pulled tightly together around the ankle. The top eyelets do not need to be pulled too closely together. The laces should not be tied around the skate (leg), as this could cause a lack of blood circulation to the feet.

Skates should be sharpened regularly to allow quick stops and turns. The sharpness of the skates can be tested by executing quick stops or tight turns. Off the ice, scraping a fingernail on the edge of the skate blade or placing a coin on the bottom of the blade to see how much hollow there is in the blade will tell you if the skate blade is still sharp.

SKATING TECHNIQUES

FORWARD STARTING
Front Start
- The body weight is over the drive leg.
- The drive leg is rotated outward at an angle of 90 degrees to the direction of the motion.
- The feet are a shoulders' width apart.
- The body leans forward, and the center of gravity shifts forward.
- The initial strides are short and quick without gliding, and the feet are lifted off the ice slightly.
- As the number of strides increases, the push is to the side rather than to the back.

Crossover Start
- The skates are slightly closer together than in the front start.
- The skates are parallel and perpendicular to the direction of motion.
- The lean of the body and the head and shoulders are toward the direction of motion.
- After the crossover, the outside skate is placed at an angle of 90 degrees to direction of motion.

FORWARD SKATING
A solid, well-balanced stance is important in skating.

- The feet should be a shoulders' width apart.
- The foot of the drive leg (back leg) is turned outward for a lateral thrust (to the side, not to the back).
- The drive leg is fully extended at the hip, knee, and ankle joint.
- The knee of the drive leg is flexed beyond the toe of the skate.
- The trunk and glide leg should form an approximate 90-degree angle.
- The drive leg should be recovered close to the ice in a circular motion, passing under the center of gravity.

DRIVE LEG

GLIDE LEG

The skater should allow for a natural arm swing but not overswing the arms to cause overshift, which will interfere with the forward motion. The skater should try to develop a smooth action stride with maximum thrust from the drive leg. Excess motions are a waste of energy and may cause a reduction in the forward speed.

FORWARD STOPPING
Two-Foot Stop
- The knees are bent, and the skates turn to a 90-degree angle to the direction of motion by the rotation of the hips.
- The skates are staggered six to eight inches apart. The inside skate is slightly beyond the outside skate (to arch).
- The weight should be distributed as evenly as possible on both skates.
- The stop is executed on the outside edge of the inside skate and the inside edge of the outside skate.

One-Foot Stop
The front leg stop is similar to the two-foot stop except all the weight is on the front leg (inside edge). The back leg is off the ice, ready to initiate the next stride.

The back leg stop is rarely used, as it puts the player in a vulnerable position to be hit (off balance). The weight is on the outside edge of the back leg.

FORWARD CROSSOVER
Players use the forward crossover to accelerate while changing direction.
- The head, shoulders, and arms are rotated in the direction of movement.
- The body leans toward the inside, with the trunk bent forward and the knees bent.
- The weight transfers from the inside to the outside leg.
- The outside leg drives with an extension of the hip, knee, and ankle.
- Following the extension of the outside leg (inside edge), the outside leg crosses over the inside leg (outside edge).

BACKWARD SKATING
- The knees are bent and a shoulders' width apart.
- The toe of the drive leg is rotated inward to a 90-degree angle to the direction of the motion.
- The drive leg extends in the sequence of hip, knee, and ankle (inside edge) in a semicircular motion.
- The extension is not full, which allows for a quick recovery.
- The glide leg is flexed to allow for a longer push by the drive leg.
- During the extension of the drive leg, the weight is transferred to the glide leg, which is ready to become the drive leg.

BACKWARD STOPPING
One-Foot Stop
- The back skate rotates outward in a semicircle before stopping at a 90-degree angle to the desired direction.
- The weight of the body is on the rear leg and the front part of the skate.
- The knee of the back leg is flexed, ready to extend for movement in the opposite direction.

Two-Foot Stop
- Both skates are rotated outward at 180 degrees with heels close together.
- Both legs are flexed, with pressure on the front part of the blades (inside edges).

BACKWARD TURNING
Two-Skate Quick Turn
- Both skates turn in the desired direction.
- The skate on the side of the turn is slightly ahead.
- The head, shoulder, and arms are turned in the desired direction.
- The knees are bent, and the weight is on the back of the blades (outside edge of the front skate, inside edge of the back skate).

Forward to Backward
- The weight is placed on the glide leg opposite the intended pivot side (right skate if turn is to the left).
- At the end of the stride, the player straightens up and rotates the left skate outward at 180 degrees, bringing it to the other side of right glide skate.
- The head and shoulders rotate to the left, and the right skate rotates 180 degrees and is then parallel to the left skate.

Backward to Forward Heel-to-Heel Pivot (Mohawk Turn)

- The skates are brought close together.
- The weight of the body is brought over the glide leg.
- The head, shoulders, and arms are turned in the desired direction.
- The pivot skate is raised slightly off the ice, rotated in the desired direction, and placed back on the ice.
- The glide leg pushes and transfers the weight to the pivoting leg, allowing for rapid acceleration with short strides.

Backward to Forward Crossover

- The skates are brought close together with the arms close to the body.
- The body weight shifts over the glide leg.
- The other leg crosses over with the blade (inside edge) at a 90-degree angle to the desired direction.
- The crossover is short and close to the ice.

SKATING AND TURNING DRILLS

Note that these drills can be done with players skating backward or forward.

1. Figure Eight

Have players skate around the rink, going behind the nets and moving in both directions.

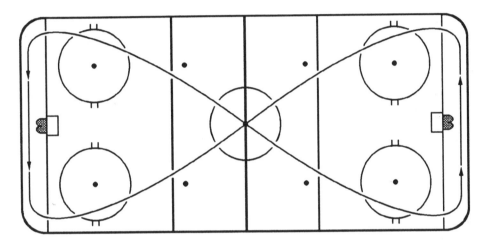

2. Small Figure Eight

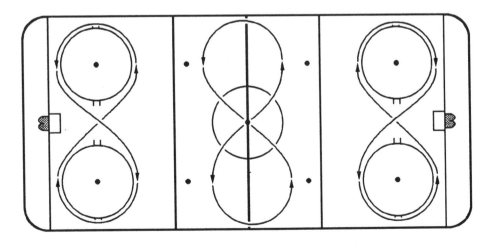

3. Circle Skate
Players skate in circles in five groups, changing direction forward and backward.

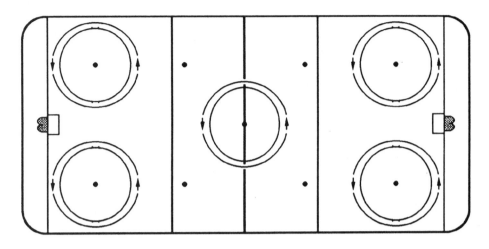

4. Skate the Circles—Two Groups

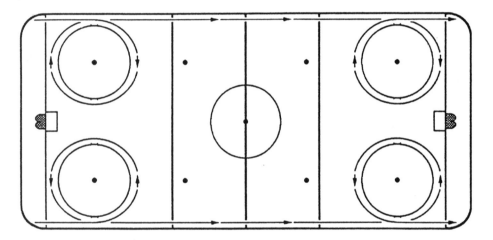

5. Skate the Circles—One Group

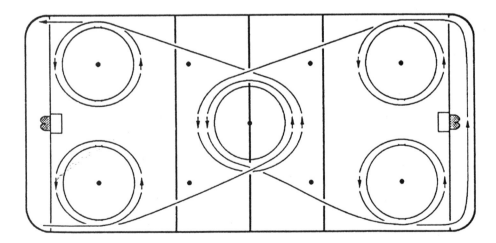

6. Weaving Through Markers

(a) With the pylons in a zigzag position, players skate forward through the markers and then skate backward through the markers.

(b) Players skate forward clockwise around the markers, then backward clockwise around the markers, then forward counterclockwise around the markers, and then backward counterclockwise around the markers.

(c) Players deke around each pylon using a sharp turn both right and left.

(d) Players skate forward then backward through the markers in a straight line.

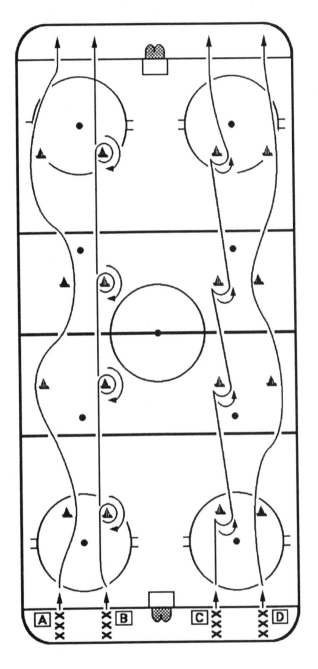

41

7. Zigzag Drill

All players skate forward stopping at each point (1 through 7) up the ice. The second player leaves when the first reaches the blue line. All players stay at one end when they complete the drill, then reverse directions.

Variation: All players skate forward to points 1, 3, 5, and 7 and backward to points 2, 4, and 6.

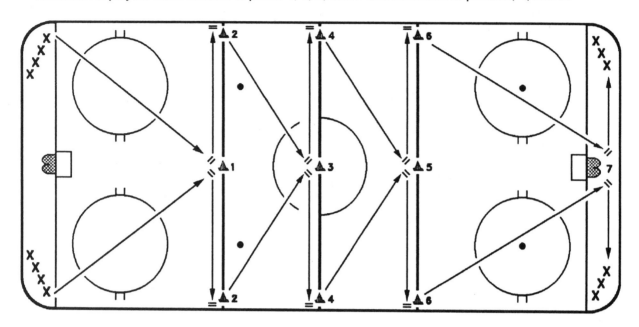

8. Overback Drill

Players skate forward across the blue line, stop, skate backward to the top of the face-off circle, pivot toward the other group, skate to the corner, stop, and then move into the back of the line.

Note that you must have groups 1 and 4, and 2 and 3 switch sides halfway through the drill to be sure the players work on stopping and turning both ways.

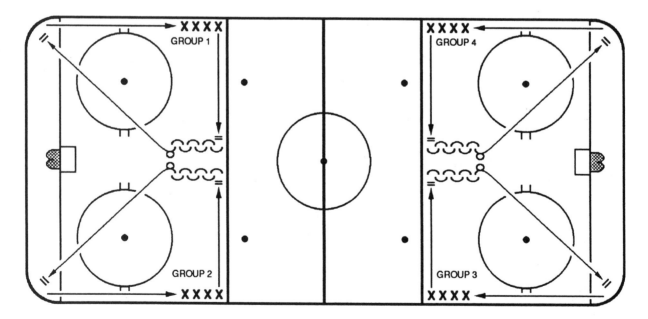

9. Skating Agility

Three forwards and two defensemen skate down the ice. The wingers cut at the far blue line and skate directly to the net and back to the blue line twice. The center skates to the crease and moves laterally side to side twice. The defensemen skate to the far blue line and cross-step to the pylons three times. After this skate, the players skate the length of the ice to the starting position.

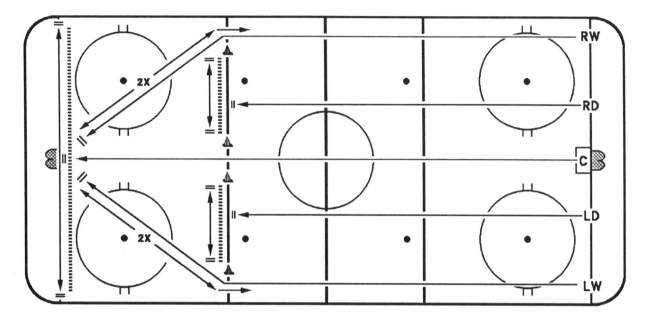

10. Forward and Backward

Players skate forward; on the whistle, they skate backward. Have them turn the opposite way each time in order to practice the movement in both directions.

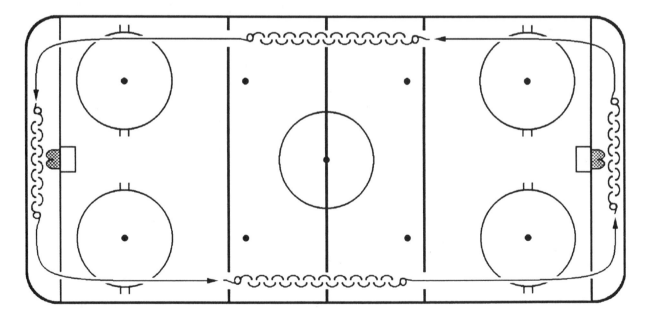

11. Skating Agility Variation
This drill is done the same as 9, except the players skate around the outside of the rink and change directions at the blue lines.

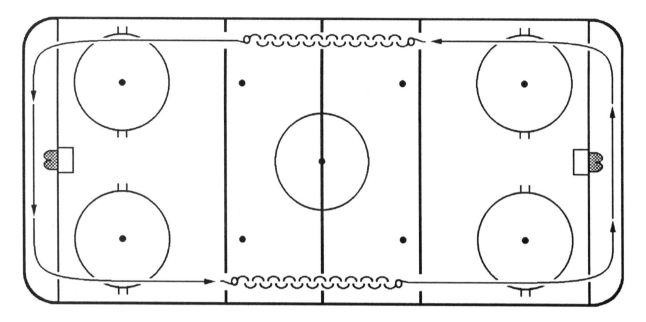

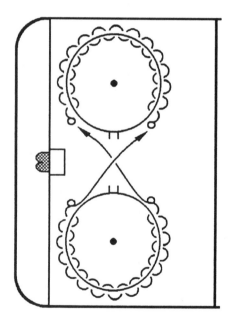

12. Circles
Players skate backward around the circles and forward between the circles.

13. Between the Blue Lines (not shown)
Players skate forward straight up and down the rink, skating backward between the blue lines.

14. Turns Between the Blue Lines (not shown)
Players skate around the rink doing 360-degree turns, as many as they can, between the blue lines.

AGILITY DRILLS

1. Wave Drill

On the coach's hand signals, players move forward, backward, and sideways, keeping their heads up and staying up on toes.

2. Shadow Drill (not shown)

Players work with partners. One player skates forward, the other backward. The offensive player moves and the defensive player must react to the offensive player.

3. Lateral Drill

Players skate backward, moving laterally side to side across the ice.

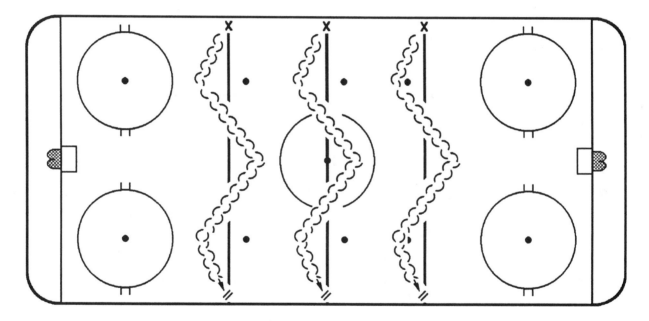

4. Knee Drops (not shown)

Players skate around the rink, and at the red and blue lines they drop down on both knees and quickly recover. Then they skate around the rink, and at the red and blue lines they drop down on one knee and recover (alternate knee each time).

6. PASSING AND RECEIVING

STICKHANDLING AND PUCK CONTROL

CHOOSING A STICK
It is very important that each of your players choose a stick that feels right and is correct for his skating and puckhandling style. The thickness of the shaft varies from manufacturer to manufacturer. Be sure each player picks one that allows him to close his hands completely around it.

LENGTH OF STICK
The length of the stick varies with the individual. In general, the stick should reach the player's chin in shoes and the player's collarbone on skates. The style of skating is also a very important consideration in choosing a stick, as some players skate with the upper body in a more upright position than others.

LIE OF STICK
Lies of sticks normally range from four to seven, with five and six being the most common. The player's skating style is important. More upper body lean means a lower lie stick is appropriate and less upper body lean means a higher lie stick. A test for the proper lie of a stick is to have players stand at a normal stance with the stick on the ice in front of them. If the heel of the blade is off the ice, a higher lie should be used. If the toe of the blade is off the ice, a lower lie should be used. When a player is skating, check if the heel or toe of the stick is off the ice. If so, the stick has the incorrect lie.

WEIGHT OF THE STICK
The stick should feel comfortable to the player, as each individual has a different preference. As a general rule, the stick should be stiff but not whippy. Bigger, stronger players often need longer, heavier sticks.

CURVED STICK
Young boys should not use a curved stick. Some stick manufacturers have reintroduced the straight blade stick. When all passing, stickhandling, and shooting fundamentals have been mastered, older boys should be allowed to experiment with a curved blade. The curve is measured by the distance of a perpendicular line measured from a straight line drawn from any point of the heel to the end of the blade.

The rules for most leagues state that the curve should be no greater than half an inch. All instructors and coaches should be alert to pick out boys who are having difficulty with passing, stickhandling, or shooting. A curved stick may be one of the reasons for these problems. Backhand passing and shooting are the skills most affected by the curved stick.

TAPING THE KNOB OF THE STICK
Taping the knob depends on the grip and feel desired by the player. If his upper hand is on or over the end of the stick, the knob is usually smaller. If his upper hand does not reach the end but rests against the knob, larger amounts of tape are usually used. White tape (as opposed to black friction tape) should be used on the knob to prevent the glove palm from deteriorating.

TAPING THE BLADE OF THE STICK
Taping the blade is usually a matter of choice. Some players now use little or no tape on the blade. Generally, the stick is taped from heel to toe without large amounts of overlap. The use of talcum powder or rubbing the blade of the stick on the bottom of a shoe is sometimes used to take the stickiness off the tape. White tape is easier to apply, adheres better, and is now preferred by many players.

PASSING AND RECEIVING

PASSING
The puck is cradled with the blade of the stick slightly over the puck. The puck should be in the center of the blade or slightly to the heel of it. The weight shift moves from the back foot to the front foot with a sweeping motion of the stick blade on the ice. Instruct your player to push with the lower hand and pull with the upper one. The puck should be released with the blade at a 90-degree angle to the direction the puck is traveling. Remind your player to lead the man and make passes quickly.

RECEIVING

To be in position to receive a pass, the player keeps the stick blade on the ice or just slightly off. The hands are tight on the stick but arms remain loose. The player should give with the blade of the stick and tilt it toward the puck. The blade of the stick is turned to the direction the puck should go.

TYPES OF PASSING

FOREHAND SWEEP

The stick blade is on the ice, and the puck remains in contact with it until it is released. Body weight transfers from back to front leg and the follow-through is low.

BACKHAND SWEEP

The same fundamentals used in the backhand sweep are used in the forehand sweep, except the puck is moved on the backhand side. The puck begins well on the backhand side and the weight shifts from the back foot to the front foot. The backhand sweep is a more difficult pass and requires a low follow-through.

SNAP PASS

The snap pass is similar to the forehand sweep. The stick is brought back slightly from contact with the puck in a sweeping motion and snapped. It is a quick, hard pass.

FLIP PASS (SAUCER PASS)

The flip pass is used to pass over an opponent's stick. The puck spins off the stick from the heel to the toe. The puck should be approximately four to six inches off the ice and land flat in a spinning motion. It must land before the receiver's stick. Players should lead the receiver more than usual, as the pass is slower.

DROP PASS

To make a drop pass, the offensive player skates in front of the defensive player and drops the puck to his trailing teammate. The puck is dropped from the forehand or backhand position but is not passed back, as this allows the trailer to skate into the puck.

BACK PASS

This pass differs from the drop pass because the puck is passed back to a teammate. The puck can be passed back from the forehand or backhand side. The trailing teammate is usually 10 to 15 feet behind.

BOARD PASS

The board pass is used by defensemen behind the net or by any player attempting to pass by a defensive man with a teammate slipping behind. The pass should be low and not too hard, so the rebound will be easy to handle. As the puck rebounds, the angle of incidence equals the angle of reflection.

BANK PASS

This pass is used by a forward driving down the boards in the offensive zone. The forward bounces the puck back off the boards to a trailing player or passes off the boards to another defenseman behind the net (a defense reverse). The pass is executed by bouncing the puck off the boards backward to be picked up by a trailing player. The puck is kept on the ice and is at a sharp angle without being passed too hard.

ONE TOUCH PASS

The player redirects a pass without stopping or cradling the puck.

TYPES OF RECEIVING

OFF SKATES

The weight is put on the nonreceiving skate. The blade of the receiving skate is turned with the toe pointing slightly in. The puck is deflected up to the blade of the stick.

IN THE AIR

The player should attempt to knock down a low pass in the air with the blade of his stick in a downward slapping motion. He should attempt to bunt down a pass high in the air with his glove or body.

TOO FAR AHEAD

The arms are extended completely and the stick is extended in one hand. A player may go down on one knee and extend the stick flat on the ice if the puck is coming from behind at an angle.

OFF THE BOARDS

If no defensive man is in the area, the player should start skating and pick up the puck while moving. Otherwise, he must stop and/or deflect the puck with the back skate onto the blade of the stick.

PASSING DRILLS

1. Stationary
In a stationary position, players pass a puck with a partner across the ice. They lengthen the distance of the passes in stages. Players pass over a stick for flip passes.

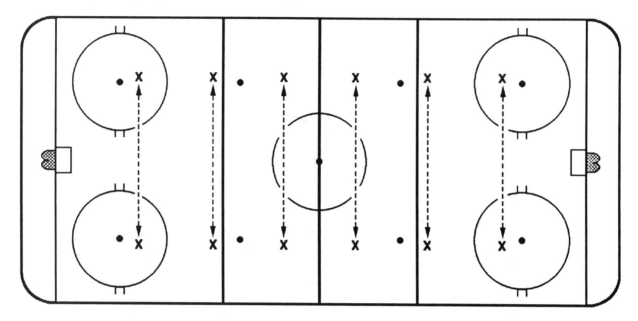

2. Circles
Players pass in circles, across and around. This drill is the same as 1 except the passing player follows the pass and replaces the receiver in his line.

3. Interceptor (not shown)
Players pass in a circle with one man in the center attempting to intercept the passes.

4. Pepper Passing
Players keep the puck moving as quickly as possible.

5. Pairs
Players pass in pairs around the ice using both forehand and backhand passes.
Variation: Players pass in pairs around the ice deliberately aiming passes at the skates.

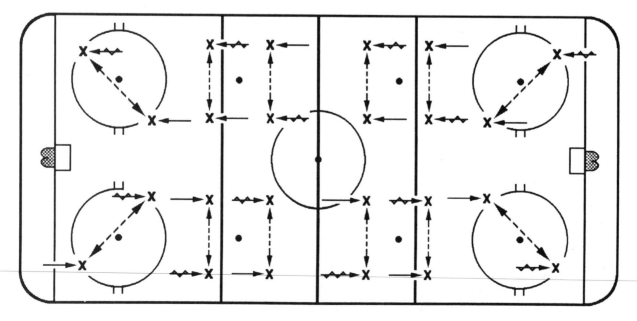

6. Two Pairs Passing

Players pass in pairs down the ice. They stop at the far end and return in the opposite direction when the drill is completed. Forehand passes then progress to backhand passes.

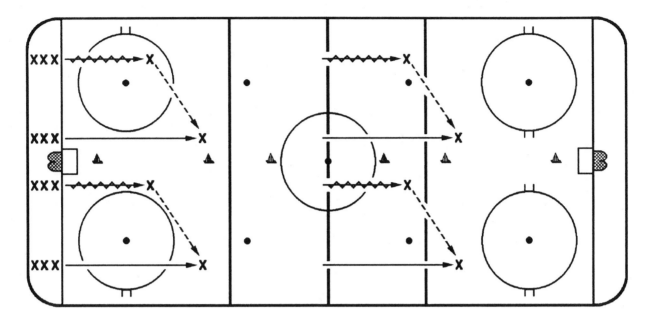

7. Two Pairs Passing Variation

This drill is the same as 6 except the pylons are put in a line between the two passing players.

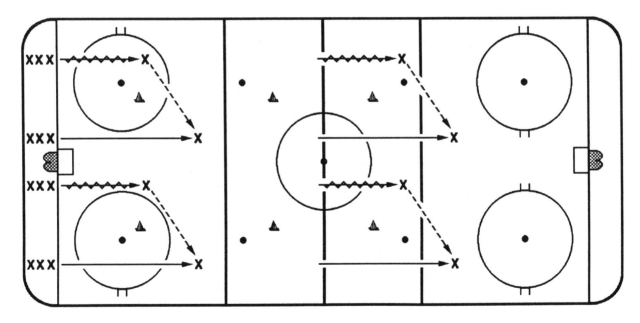

8. Give-and-Go

The player with the puck passes to a stationary man who returns the pass.

   Variation: Two players start at the X2 position. After X2 returns the pass to X1, he joins the back of the X1 line. X2, who shot on goal, returns to the X2 position.

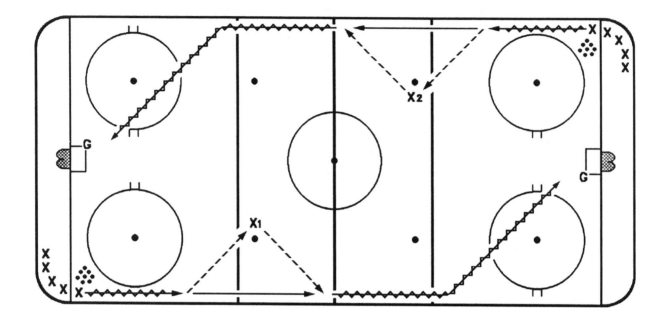

9. Two-on-None

This two-on-none passing drill works in both directions.

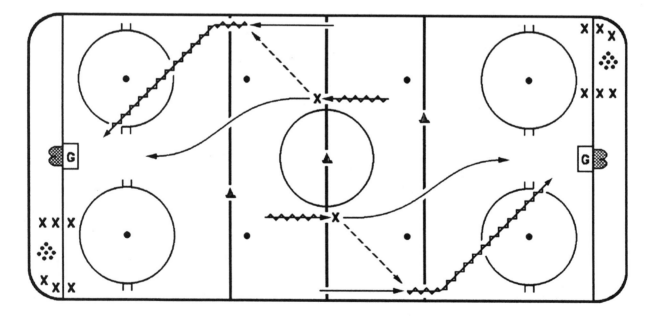

10. Wide Ice

This two-on-none drill works in both directions. This is a variation of 8 in which only one group must wait until the two-on-none is finished from the other direction. Passes are longer and more accuracy is required than in 8.

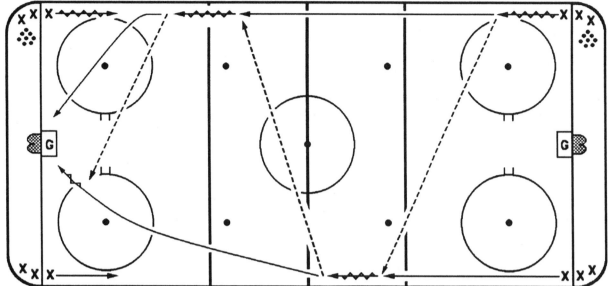

11. Defense Behind the Net

This drill is the same as 10 except a defenseman starts the two-on-one from behind the net and passes to the forward. The defensemen operate out of both ends. The defenseman who starts the play goes to the blue line, stops, and skates backward to the goal line.

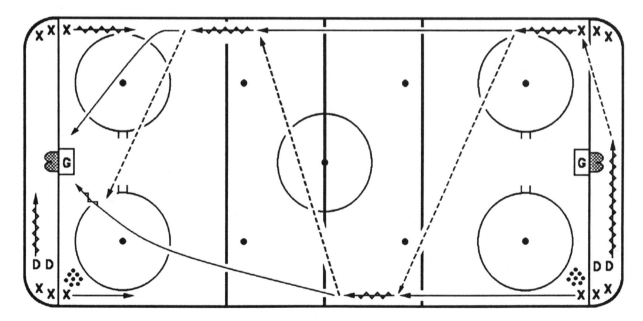

12. Three-on-None in Both Directions

Groups of three, passing one puck between them, spread out after passing center ice.

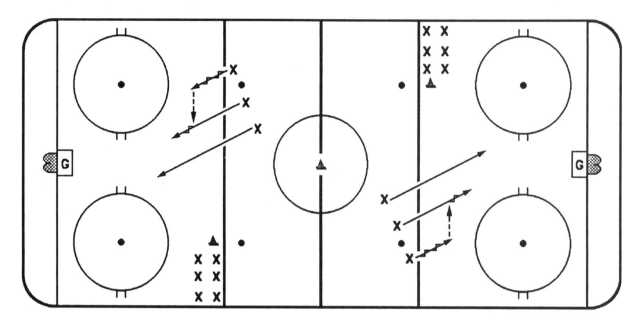

13. Passing Off the Boards

The player skates the length of the ice passing off the boards and receiving his own pass back.

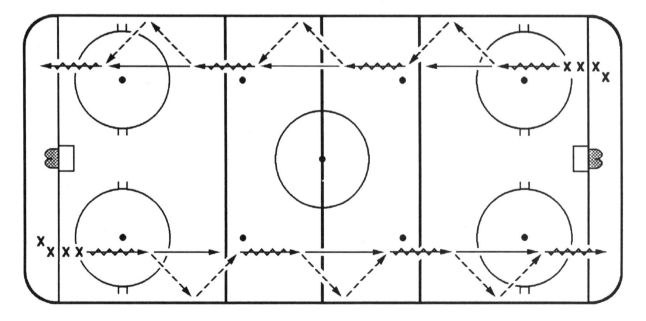

14. Pairs

In this drill players pass off the boards working in pairs. Two players alternate passing off boards and receiving the pass.

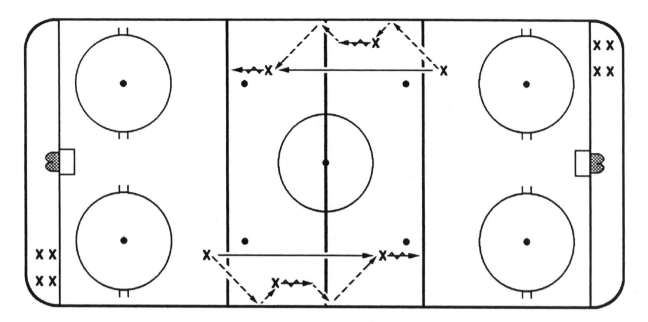

15. Keep Away

Skaters play keep away using the three zones of the rink, with three to four players on a team.

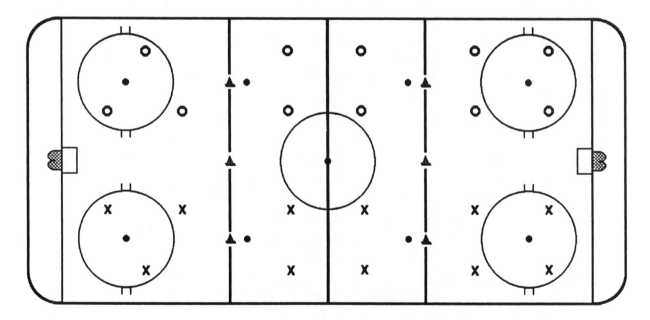

Additionally, all two-on-one, three-on-one, and three-on-two team play drills involve passing and receiving.

7. SHOOTING

Accuracy and getting the shot away quickly are key factors in goal scoring. The speed and power of the shot depend on the strength, mechanics, and coordination of the shooting movement. Note the following shooting principles.

- The puck should be placed in the middle to the heel of the blade. Any deviation from this position will result in a loss of power and accuracy.
- The base of support (i.e., the relationship of the puck and the skates) is very important in obtaining maximum velocity in shooting. Shooting should be performed at the base of support between the two skates. The puck should be released at a 90-degree angle to the intended direction.
- The lower arm provides the pushing action while the upper arm provides the pulling motion. Upper body rotation is very important in shooting. Strength in the arms, shoulders, and wrists is essential in shooting.
- Getting the shot away quickly is important, and therefore a player should be able to shoot the puck off either foot.
- The follow-through should be toward the net and the shooter should be ready for any rebound and maintain balance to receive a possible body check.
- In shooting, the force exerted on the stick is downward and forward, throwing the puck forward.

TYPES OF SHOOTING

FOREHAND
- The lower hand is a comfortable distance from the upper hand (usually 12 to 18 inches apart).
- The puck is brought back to the side and opposite or slightly behind the rear skate.
- The body is at a 45-degree angle to the direction of the puck.
- The puck is in the middle to the heel of the blade of the stick, which is slightly cupped.
- The lower wrist is extended and the upper wrist is flexed.
- The puck comes forward in a sweeping motion.
- The weight shifts from the rear foot to the front foot, and the puck is released from the front skate at a 90-degree angle to its intended direction.
- The arms extend, the upper body rotates quickly, the lower wrist flexes, and the upper wrist extends.
- The turning of the stick blade follow-through determines the height of the shot. If the blade is turned over the puck, the shot is low. If the blade is turned under the puck, the shot is high.
- Balance should be maintained at all times to receive a possible body check.

BACKHAND
The backhand shot is often neglected because players tend to use the curved stick. The shot is valuable coming off a shift to the backhand side and cutting toward the net. The shooting principles for the backhand shot are similar to those for the forehand shot, and the follow-through is important.
- The puck is drawn to the backhand side and the lower wrist is in a reversed or flexed position.
- The weight shift is from back to front foot.
- The upper body rotates quickly, and the lower wrist extends.

SNAP
The snap shot is a valuable shot, as it is quick and accurate from 30 feet away.
- The stick blade is at a 90-degree angle to the desired direction of the puck, and the puck is cupped in the middle of the stick blade.
- The stick is drawn back about one inch from the puck.
- The wrists are extended and flexed when the stick blade hits the puck. The follow-through is short.

SLAP
The slap shot should be developed after the forehand and snap shots have been mastered. The slap shot is valuable because the puck can be shot at a greater speed from a greater distance. Accuracy and quickness of release are sacrificed for velocity.

- The body is parallel to the desired direction of the puck and the puck is close to the heel of the skate.
- The lower hand is shifted down the shaft of the stick until fully extended.
- The stick is drawn backward to shoulder height with the lower arm rigid and the eyes focused on the puck.
- On the downswing, the weight shifts from the back leg to the front leg.
- The stick contacts the ice just before it hits the puck, usually one-half to one inch from the puck. The puck is struck at the middle of the blade.
- The wrist moves from extension to flexion, and pressure is exerted downward on the ice as contact is made with the puck.

FLIP

The flip shot is used to get the puck up in the air quickly when clearing the puck from the defensive zone, lifting the puck over a fallen goaltender, or flipping the puck into the offensive end.

- The lower hand is moved further down the blade than usual.
- The blade of the stick is open, the puck is lifted in a scooping motion, and the follow-through is high.
- The flip shot can be executed with a forehand or backhand motion.

TIP-INS

Many goals are scored by a player changing the direction of a shot using the blade of the stick. It is important to get in a good scoring position for a tip-in, in order to prevent the opposition defenseman from tying the player up. The forward should attempt to block the goaltender's vision by moving in front of the goal crease.

- The player should keep his feet in an open stance to avoid being knocked down by opponents. He should angle the blade of the stick down to deflect the puck downward and angle the blade of the stick upward to deflect the puck upward.
- The player must keep a tight grip on the stick for all deflections and maintain a low balance stance.

SHOOTING OFF EITHER FOOT

Players should be able to shoot the puck off either foot in order to get the shot off quickly. The shot is used to execute a quick shot. All good goal scorers are able to shoot the puck off either foot as in many cases there is no time to relocate the footing when receiving the puck in a shooting position.

- The weight is on the foot nearest the puck.
- The speed of the shot comes from the arm, wrist, and shoulder action, with little or no body rotation.
- The follow-through is short, as the player is not in a stable position and is vulnerable to a body check.

ONE-TIMER

The ability to take a pass and shoot in one motion when receiving a pass is a skill that top scorers have. The blade of the stick is lifted off the ice and is brought forward as the pass is received out in front of the base of support similar to the skills of a slap shot with a short back swing.

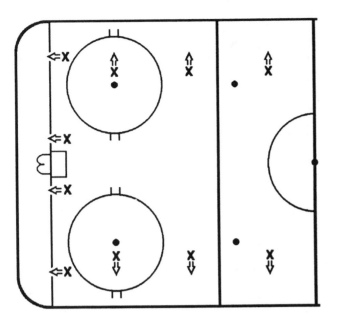

SHOOTING DRILLS
1. Against the Boards Stationary
Combination drills may be executed combining many types of shooting drills using the entire ice surface whenever possible. Have players rotate from group to group. Be innovative. Shoot against the boards in a stationary position. Have them shoot 10 high shots, 10 low shots, then alternate high and low shots. Mark the low and high spots on the boards and have the players shoot for the marks. Use half-ice or full ice.

2. Moving from the Middle
Players shoot against the boards from a moving position, working from the center of the ice. Use half-ice or full ice.

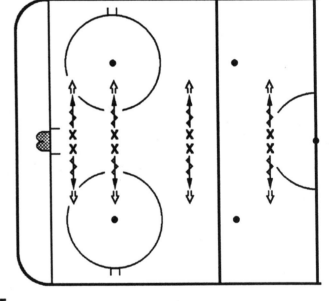

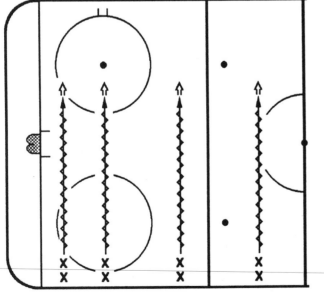

3. Moving Across the Ice
Players shoot against boards starting from one side and moving to the other side. For large numbers, divide players into two groups. Use half-ice or full ice.

4. Skating the Length of the Ice

Divide the players into two groups. Players skate the length of the ice and shoot on the goaltender from the slot area. The shot area can be marked by pylons on the ice. Have players switch sides halfway through the drill. The drill can be varied with the give-and-go drill.

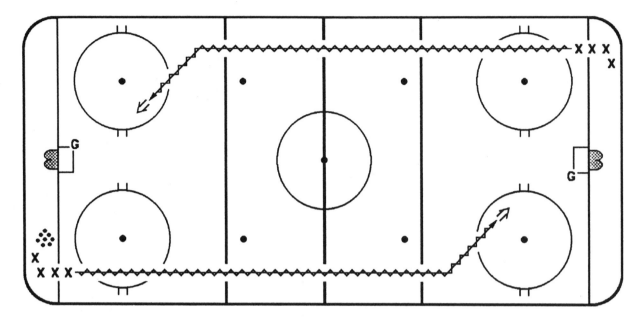

5. Around the Pylons

This drill is the same as 4 except players cut around pylons and shoot. This drill can be varied with the give-and-go drill.

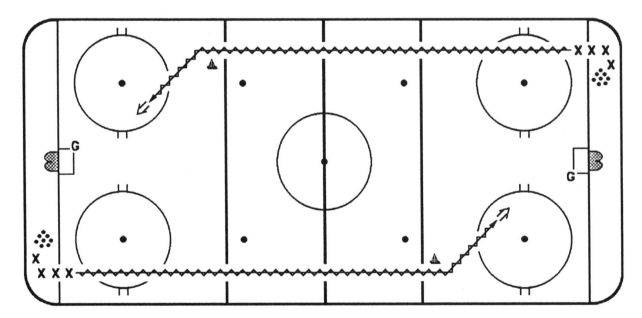

6. One-Way Shooting

Divide the players in half in two corners at the same end of the rink. Have players alternate shooting from the right and left side. This drill can be useful if only one goaltender is available for practice. Players should shoot from both sides. The drill can be varied using pylons and the give-and-go drill.

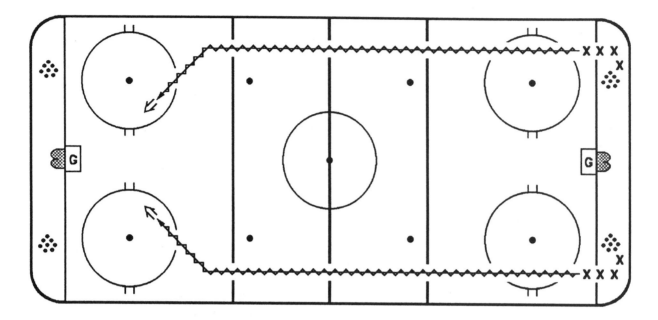

7. Cross-Ice Pass and Shoot

Players start at the same time from opposite corners, each carrying a puck. Between the blue lines, each player passes the puck to another player, continues, and shoots after receiving the pass. The players move to the opposite corner after shooting.

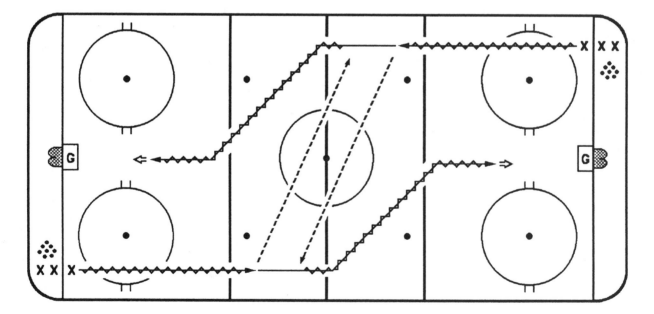

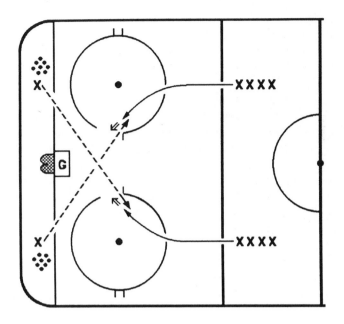

8. Pass Out Shooting
A player in each corner passes the puck alternately to the players skating in on goal. Players should follow the puck after shooting and go for a second shot if a rebound comes out.

9. Pass Out Shooting Variation
In this variation on 8, after shooting the puck, the player goes to the corner the pass came from. The player passing the puck then goes to the end of the line on the same side of the rink.

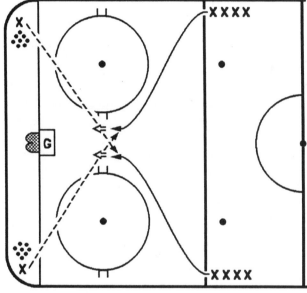

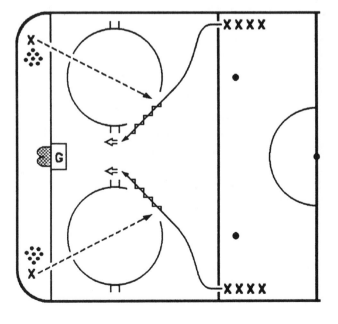

10. Pass Out Shooting Variation
This drill is a variation of 8 in which the pass comes from the same side instead of from the opposite side. The player goes to the corner from which he received the pass.

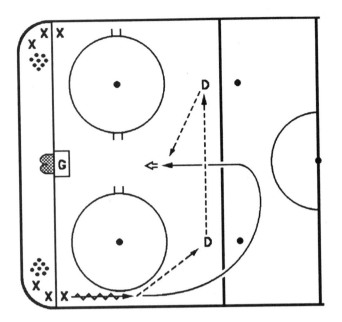

11. Defenseman to Defenseman

A player skates from the corner and passes to the nearest defenseman. The defenseman passes the puck to the other defenseman, and then back to the forward. The forward then goes in, shoots to the goaltender, and moves to the other corner. The next forward up moves from the other corner. The defensemen stay in the same positions for this drill.

12. Defenseman to Defenseman Variation

The pass goes from X1 to X2 and then to X3, who goes to the line in the corner after a shot on goal while X2 goes to the position of X1. X1 goes to the shooting line. This drill differs from 11 because all players rotate, playing all positions.

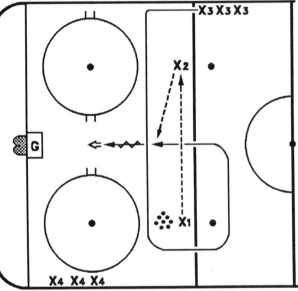

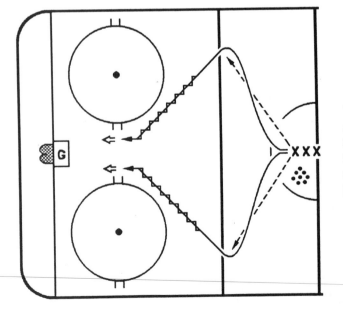

13. From Center Ice

A player receives a pass from the center, cuts in, and shoots from the wing. The puck is returned to the center. The next player swings to the opposite side and receives a pass from the next player in line.

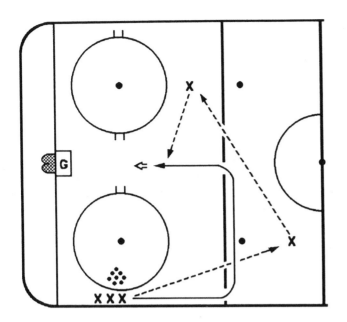

14. Pass, Return Pass, and Shoot

The player skates from the corner and passes the puck to one stationary man, who passes to the other stationary man, and then a return pass is made to the forward.

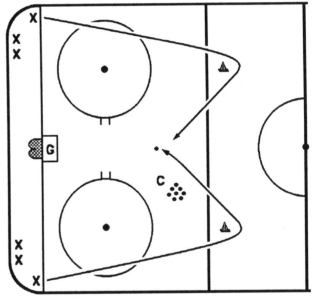

15. Race for the Puck and Shoot

Players must start at the same time. They round the pylons, and the first player then shoots on net while the other player tries to check him.

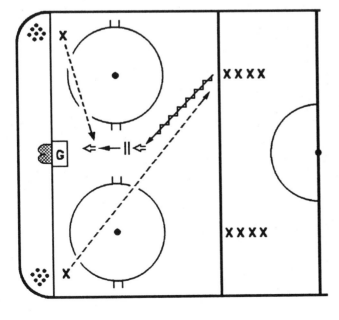

16. Pass Out Variation

After the player has taken the first shot, he stops in the high slot, receives a second pass out from the opposite corner, and then shoots again.

Variation: X moves while trying to take a second shot.

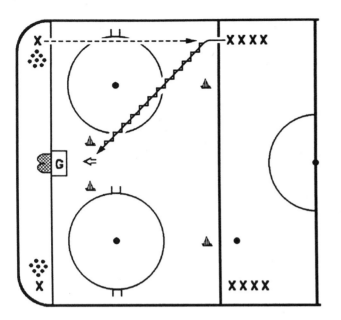

17. Backhand Drill

This drill is the same as 16 except the pass comes early from the corner, and the player cuts around a pylon and shoots from his backhand side from the slot area.

18. Rebound Drill

This is another variation of 16. A player from the opposite line trails the shooter and picks up and shoots any rebound. Alternate the shooter and the rebounder each time.

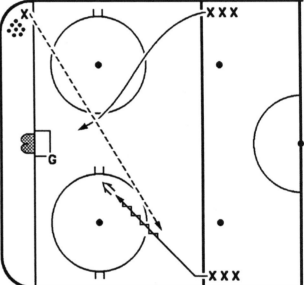

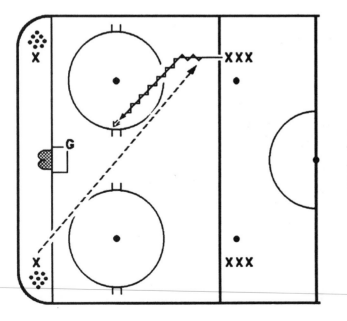

19. Along the Ice Drill

This is another variation of 16. In this drill the goaltender is without a stick and all shots are along the ice.

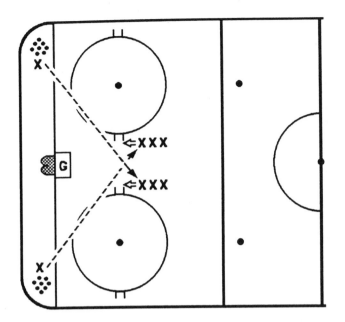

20. Stationary Pass Out Drill

Players are stationary in the slot and shoot as soon as the puck is passed out. Alternate their pass outs.

Variation: Players pass from one corner and shoot, then pass from the other corner and shoot.

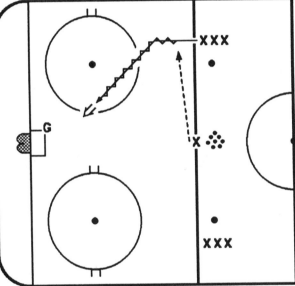

21. Pass Across Drills

Drills 7 through 11 can be performed with passes coming across instead of from the corner.

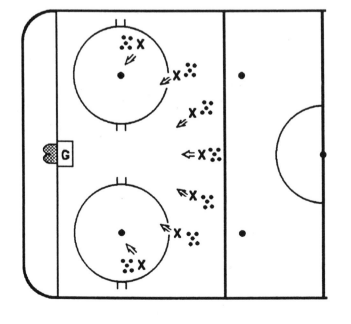

22. Semicircle Drill

The players are stationary in a semicircle starting from the blue line. The players shoot in rapid succession. After each player has shot one puck, he retrieves it and moves in five feet, using wrist shots only.

Variation: Players shoot alternately rather than in succession (left side, right side, next left, and so on).

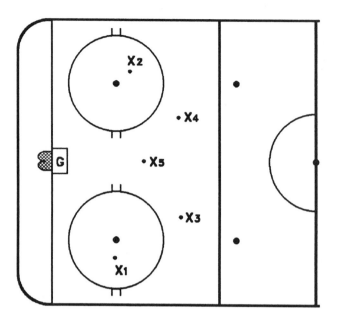

23. Shoot by Numbers
Each player has a puck, and shots are from different angles. The players shoot by numbers in order. The goaltender should know the order as well. Move players into different positions to create new angles.

24. To the Slot
Pucks are passed from different angles with the last shot chased by a checker. Rotate positions.

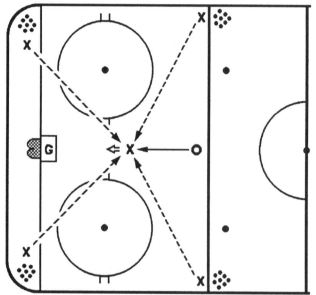

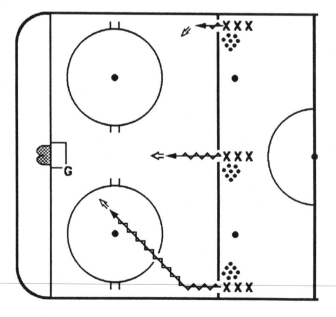

25. Three-Line Shooting Drill
The players form three lines and move with a puck simultaneously. One winger shoots from the blue line, the center shoots from the high slot straight out from the goal, and the other winger shoots from an angle at the bottom of the circle. The players alternate lines. Halfway through the drill, the long shots come from the opposite side.

26. Moving Slot Drill

The center skates to the center line and passes to the winger. The winger moves down the boards and passes the puck back to the center (after he passes the pylon), who then shoots from the slot area, one-timing it (shooting without stopping). The forwards alternate positions of the center and wing. Work with the center and one winger alternating from one side to the other.

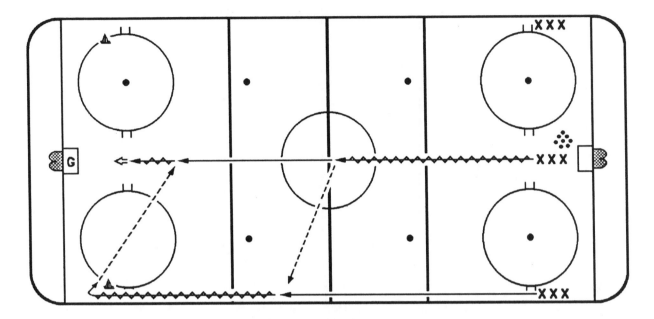

27. Chase the Rabbit

In this drill on shooting under pressure, the puck carrier says "go," skates the length of the ice outside the pylon, and shoots with the checker starting two steps behind him and on the inside of the pylon.

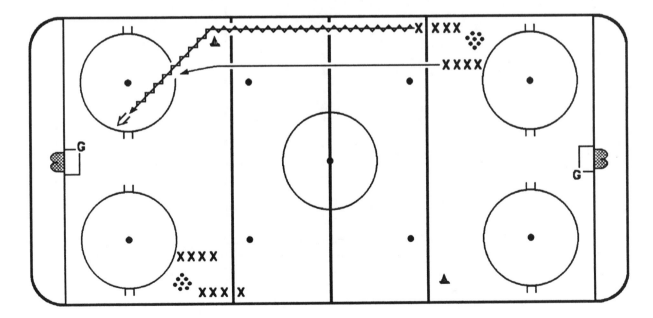

28. Shooting Under Pressure

In this variation of 27, the shooter receives a pass from center ice.

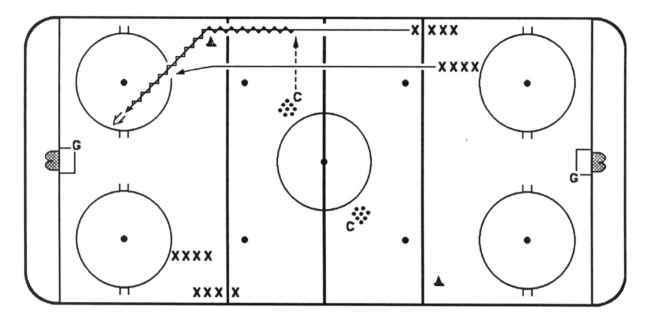

29. Shoot and Chase

The player skates the length of the ice, shoots, and then chases the player coming from the side as he skates the length of the ice and shoots. Players work both sides of the ice.

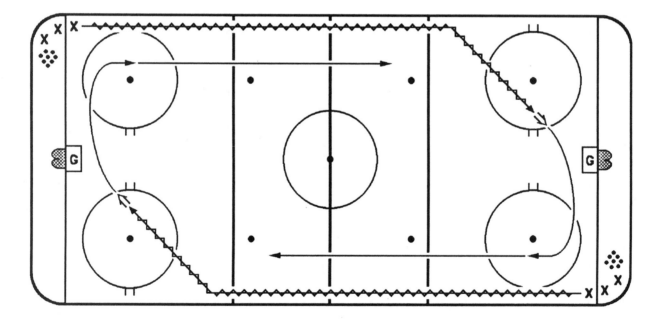

30. Shooting Under Pressure Variation

The player skates from the corner with the puck, cuts around the pylon, and shoots. As soon as the puck carrier hits the far blue line, the checker from the opposite side cuts across and attempts to stop the player from shooting.

Variation: A pass is made from the neutral zone to the player coming up the ice.

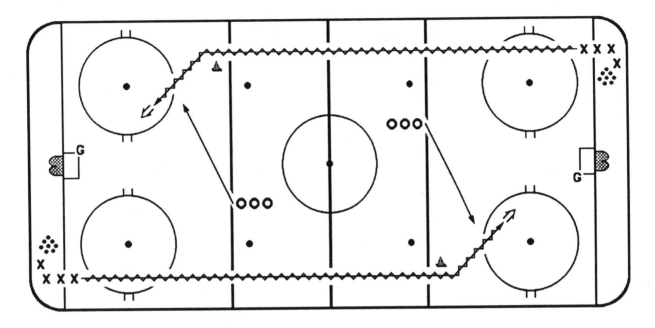

31. Continuous Shooting Drill

The player skates down one side, cuts around the pylon, shoots, goes for the rebound, turns, receives a pass going in the opposite direction, skates down the center of the ice, and shoots. The shooter works the drill from both directions.

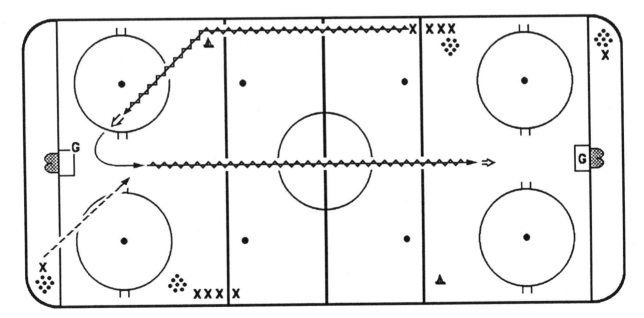

32. Group Shooting Drill

The first player in group 1 skates diagonally across the ice, receives a pass from the first player in group 2, skates around the pylon, and shoots on goal. Group 1 player moves to group 4, and group 2 player moves to group 3. The type of shot can be predetermined. Players work the drill from both directions.

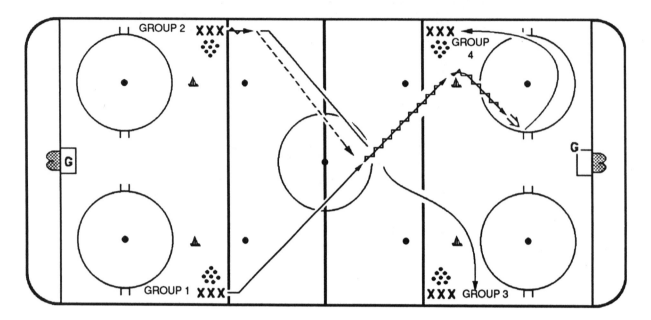

33. Horseshoe Drill

The player passes the puck to a player who has come from the other side of the rink and skated around the center circle. The player receiving the puck goes in for the shot. After passing the puck, the player skates around the circle and receives a pass from the other side. The players return to the same side they started on.

Variation: Have two men starting together for a two-on-none. Then progress to three men starting at the same time to create a three-on-none.

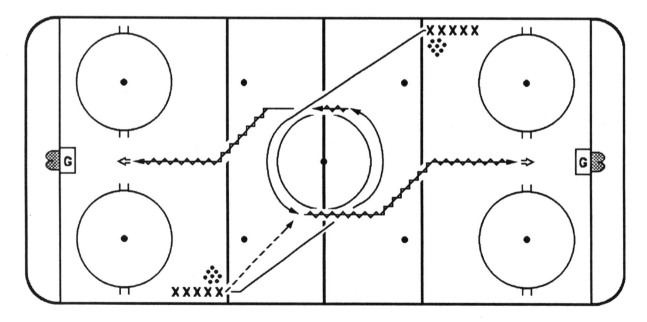

34. Horseshoe Variation

The puck is passed from corner to corner and then passed to the player skating around the center circle from the other end. The player receiving the pass then goes in and shoots. The players rotate, following the puck. After shooting, the player returns to the corner where he started.

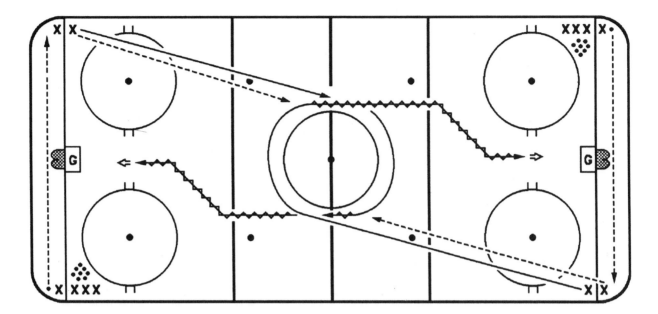

35. Horseshoe Variation

This is a variation of 33. After taking the pass, the player skates backward to the blue line, turns, skates forward, and shoots at the net.

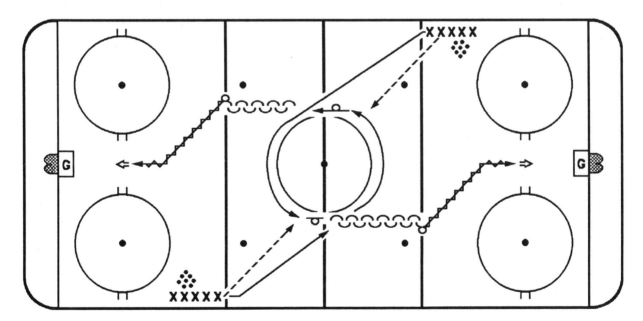

36. Horseshoe Variation

In this variation of 33, the puck is passed from the forward to the defenseman, then from defenseman to defenseman, and back to the forward, who then goes in and shoots on the goal. The forward returns to the same line he started in.

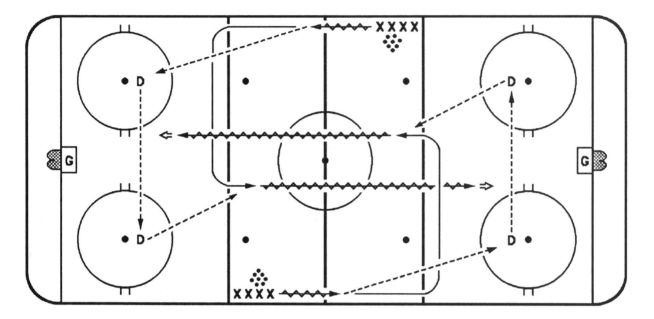

37. Shoot and Pass

The player skates in on the net, takes a pass from the preceding player, picks up a puck in the corner, and passes the puck across to the next shooter. A pylon may be added for the player to skate around before shooting.

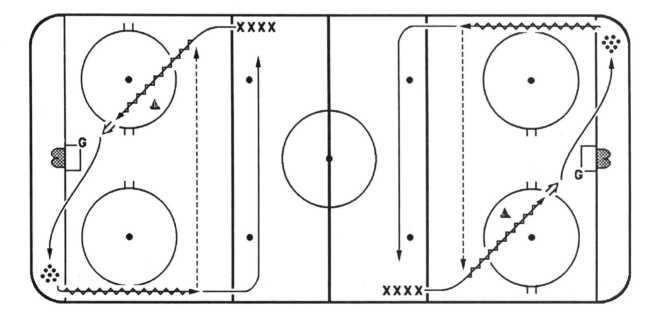

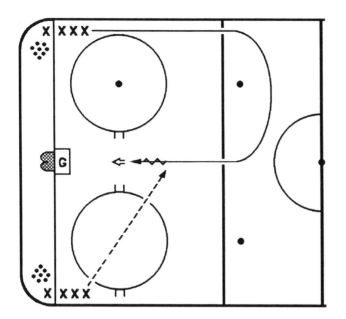

38. Out of the Corners

The player shooting the puck comes out of one corner, cuts in the middle of the ice at the blue line, receives a pass from the opposite corner, and proceeds to shoot on the goaltender. The player passing the puck then becomes the next shooter and receives a pass from a player in the opposite corner.

39. Tip-in Drill

Tip-ins should be executed from a stationary and moving position and from the short or long side. The drill can be run faster by having the defensemen shooting directly from the blue line without receiving a pass out. All shots should be on the ice or low.

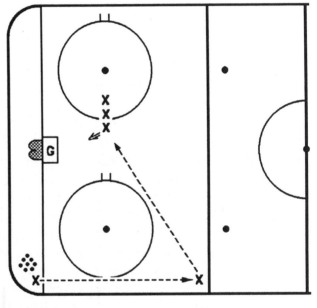

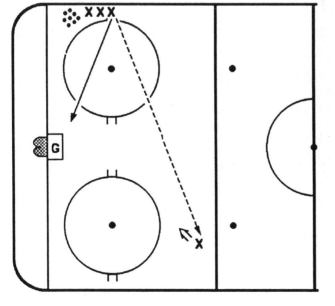

40. Tip-in Variation

Player passes the puck from the far side and moves for the tip-in.

41. Tip-in Drills for Young Players

Much time can be wasted with young players when they attempt to tip-in pucks shot inaccurately from the blue line. A variation for tip-in drills can be worked in pairs with one player shooting the puck at the boards and the other player tipping the puck to the boards at certain spots. The shooter should be 15 feet away from the tipper. They should change positions every few shots and tip from both sides.

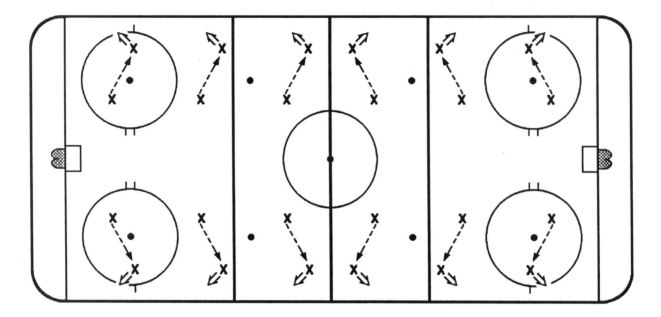

42. Flip Shot Drill from Defensive End

Players skate around the net and flip the shot high in the air down the ice. They should try not to let the puck go over the goal line. This drill may be executed from the backhand and forehand side.

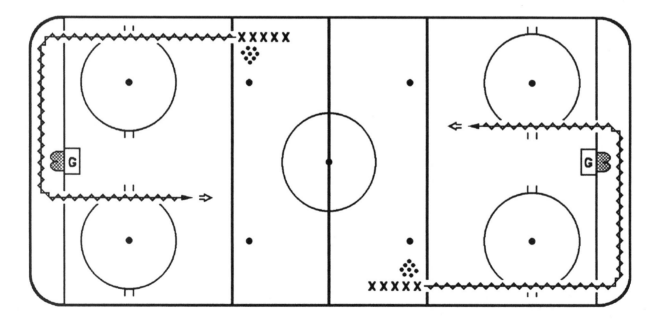

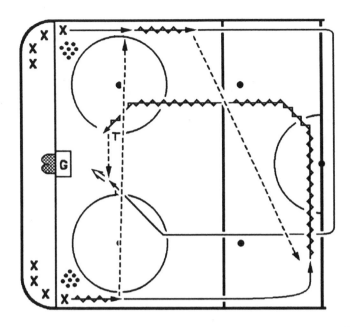

43. Two-on-None from the Corners
Players skate from two corners, pass the puck diagonally across, turn, and work a two-on-none. The players return to the opposite corners.

44. Two-on-None Behind the Net
The puck is passed to the player at the blue line. The forward goes behind the net and receives a return pass for the two-on-none.

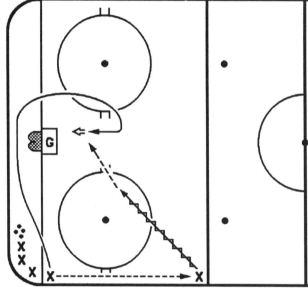

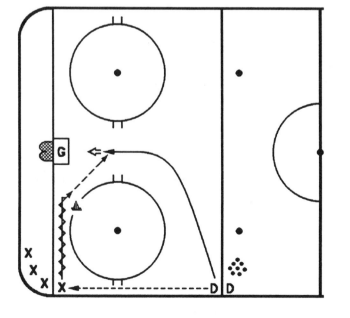

45. Defenseman Breaks to the Net
The defenseman passes the puck to the forward. The forward then skates around the pylon and passes to the breaking defenseman for a shot on goal.

46. Flip Shot Drill for Shooting in the Offensive End

Players skate to center ice and flip the shot into the offensive end toward the goal or in the corner.

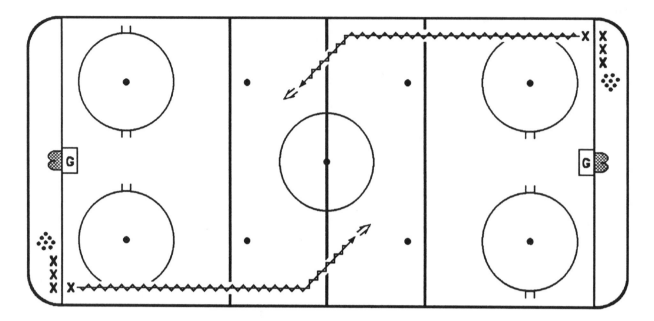

47. Horseshoe Rebound Drill

The first player shoots and goes to the corner. The second player follows for a rebound and then turns and takes a pass. He skates to the other end and shoots. The person giving the pass follows the shooter for the rebound, turns and takes a pass, and skates to the other end and shoots.

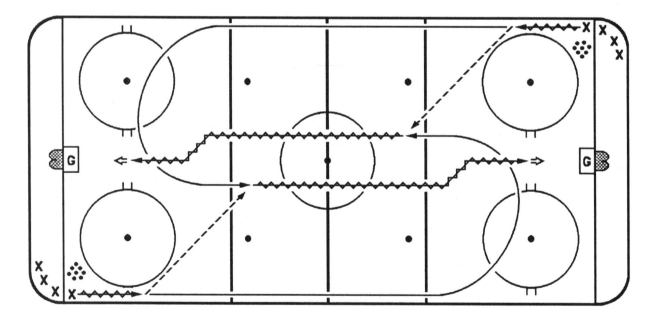

8. STICKHANDLING AND PUCK CONTROL

Stickhandling is important for a one-on-one, for maneuvering at close quarters, or when playing close in on a goaltender. The puck is passed whenever possible, and stickhandling should not be used in open ice or on a breakaway. Players should remember the following points whenever practicing stickhandling and puck control:

- Keep your head up. Your peripheral vision allows you to keep the puck in view.
- Cup the puck in the center of the blade, cushioning it while you stickhandle. Be sure to roll your wrists.
- Slide the blade of the stick along the ice but do not bang it. There should be little or no noise created by the stick's hitting the ice.
- Try not to shift your lower hand down, as it will tip off the opposition that you are about to change to a shooting position.

BASIC STICKHANDLING TECHNIQUES

SIDE-TO-SIDE STICKHANDLING
Stickhandling should be done with the puck in front of the body. The puck should be moved from side to side, from forehand to backhand. The skater's weight is over the top of the puck. That is, if the puck is off to his right, then his body weight should be to the right. The same goes for the other side.

BACK-TO-FRONT STICKHANDLING
This is the same as side-to-side stickhandling except that the puck is moved off to the side of the body.

BACKWARD STICKHANDLING
This is the same as side-to-side and back-to-front stickhandling except the skater is skating backward. The puck must be drawn toward the body in the side-to-side action, or the player will lose control of it. This is an essential skill for the defensemen. The head must be kept up.

STICKHANDLING WHILE CUTTING IN
The player should keep his feet moving when turning and try to eliminate gliding.

DRILLS FOR STATIONARY AND MOVING STICKHANDLING

1. Stationary Stickhandling (not shown)
Direct the team into three lines, each 10 feet apart. Have the players watch the coach's hand. If his arm is straight up, they stickhandle in front. If his arm is to one side, they stickhandle to that side.

2. Stickhandling While Moving (not shown)
Divide the players into three lines, each 10 feet apart. Have them stickhandle down the ice at half speed. This is a puck control drill, and skating speed is not essential.

3. Stickhandling While Stationary and Moving (not shown)
Players start stickhandling while stationary, and then they move on the instructor's command at half speed. They stop on command and continue stickhandling in a stationary position. Then they repeat these movements for the length of the ice.

4. Stickhandling Around the Rink (not shown)
Players skate around the rink in one direction outside the pylons. They change direction halfway through the drill.

5. Stickhandle and Breakaway (not shown)
Players stickhandle to the red line and then push the puck to the goal line, eliminating stickhandling in open ice.

6. Stickhandling in Both Directions (not shown)
Two groups skate in opposite directions. The players must keep their heads up to avoid collisions.

7. Stickhandling in All Directions (not shown)
All the players have pucks and stickhandle in all directions. You may divide them into three groups, divide the ice into three areas, and have each group keep the puck in a separate area.

8. Backward Stickhandling (not shown)

Players perform drills 1 through 7 while stickhandling backward.

9. Forward-Backward Stickhandling (not shown)

Players skate forward while stickhandling and then stop and stickhandle while stationary. Then they skate backward while stickhandling. Use a whistle or a verbal command to signal them to change direction. This drill can be done in lines across the ice or while the whole group is skating around the ice.

10. Forward-Backward Stickhandling (not shown)

Players stickhandle forward to the red line, backward to the blue line, forward to the far blue line, backward to the red line, and forward to the end of the rink.

11. Stickhandling Changing Direction

Set pylons in a straight line, with four pylons in each of four lines. Players skate through the pylons, first without and then with the pucks.

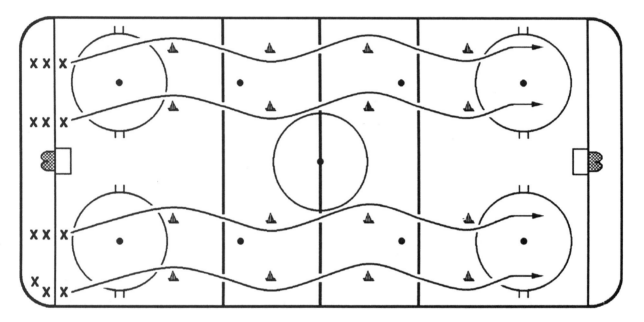

12. Stickhandling Changing Direction Variation

In this variation of 11, the player stickhandles forward to the first pylon and then stickhandles backward to the second pylon, and so on. Have each player execute the drill without a puck first.

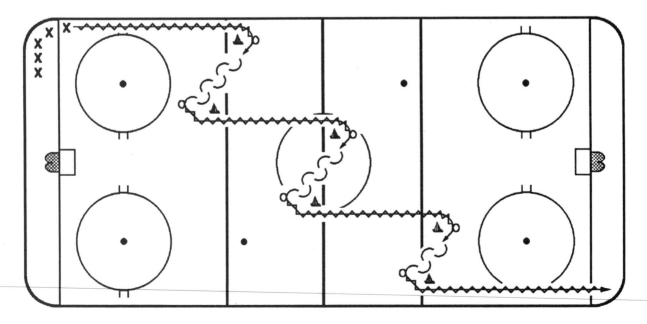

76

STICKHANDLING AROUND A PLAYER

It is important that a player knows when to stickhandle and when to pass to beat a player. Many plays are broken up by the defending team when a player attempts to stickhandle around another player instead of passing.

Generally, a player should attempt to stickhandle around a man when he does not have a teammate in a position for a pass, when the player is in close quarters and a pass cannot be made, or in a one-on-one situation with no trailing teammate. A cardinal sin in hockey is for a player to attempt to stickhandle around an opposition player in his own end of the rink or if he is the last man. He must ascertain the defender's speed and direction and whether he is sweeping his stick, looking down at the puck, off balance, or reaching slowly, as all of these positions can be taken advantage of. Discourage players from using the same move all the time (e.g., going to backhand side). Encourage them to analyze the situation and make an appropriate move. A discussion of moves for this situation follows.

FOREHAND SHIFT

The puck is shifted to the forehand side. The arms are fully extended, and the puck is brought out slightly back and away from the defender. The body is used as much as possible to protect the puck. The head is kept up. Speed is important in this move. As the skill is learned, the player should set up the move with a slight move to the backhand and/or a head-and-shoulders fake to the backhand side. As an advanced skill, the player's lower hand can hold the stick while the upper hand is used to ward off the defender.

BACKHAND SHIFT

The puck is shifted to the backhand side. The arms are extended. The body can be used to protect the puck. The head is up. The move can be set up with a fake to the forehand side.

SLIP THROUGH

The puck is pushed forward between the defender's stick and skates or between the skates. The defender should have slowed down, the stickhandler's head should be down, and a large space should be between his legs or between his stick and skates.

SLIP ACROSS

In the slip across, as opposed to the slip through, the puck travels across the forward direction instead of straight ahead. The player sets this move up by shifting to one side to get the defender to shift weight on that side. The puck is slipped across between the defender's skates and the heel of the stick. The player shifts directions and picks up the puck on the other side of the defender.

DOUBLE SLIP ACROSS

This is an advanced skill. It works the same as the slip across except the puck is slipped across a second time and ends up on the same side as the original shift.

FAKE SHOT

This shot involves a shift to backhand or forehand. An initial slap or wrist shot motion is executed. A shoulder drop or lower hand side is beneficial. The puck is then shifted to the forehand or backhand side. This move is especially useful when the defender has slowed down or stopped in his defensive zone.

SPIN AROUND (DELAY)

The player stops quickly, close to the defender. The puck is kept away from the defender on the forehand side. The player spins 180 degrees with the puck on the backhand and accelerates forward quickly or passes.

PUCK OFF BOARDS

This is used to advantage when the player is moving out of his own end and a defender, usually a defenseman, is standing still. The puck should be shot off the boards at approximately 45 degrees and at only moderate speed (the puck will come off the boards at the same angle it hits the boards: angle of incidence equals angle of reflection). The player skates around the defender on the off-board side and picks up the puck.

CHANGE OF PACE

The player skates under control at three-quarter speed. Just as he reaches the defender, the player accelerates. This move is especially useful when a defenseman is skating backward slowly and there is room for the player to move on either side.

DRILLS FOR STICKHANDLING AROUND A DEFENDER (ONE-ON-ONE)

1. Across the Ice Against a Stationary Object

First have the player practice the stickhandling move against a pylon. Next have the player practice stickhandling against a stationary player without a stick and then against one with a stick.

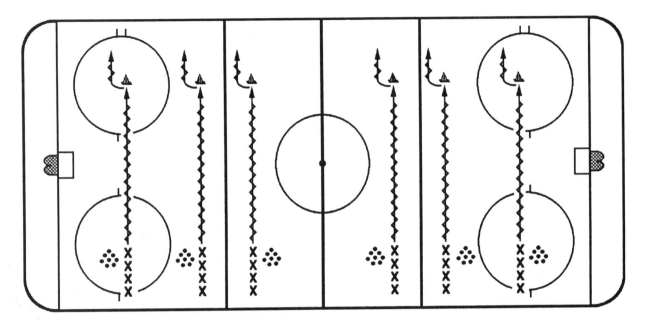

2. Across the Ice in Pairs

One player acts as an attacker and the other acts as a defender. They change positions coming back across the ice. Have them execute the drill at half speed and passively at first. This allows the player to beat the defender with a move. Then have them execute the drill at full speed. If you have a large number, divide pairs into two groups, and have one group move across the ice with the other group following.

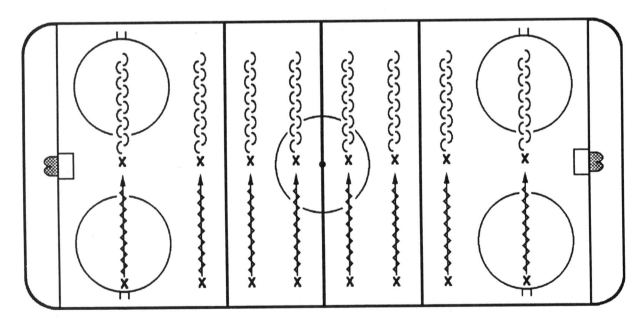

3. Both Directions

The defender is with the puck on the blue line. The offensive man is at the top of the face-off circle. The defender passes the puck to the offensive player, and the one-on-one begins. They change positions moving back in the opposite direction, with the forward acting as a defenseman and vice versa.

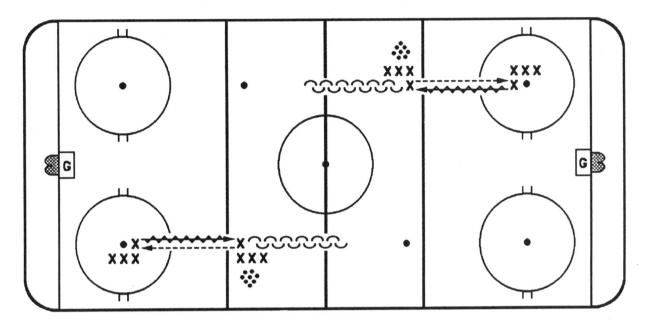

PUCK CONTROL USING THE SKATES

Controlling the puck with the skates is difficult and requires long hours of practice. Russians and other European players are highly skilled in this area and make use of soccer for carryover application of this skill. Soccer, ball hockey, lacrosse, etc., are all helpful for stickhandling and puck control. Kicking a ball on the ground is also helpful. The Europeans make great use of off-ice drills and games to develop these skills.

BETWEEN SKATES

The puck is passed from one skate to another, with the player always kicking the puck in a forward direction.

SKATE TO STICK

The puck is kicked ahead to the stick. This is practiced with both skates.

STICK TO SKATE TO STICK

The puck (in front of the body) is passed directly back to the skates and returned to the stick from the skates.

OVERSKATE THE PUCK

The player deliberately overskates the puck. He brings one skate behind the other and kicks the puck up to the other skate. This is practiced with both skates.

STICK TO BACK SKATE TO STICK

The puck is drawn back and to the side of the body and then passed back to the back skate. The puck is kicked up as in overskating the puck.

DRILLS FOR PUCK CONTROL USING SKATES

1. Slow Speed (not shown)

Players skate around the ice at slow speed practicing various skills.

2. High Speed (not shown)

Players skate around the ice at high speed practicing various skills.

3. Length of the Ice (not shown)

Players skate the length of the ice practicing skills.

4. Skate Around the Pylons (not shown)

Players skate around the pylons using only the skates to control the puck.

5. Three Groups

Divide players into three groups and divide the ice into three sections. Have three games in which the players do not use sticks. A team scores by holding the puck against the opposite side boards.

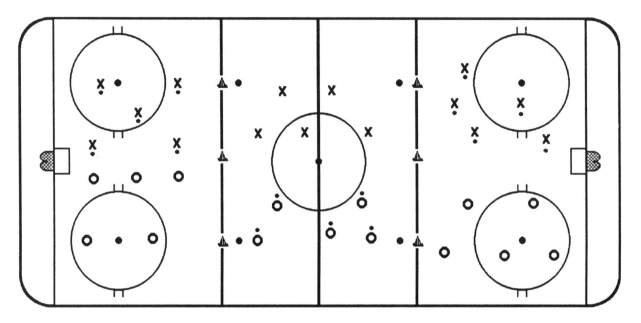

DEKING THE GOALTENDER

When a player breaks in alone on a goaltender, he must decide whether to deke the goaltender or shoot. When the goaltender is far out in the crease is an ideal time to deke the goaltender. Remind each player not to telegraph his moves by dropping his head or shoulder or slipping his lower hand down the shaft to indicate a shot. He must make his move quickly. Discuss the following types of dekes on the goaltender with players.

BACKHAND SHIFT

This was described previously. The puck is moved completely around the goaltender.

FOREHAND SHIFT

This was also described previously. The puck is moved completely around the goaltender.

HALF BACKHAND SHIFT

The puck is shifted to the backhand side and then slipped between the goaltender's legs.

HALF FOREHAND SHIFT

The puck is shifted to forehand side and then slipped between the goaltender's legs.

BACKHAND-FOREHAND SHIFT

The puck is moved to the player's backhand side and then quickly moved to his forehand side. This maneuver is effective when the goaltender moves with the first shift.

FOREHAND-BACKHAND SHIFT

This deke is the opposite of the backhand-forehand shift.

BACKHAND DRAG

The player approaches the goaltender on his backhand side at a sharp angle. The player starts to cut across the front of the net. The puck is dragged behind with the player's top hand only on the stick. The puck is slipped in on the short side by the post.

FAKE SHOT AND SHIFT

The player fakes the shot to one side by dipping his shoulder. The player should shift to the other side when the goaltender makes a move.

DEKING DRILL
Breakaway Drill
Line up players in three lines and have them break in on the goaltender one at a time. Have the players switch lines as they come back.

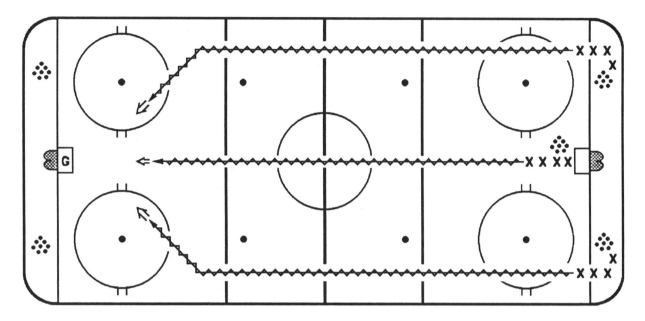

9. CHECKING

Checking is a very important aspect of hockey, and in many cases it is neglected in practice sessions. Playoff hockey puts stress on checking, but the checking skills should be used in every game.

STICK CHECKING

In all stick checking, the checker should watch the man, not the puck.

POKE CHECK

The poke check is often used in one-on-one situations or with forechecking forwards. The elbow of the arm holding the stick is bent and close to the side. The head is up and one hand is on the stick. This move must be used when the opponent is in close range. The arm holding the stick extends quickly. The body is kept in a stable position and there is no lunging at the opponent. The arm and blade of the stick do the checking. The stick is held in until the opponent is in close range.

STICK LIFT

The player approaches the puck carrier from behind and to the side of the puck. He lifts the opponent's stick at the shaft near the heel of the stick. He takes possession of the puck.

STICK PRESS

The stick is pressed down over the opponent's stick or lower arm. The approach is the same as the stick lift. Upper body strength is also important in this move.

SWEEP CHECK

The checker approaches the puck carrier from the front in a semicrouched position. The stick is swept in a flat position to knock the puck from the offensive player's stick. The head is kept up in anticipation of a body check that may result if the sweep check fails.

HOOK CHECK

The hook check should be used only when the puck carrier cannot be fully overtaken. The player approaches the puck carrier from behind with one hand on the stick. He goes down on the inside knee, extending the arm holding the stick after obtaining the puck. The weight is on the other skate so a quick pivot can be made. The blade of the stick is turned flat on the ice toward the puck, and the puck is hooked back. He regains balance, gets up off his knee, and resumes skating stride.

DIVING POKE CHECK

This check is used as a last resort, when the offensive player is in a breakaway situation. The player skates as close behind the player as possible. He keeps inside of the puck carrier and approaches from an angle. The player leaves his feet in a diving motion when the offensive player reaches 30 to 40 feet from the net. He extends his arms and puts the stick flat on the ice. He aims the stick and his body at or ahead of the offensive player's stick and attempts to knock the puck away. The player should not knock the opponent's feet away, as this could cause a tripping penalty and/or penalty shot.

BODY CHECKING

It is important in all body checking that the head is up and the eyes are on the opponent's chest area, not on the puck. A player's getting the proper handle and speed when checking an opponent will allow him to take an opponent out of the play regardless of size. Agility and balance, including lateral and backward skating ability, are essential in good checking.

SHOULDER CHECK

A player should be able to use either shoulder. The point of the shoulder hits the opponent's chest. Knees are bent and extend on contact. The skates are turned outward and dig in a shoulders' width apart. The drive is off the back leg. One hand is on the stick with the other flexed to the side. The hand is close to the body to prevent injury. The push is up and through on contact. The head up, and the player should not commit too early. The player should watch for an opponent with his head down; this is a good time for the shoulder check.

RIDING THE MAN OUT OF THE PLAY

This check is used mainly along the boards. The checker stays between the offensive man and the goal and is even with or slightly ahead of the man. Body contact is made with the side of the upper body and hips. If possible, the inside arm is extended across the body of the offensive man. The players cuts the offensive man off and angles him toward the boards. He rides the man off and goes for the puck.

HIP CHECK

This check is used mainly by defensemen along the boards. When mastered, it is an effective mid-ice check. The check is started by the player's skating backward, usually with one hand on the stick. He pivots and pushes off the far side foot and moves into a low crouch position. He swings his hips at a 90-degree angle and drives sideways into the puck carrier. Timing is extremely important in this skill.

STICK LIFT AND SHOULDER CHECK

The checker places the bent inside knee in front of the opponent and places the stick under the opponent's and lifts upwards. Make contact with the shoulder and/or hip and pin the opponent's arm and stick against the boards. Gain possession of the puck with the stick or the skates.

PINNING TECHNIQUE

The checking player turns the opponent towards the boards by driving the arm and shoulder under the opponents outside arm from the side. As the opponent rotates towards the boards, the checker pushes with the legs and hips. Place the inside leg between the opponent's legs and push up and pin.

ROLLER CHECK

The checker pushes the opponent with the forearm or shoulder along the boards so that the opponent's hip and shoulders make contact with the boards. The checker should try to make contact with the near shoulder of the opponent forcing the player being checked to rotate inwards towards the boards.

BACKCHECKING

Backchecking is an essential skill for all forwards. It assists the defensemen by allowing them to stay up and force the play. The backchecker should stay at least one stride ahead of the offensive man and within a stick's length away. The man, as well as the puck, should be watched using peripheral vision. The checker should not let the offensive player get ahead of him. As the man moves closer to the goal, the checker moves tight with the opponent's forward progress. He always stays in the lane; he should not chase a puck carrier into the center area and leave his check, as the defensemen will pick up the center area.

FORECHECKING

Forechecking (one-on-one) is an important defensive skill and can also become an offensive skill if possession of the puck is gained in a scoring position. The forechecker must always keep his head up and play the man, then go for the puck. The stick may be held in one hand in order to poke the puck away. The man should be angled toward the boards and his skating space cut off. The player should not approach the offensive man straight on or chase the man behind the net unless he is very close to him. Agility is important. A good forechecker can stop quickly, change direction, pivot, skate backward, sweep, and poke check effectively.

TAKING A CHECK

It is important that all hockey players be able to take a body check to prevent injury or to recover quickly to get back into the play. When an opponent is moving toward a player to body check, the player taking the check can tense his muscles and gain momentum by moving toward him. As momentum equals mass times velocity, the smaller the player, the more important speed is in head-on contact. It is important to spread the body check force over a large area against the boards. Consequently, the whole body should be against the boards, and the body should give on contact and spring off the boards from the check. A player should keep in a semicrouch position and should not use the hand or wrist to cushion a blow. He must learn to fall properly, quickly regain his feet, and start skating again.

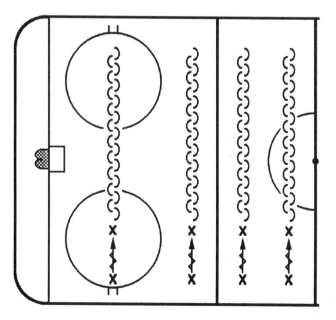

CHECKING DRILLS
1. One-on-One Drill Moving Across the Ice
Players practice using the various types of stick and body checks. They work at half speed passively and then work at full speed, using the full length of the ice.

2. One-on-One Drill Using the Length of the Ice

This drill is the same as 1 except in this drill there is no more space in which to maneuver. Players switch from offense to defense.

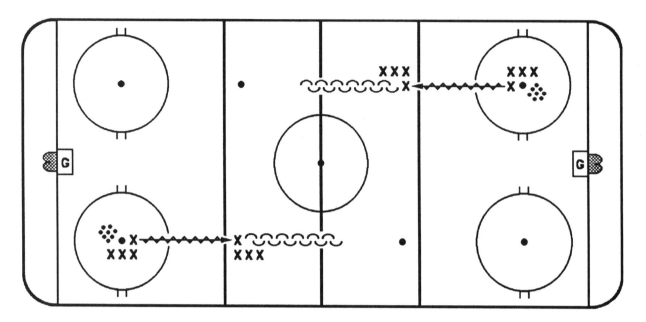

3. One-on-One Swing Drill

The forward skates to the far blue line, turns, and receives a pass from the opposite side. The defenseman skates forward around the center circle and turns backward. The forward goes one-on-one against that defenseman. The player who passes the puck then goes around the center circle and turns backward. The forward starting beside him skates inside the far blue line and takes a pass from the defenseman.

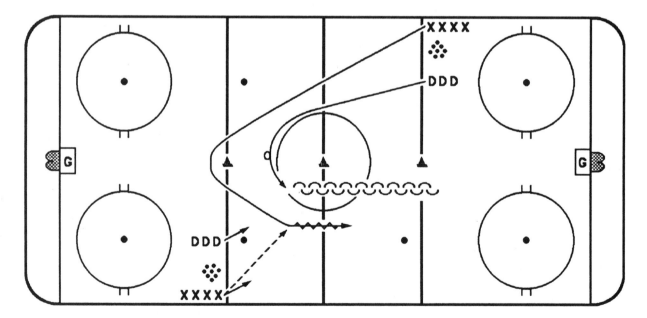

4. Checking the Player Stopped Behind the Net

The puck carrier carries the puck behind the net and stops. The checker stops in front of the net. The puck carrier then moves to either side, and the checker moves with him. The puck carriers then become the checkers, and the checkers become the puck carriers.

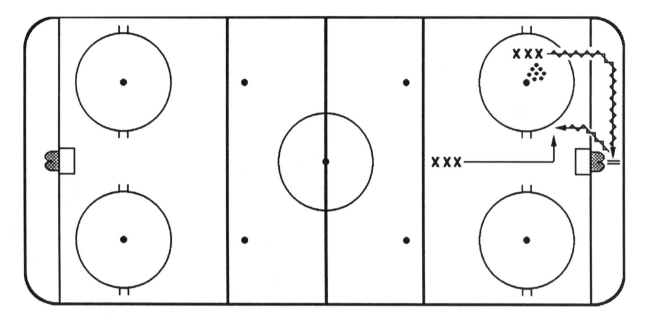

5. Checking the Player Moving Behind the Net

This drill is the same as 4 except in this drill the puck carrier does not stop behind the net but moves out the far side. The checker moves in at an angle and attempts to force the puck carrier to the corner.

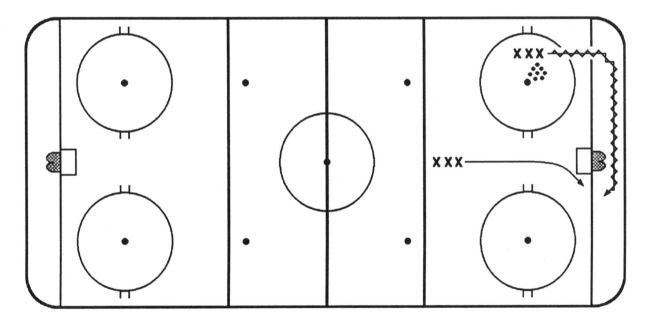

6. Backchecking

On a command, the player starts down the boards with the checker starting slightly behind. The player receives a pass from a center, cuts around the pylon, and moves in on the goaltender. The checker stays on the inside of the pylon and attempts to check the offensive player. The drill is worked in both directions.

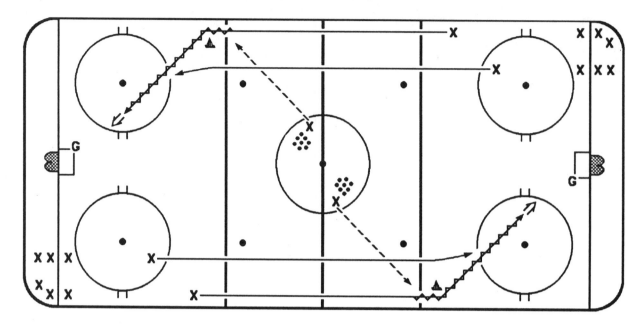

7. Chase the Rabbit

The puck carrier says "go," skates to the outside of the pylon the length of the ice, and shoots, with the checker starting two steps behind him and to the inside of the pylon.

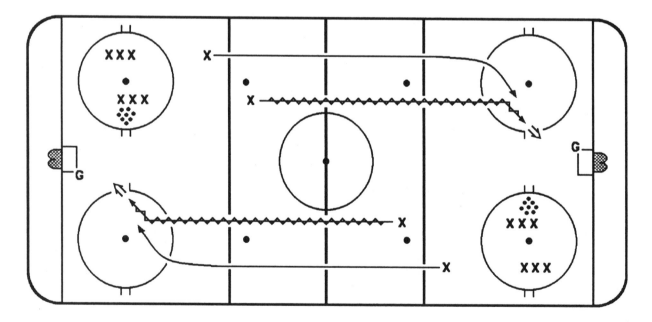

8. Body Checking
Players work in pairs around the boards taking and giving body checks.

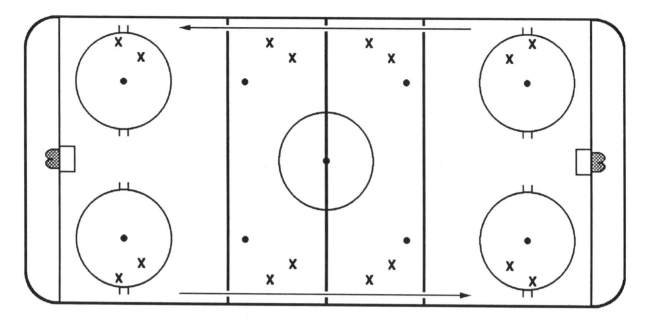

9. Failing Drill
Players practice failing front rolls, failing side rolls, failing to one knee, and recovering the skating stride. Have them do a different maneuver between each set of lines.

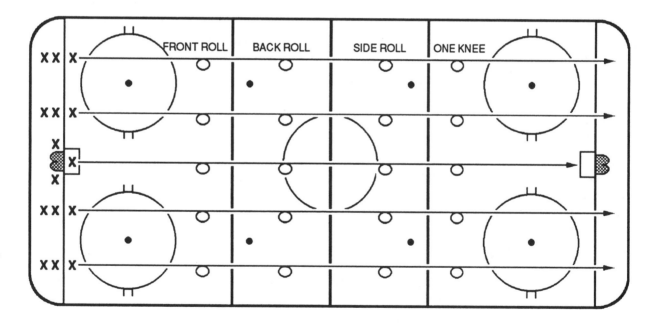

10. Diving Poke Check Drill (not shown)
Players practice leaving the feet and diving at an angle at a puck carrier in the clear who is cutting in from the boards.

10. OFFENSIVE TEAM PLAY

The objective of offensive team play is to move the puck as quickly as possible toward the opponents net to attempt to score a goal. The Canadian Hockey Association outlines four basic principles to achieve this objective:

Principle #1   Pressure
Principle #2   Puck Control
Principle #3   Support
Principle #4   Transition

Principle #1   Pressure
The principle of pressure means that all offensive team play is based on quick player or puck movement. Every move is made with speed and the concentration of the attack.

Principle #2   Puck Control
All offensive team play must set out to control the puck from the defensive zone to the offensive zone of the ice. Puck protection skills such as quick movements, driving to the net, crossing, keeping the feet moving, delays, etc., all allow the offensive team to keep control of the puck.

Principle #3   Support
The players without the puck are critical for successful offensive play. Giving the offensive player at least two passing options (triangulation), filling the mid lane of the ice, having balance and numerical advantage (three-on-two, two-on-one, etc.) to the attack, and moving at high speeds allows for support of the puck carrier.

Principle #4   Transition
The team on defense must be prepared to quickly counterattack when possession of the puck is gained. The players must quickly change from defense to offense using quick passes and speed to accomplish this.

OFFENSIVE TERMS USED IN TODAY'S HOCKEY

Triangulation: the puck carrier has two other players to pass to entering the offensive zone. One player goes to the net while the third player supports.

1, 2, 3 Principle: the puck carrier attacks with speed, the second player goes to the net, and the third player stays high for support.

Numerical advantage: always try to outnumber the defensive team when on the offensive such as three-on-two, two-on-one, etc.

Mid Lane: all three lanes of the ice should be occupied if possible. As a player leaves a lane another player crosses over to fill that lane. The middle lane of the ice is always occupied.

Width and Depth: use the width of the ice as well as filling the areas behind the puck carrier. Spread the play out over a larger area of the ice.

Crossing: players should use a variety of attack options and should use crossing patterns when appropriate instead of straight line play.

Delays: refers to a tight turn while controlling the puck. In this move the offensive player gains more space and time as the defensive player usually cannot react fast enough to keep a tight gap.

Quiet Zone: refers to the offensive corner away from the puck. The puck can be passed to this zone with an offensive player anticipating this move to keep control of the puck.

Stretch: means an offensive player moves high to the far red line or blue line to be able to receive a long pass.

Decoy: can be related to the stretch man as the player goes high or wide to the puck carrier but may only be used to distract the defender.

Interference or Pick: on a crossing pattern or a wide play an offensive player gets in the path of the defensive player.

Back Door Plays: players moving behind the offensive net pass the puck back out on the same side to a teammate.

Cycling: players move out of the offensive corner and bank pass back to a following teammate. This can be repeated with another offensive player moving to the corner to receive the back bank pass.

Offensive play begins when a team gains possession of the puck in its own end. Offensive play can be divided into three categories:

1. Moving the puck out of the defensive zone (breakout)
2. Moving through the neutral zone
3. The offensive zone (attack)

1. MOVING THE PUCK OUT OF THE DEFENSIVE ZONE—BREAKOUTS

The following drills demonstrate standard methods of moving the puck from the defensive zone when the puck is shot in by the opposition or when possession is gained by the defensive team, usually by the defensemen.

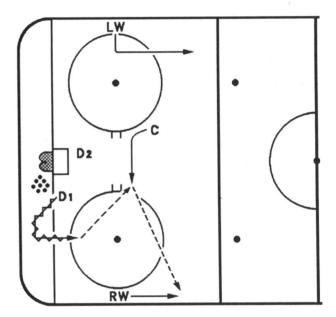

1. Quick Turn
The defenseman turns quickly with the puck. D1 can pass to the center or to the right wing or carry the puck himself. If D1 passes to the center, the center then makes a quick pass to the winger. The wingers move as soon as the defenseman turns with the puck and the center cuts across in position for a pass.

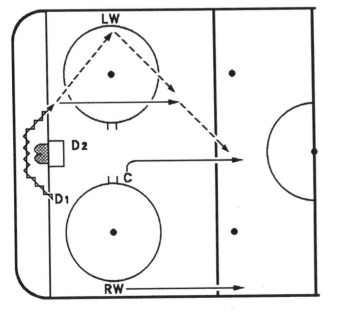

2. Behind the Net Without Stopping
The defenseman skates behind the net without stopping. D1 passes to the winger, who in turn passes the puck to the center, who has curled and is starting to break up ice.

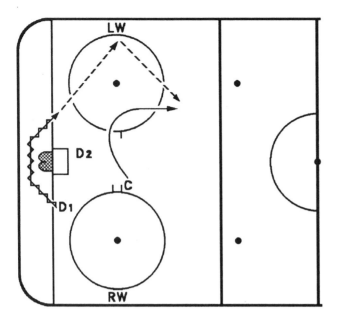

3. Give-and-Go

In this variation of 2, the defenseman skates behind the net without stopping. D1 passes to the winger, who returns the pass to the defenseman on a give-and-go. The center cuts straight up the middle of the ice. The winger takes the position of the defenseman after he returns the pass.

4. Pass to Winger

The defenseman stops behind the net. D1 passes to the winger. The winger passes to the center. D2 stations himself in front of the net.

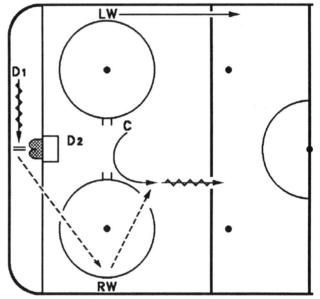

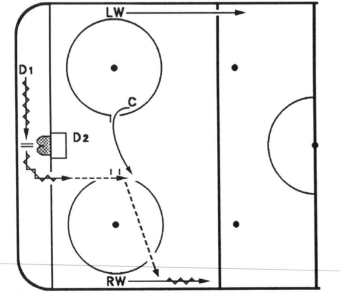

5. Pass to Center

This is a variation of 4 in which D1 passes to the center. The center passes to the winger. D2 is in front of the net.

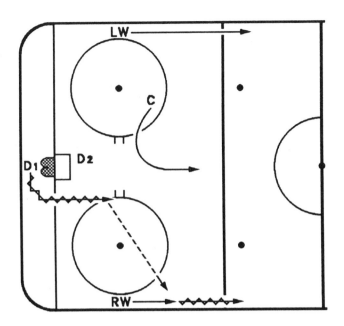

6. Defenseman Carries the Puck
This is another variation of 4, in which D1 carries the puck and passes it to the winger or the center. D2 trails the play.

7. Defenseman in the Corner
D2 moves to the corner when D1 is in full possession of the puck. The winger moves up the boards. D1 passes to D2. D2 passes to the center. The center passes to the wing.

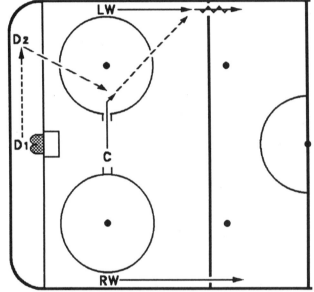

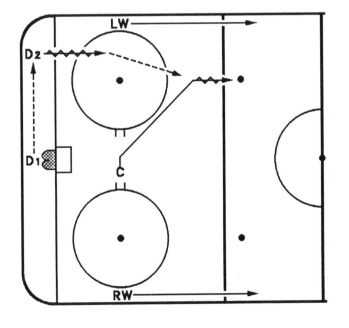

8. Defenseman in the Corner Variation
In this variation of 7, D1 passes to D2. D2 skates with the puck and then passes to the center or the winger.

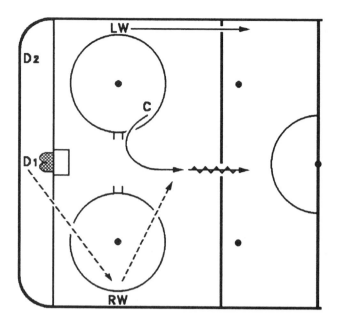

9. Pass to Offside Winger
In this variation of 7, D1 passes to the offside winger, who passes to the center.

10. Defenseman Carries the Puck
In this variation of 7, D1 carries the puck up the center of the ice and then passes to the winger.

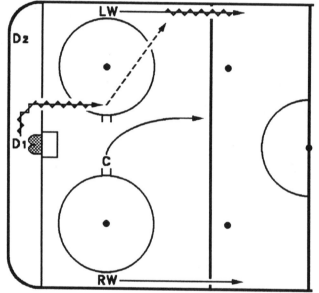

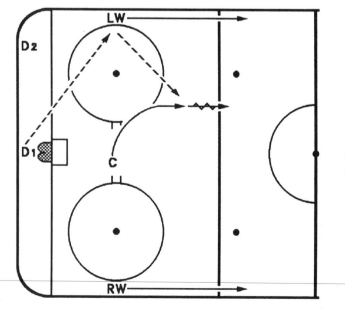

11. Defenseman Behind the Net
In this variation of 7, D1 passes to the winger on the side with the defenseman in the corner. The winger then passes to the center.

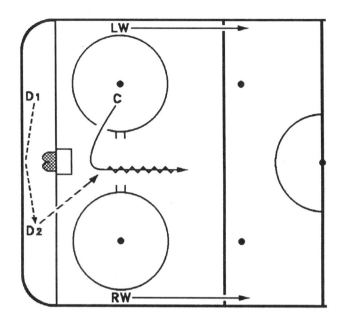

12. Off the Boards to the Center

D1 passes the puck off the boards to D2. D2 passes the puck to the center. The center passes the puck to the winger.

13. Off the Boards to the Winger

In this variation of 12, D1 passes the puck off the boards to D2. D2 passes the puck to the winger. The winger passes the puck to the center.

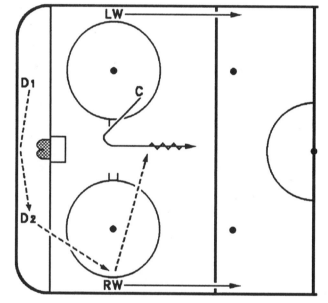

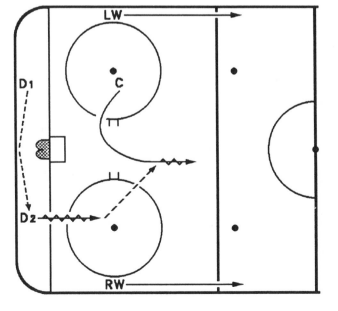

14. Carry and Pass

In this variation of 12, D1 passes the puck off the boards to D2. D2 skates with the puck and then passes to the center or winger.

93

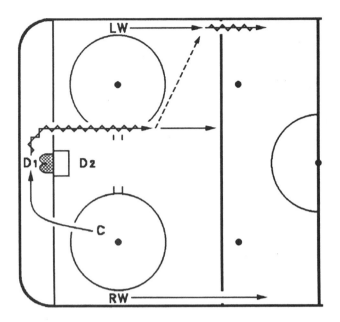

15. Center Behind the Net
D1 stops behind the net. The center comes behind the net and picks up the puck. The center moves up the middle of the ice and passes to the winger.

16. Pass Back
In this variation of 15, D1 stops behind the net. The center swings wide to the corner and drops the puck back to the defensemen. The winger on the puck side pulls off the boards. The center moves up the wing. D1 passes to the winger coming off the boards or passes to the center, or D1 carries the puck.

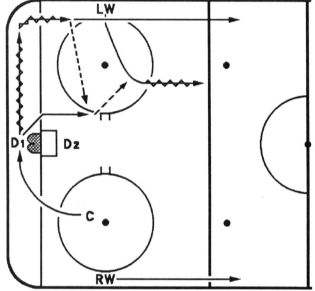

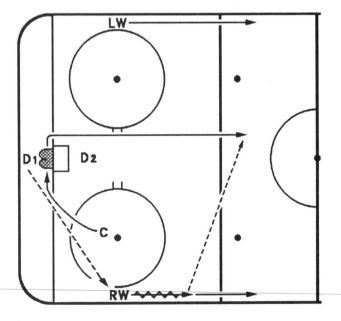

17. Leave the Puck
In this variation of 15, D1 stops behind the net. The center circles behind the net. D1 allows the center to go by but keeps the puck and passes it to either winger. The winger passes to the center.

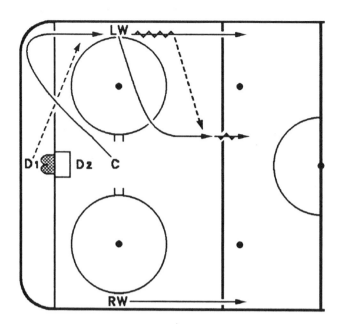

18. Center in the Corner

D1 stops behind the net. The center circles to the corner, and the winger on the puck side cuts across to the middle area of the ice. D1 passes to the center. The center passes to the winger in the middle area of the ice.

19. Winger in the Middle

In this variation of 18, D1 stops behind the net. The center circles to the corner, and the winger on the puck side pulls off the boards to the middle area of the ice. D1 passes to this winger.

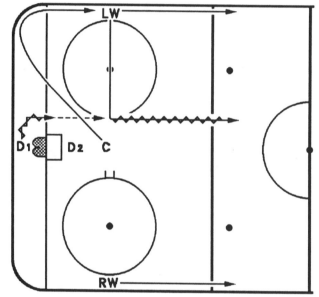

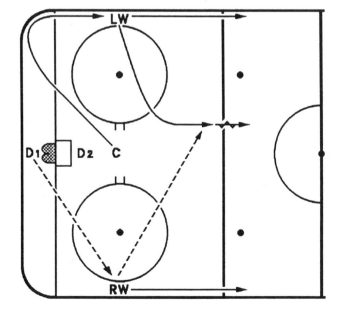

20. Pass to Offside Winger

In this variation of 18, D1 stops behind the net. The center circles to the corner, and the winger on the puck side pulls off the boards and moves to the middle area of the ice. D1 passes to the offside winger, who passes to the other winger.

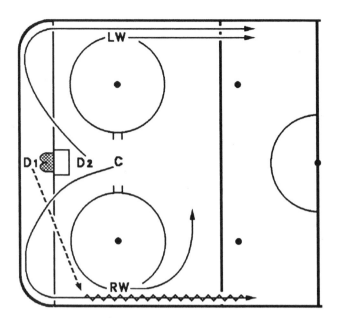

21. Double Swing

D1 stops behind the net. D2 moves to the corner. The center swings to the opposite corner. D1 passes to D2 or the center.

22. Around the Boards

The defenseman shoots the puck around the boards, and the winger picks the puck up on the move. This play is usually used from a face-off or when the puck has been shot directly in the corner and the defenseman is being chased.

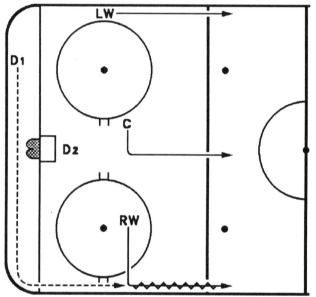

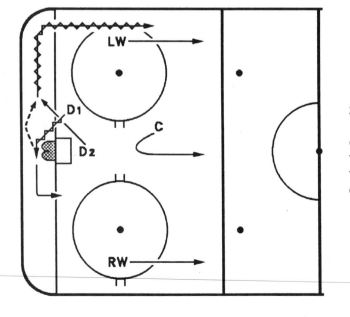

23. Defense Reverse

D1 carries the puck behind the net and is being chased by a forechecker. D1 drops the puck back to D2, who has moved from his position in front of the net. The defenseman in front of the net always calls the reverse.

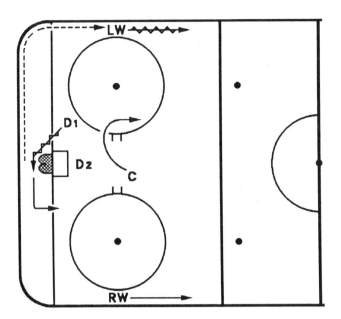

24. Reverse to the Winger
This drill is the same as 23 except the defenseman passes the puck back to the winger, who is stationed at the hash marks. The puck is passed on the ice along the boards. The winger should not be too high up on the boards. He can receive the pass moving or standing still.

25. Center Tight Turn
The center makes a tight turn at the goal line. The defenseman passes the puck to the center.

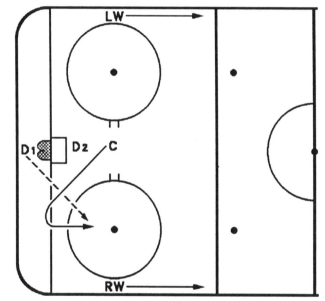

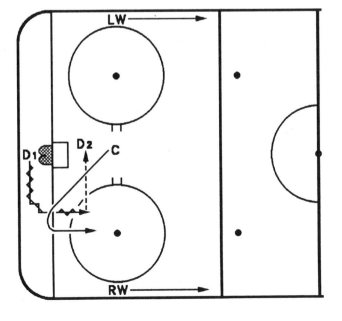

26. Center Tight Turn Variation
This drill is the same as 25 except, instead of passing puck to center, the defenseman moves out from behind the net and passes to the other defenseman. This pass must be made with caution.

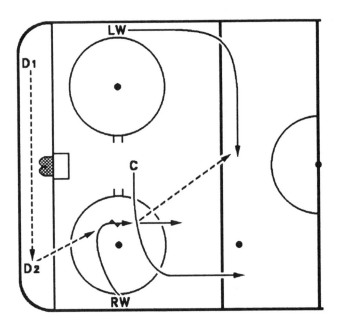

27. Center and Winger Cross
D1 passes to D2. The offside winger goes high and cuts across the middle outside the blue line.

BREAKOUT DRILLS FOR MOVING OUT OF YOUR OWN END
1. Breakouts from a Shoot-in
Line the players up by position at the blue line. The puck is shot in by the center, and the first player in each line moves in to bring the puck out. The coach designates the method of bringing the puck out of the end.

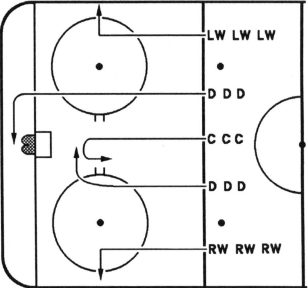

2. Five-on-Two
This drill is the same as 1 except the breakout progresses offensively the length of the ice as a five-on-two. When the offensive play is completed, another breakout starts from the opposite end with another offensive line. The defense pair who start the play follow it down the ice and then act defensively for the next five-on-two from the opposite end.

Variation on the offensive play: Have the forwards pass the puck back to the points if a direct play is not made on the net. The forwards should go to the front of the net to deflect or screen the shot coming from the point.

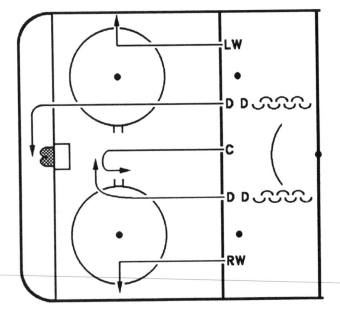

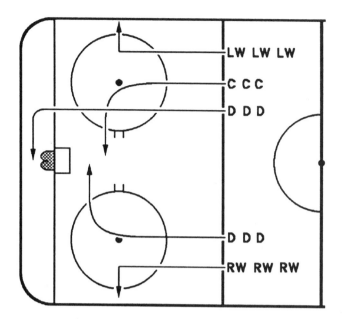

3. Centers on the Boards

The players line up in lines and defense pairs against the boards outside the blue line. The centers line up on the boards with either wing. Lines and defense pairs go in order and the puck is shot into the defensive zone by the coach. The coach states the method of bringing the puck out of the end.

4. One Forechecker

Players execute drills 1 and 3 with one forechecker moving on the puck.

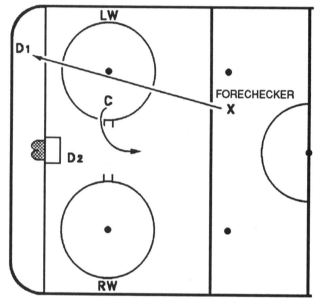

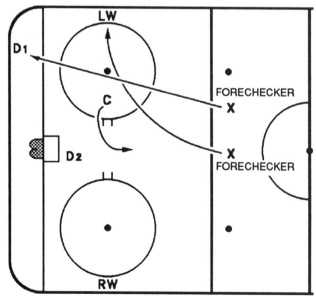

5. Two Forecheckers

Players execute 1 and 3 with two forecheckers moving into the zone.

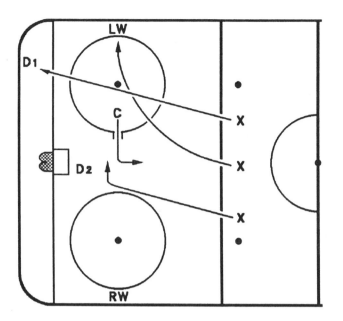

6. Three Forecheckers
Players execute 1 and 3 with a complete forward line forechecking.

7. Five-on-Five
Players work five-on-five drills with one team forechecking and the other team attempting to bring the puck out of their own end. Each team has a forward line and two defensemen. The puck is shot in by the forechecking team from the red line.

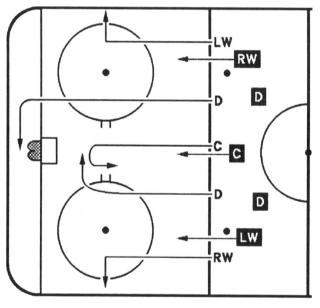

2. MOVING THROUGH THE NEUTRAL ZONE

Neutral zone re-groups have been used extensively by European teams to take full advantage of their wide ice surface. More recently, North American teams have adopted this system of play.

The Russians were probably the first to make use of the neutral zone by devising special plays for that area. Now, it's a major part of the game for all European teams and successful North American teams.

The neutral zone re-group is used offensively when a team is unable to penetrate the opposition's blue line. Instead of shooting the puck in, the offensive team keeps possession by turning back, passing the puck to the defense, and re-grouping to attack the opposition's blue line again.

After passing back to their defense, the three forwards swing back up ice, going for open space, and gaining speed for another attack.

Players have to learn to switch with their linemates so they don't all end up in one part of the ice, leaving one or more lanes wide open. They have to find the right timing so that they swing and re-group as a unit and are ready for a quick, simultaneous attack from a good position.

It's an organized system rather than a chaotic, every-man-for-himself scramble across the ice. Once mastered, it can be used by almost any team, provided the defensemen are fairly adept at handling the puck and passing well.

These are the principles of the neutral zone re-group:

- The puck is passed back to the defense. The receiver then passes across to his defense partner. They should be positioned so that they are slightly staggered, with one deeper in the defensive zone than his partner.
- As the puck is passed back to the defense, the forwards move to open ice by swinging back toward the defense.
- The forwards must skate under control with their sticks on the ice, getting themselves into position for a pass. They should fill all three lanes of the ice.
- If a forward is not open for a pass and the defense cannot move the puck up immediately, the man in possession should make a return pass to his defense partner. The forwards must then swing back again to be in position to receive a pass.
- Assuming the defense receives the pass back at the defensive blue line, the three forwards should cover the following areas: near the defense, mid-ice, and past mid-ice.
- If no forward is open for a pass, the defensemen should move forward with the puck themselves.

The progressive drills that follow can be used to teach the neutral zone re-group. The objective is to initiate the player to the idea of swinging across the ice from his wing and re-grouping with his linemates for an organized attack. This sounds simple enough but may not be a natural move for someone schooled in the straight-line, up-and-down-the-wings approach to hockey. Note that these are progressive teaching drills with no checking involved.

NEUTRAL ZONE DRILLS
1. Horseshoe
Players, including defensemen, line up along the boards. On the whistle, the first man in the line skates down the wing, swings inside the offensive blue line, receives a pass from the first player in the other line, and moves down to the other end for a shot on the goaltender. He then returns to the back of the line from which he started while the first player in the other line takes his turn.

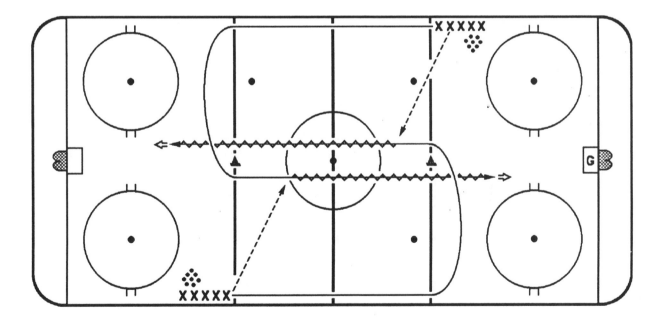

2. Horseshoe with Two Defensemen

The forward passes back to the defense and swings. In this variation of 1, two defensemen are included. They don't check but receive and give passes. They should be staggered with one deeper in the defensive zone than the other. The first forward skates across the blue line and passes the puck to the near defenseman, who then relays it across to his partner. The forward swings either in front or behind the first defenseman and up center ice to take a return pass from the other defenseman. He then goes up for a shot on goal. The drill continues, each side going in turn.

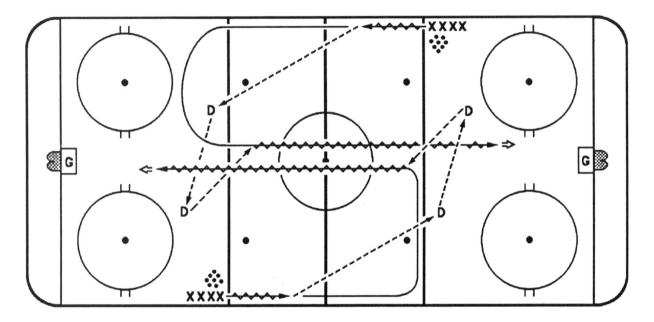

3. Two Forwards Swing from the Same Side

This drill teaches forwards to swing together so they don't interfere with each other. Each must look for open ice rather than bunching together. The first two men come down the wing and swing across, one in front of the defenseman, the other behind. The first forward passes the puck to the defenseman, who then relays it to his partner. The forward takes the return pass and goes up ice with his teammate for a shot on goal. If his teammate goes wide, he should go up the center; if the teammate chooses center, he should swing wide.

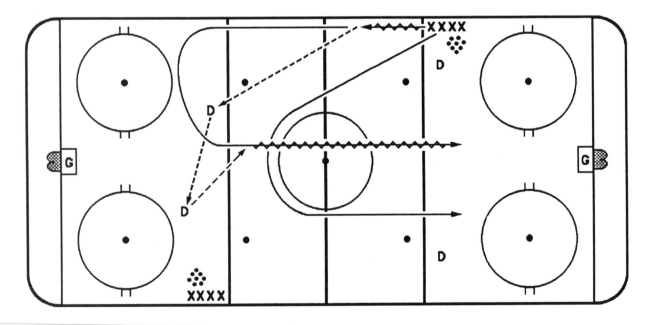

4. Two Forwards Swing from Opposite Sides

In this variation of 3, the two forwards swing from opposite sides of the rink. One swings near the defense or behind it, and the other swings in the center ice area. They alternate.

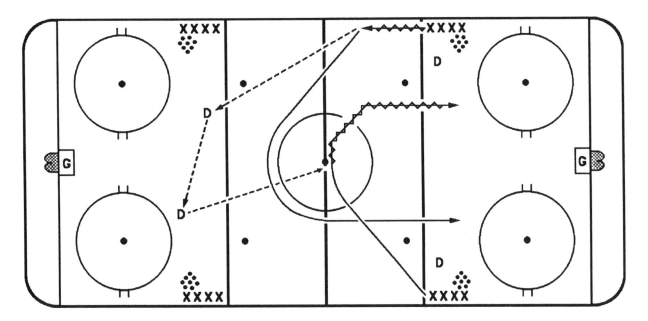

5. Three Forwards Swing

This drill combines 3 and 4 using three forwards, two from one side, one from the other. They should cover the areas near or behind the defense, the center line, and the far blue line alternately.

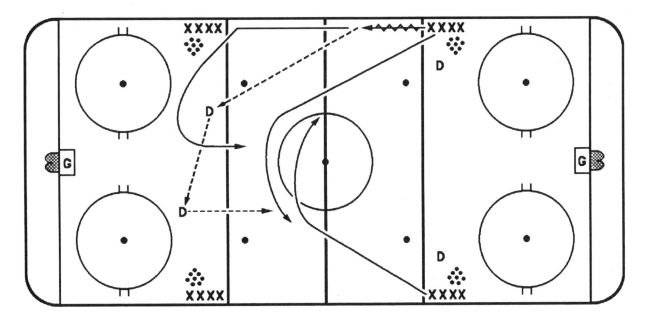

6. Two Re-groups

In this drill, the goal is attacked twice. Three forwards start at the blue line, pass the puck to the defense, swing, and receive a return pass. They skate to the far blue line, pass the puck to the defense, re-group, receive a return pass, and attack the goal three-on-none. They then return to the starting point. Forwards should try to find open ice so they're not jamming the same area at the same time.

Remember that depth is a factor. Have players swing so that zones near the defense, mid-ice, and past mid-ice are covered.

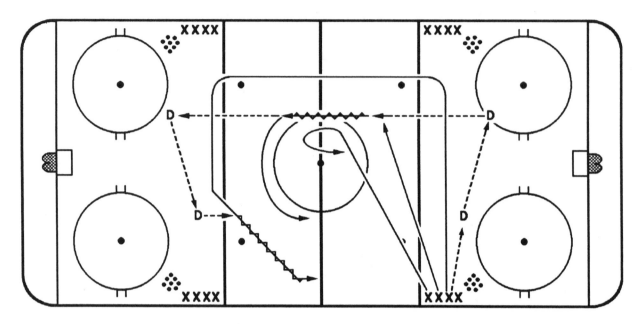

7. Breakout with Neutral Zone Re-groups

In this drill there are five players (three forwards and two defensemen) working as a unit. The forwards dump the puck in from outside the blue line. The defense retrieves it, and they all break out, five on two, using whatever system the team has been practicing. The drill continues on the opposite page.

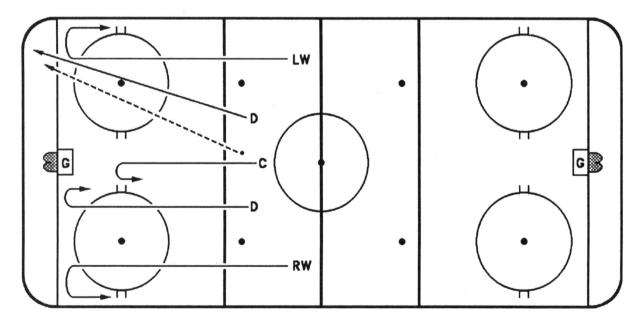

Continued: When the forwards reach the far defense, they pass to them instead of attacking, as in 6, and re-group with that defense pair. This is the first re-group. Meanwhile, the first defense pair has skated back into position for a five-on-two attack by the group that has the puck. When the forwards reach the blue line, they again pass to the defense and re-group. This is the second re-group. The forwards then skate down to attack the goal five-on-two, and the next group starts from the other end.

When they have mastered all these drills, set up a scrimmage in which they try to use the neutral zone re-

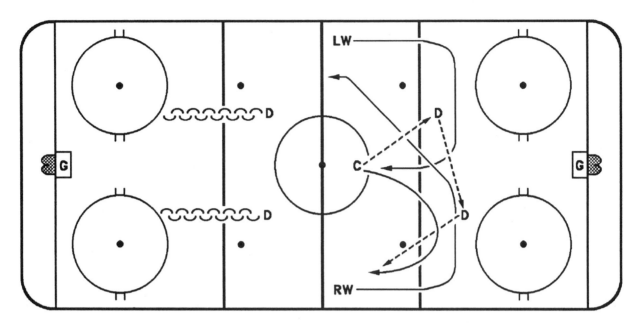

group whenever it is appropriate; that is, when they can't carry or pass the puck across the opponent's blue line. Instead of shooting the puck in, they swing back, re-group, and attack again.

To make sure the neutral zone re-group is done correctly, watch for the following points:

- When players swing, they should skate for open ice. Make sure they fill all three lanes.
- Players should think about what they are doing, be under control, and try to get into position to receive a pass.
- Although the players may swing out of their lanes, the lanes still have to be filled. This means they have to be ready to alternate (e.g., if the center moves over to the wing, that winger should move into the center, and so on).
- During the re-group, players should also cover different depths in the neutral zone, as pointed out earlier (near the defense, mid-ice, past mid-ice). This adds a dimension to the re-group systems and requires each player to read and react quickly to what his linemates are doing.

3. PLAYING IN THE OFFENSIVE ZONE (ATTACK)

Basic three-on-two plays, those plays made by the offensive team into the offensive zone, are usually made from the neutral zone just as the play approaches the opposition's blue line. The play then continues until there is a scoring opportunity.

The basic concept in offensive team play is that one forward should be driving for the net at all times to create an opening or to draw a defenseman with him. A forward other than the puck carrier and the driving man should trail the play. This is sometimes referred to as the one-two-three principle.

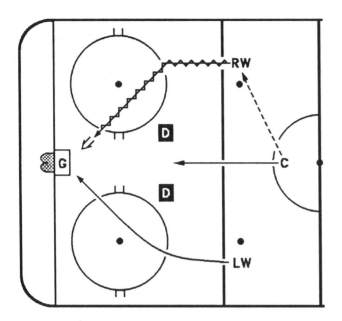

OFFENSIVE ZONE DRILLS
1. Offside Winger to the Net
The center passes to the winger, who cuts around the defenseman and shoots. The offside winger cuts to the far post for a rebound. The center trails the play in the high slot area.

2. Center Trails
The center passes to the winger. The center trails the play slightly to the side of the puck carrier. The winger goes wide to take the defenseman over. The winger passes the puck back to the center, who either shoots or passes to the other winger, who shoots.

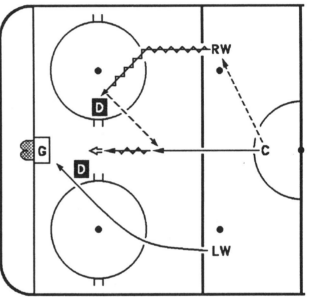

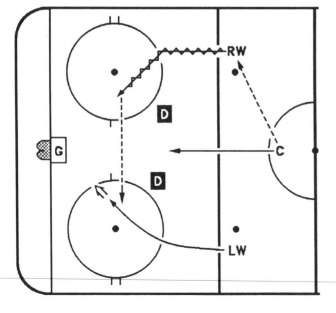

3. Winger to Winger
The center passes to the winger. The winger cuts behind the defenseman and passes across to the opposite winger. The opposite winger shoots. This play works well if the opposition defensemen are well out toward the blue line.

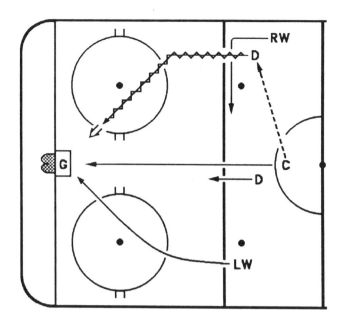

4. Winger Cuts Across

The winger, ahead of the play, skates parallel to the blue line. The defenseman on the winger's side moves quickly up the boards. The center passes to the defenseman. The defenseman cuts in and shoots or drops the puck back to the trailing center, who shoots. The left winger goes to the net for a rebound.

5. Behind the Net

The center passes to the winger, and the winger cuts wide and goes behind the net. The center trails the play and moves to the slot area. The winger passes to the center, who then shoots.

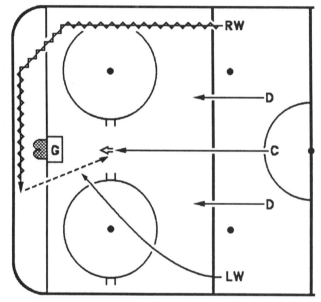

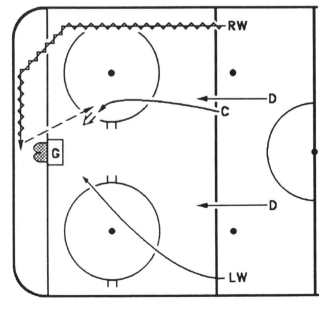

6. Pass Back on Same Side

The winger drives hard behind the net and passes the puck back on the same side. The trailing forward tries to shoot quickly, as the goalie tends to move from the post because he believes the winger is continuing behind the net with the puck.

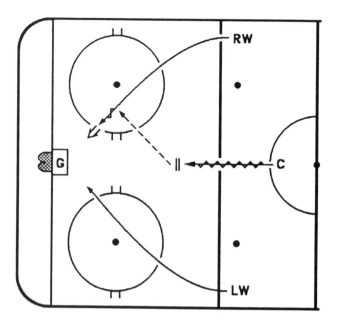

7. Center Stops

The center is slightly ahead of the winger, who cuts wide and goes to the net. The center trails the play and moves to the slot area. The winger passes to the center, who then shoots.

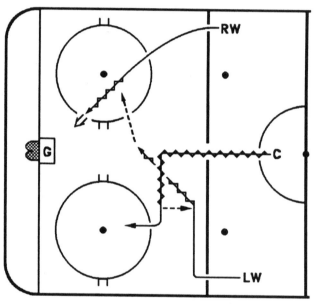

8. Cross-and-Drop Pass

The center is ahead of the wingers when crossing the blue line. The center cuts across to either wing. The winger on that side cuts behind the center. The center drops the puck back to the winger. The winger passes to the offside winger, who is cutting for the net. The offside winger shoots.

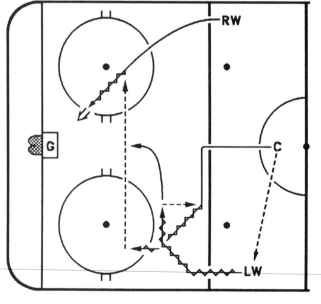

9. Cross and Pass

The winger cuts across over the blue line. The winger takes a pass from the center and cuts toward the middle of the ice in front of the defenseman. The center cuts behind the winger and is in a position to go wide with a return pass. The offside winger may cut wide or cut toward the center of the ice.

10. Bank Pass
X leads the play over the offensive blue line and back board passes the puck to X2. X2 must be inside the blue line to receive the pass.

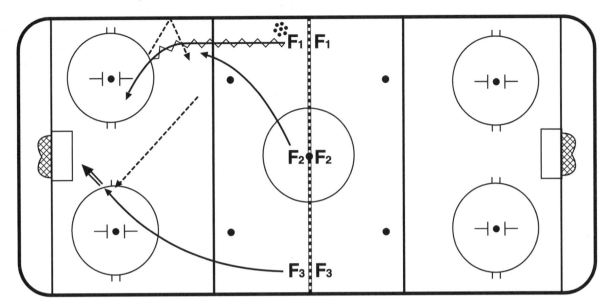

11. Delay
The forward skates hard into the offensive zone and then does a tight turn (delay) and passes off or then drives again for the net.

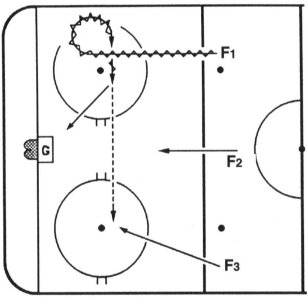

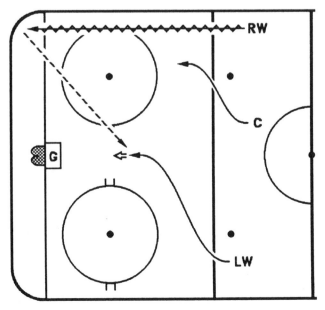

12. Offensive Triangle
The winger moves into the offensive corner for the puck. The center trails the winger on the boards. The offside winger moves for the slot area.

13. Offensive Triangle Variation

In this variation of 6, the winger may pass to the off-side winger or to the center. If the center receives the pass, he can shoot or pass to the offside winger who is moving to the net.

The winger and center on the puck side may alternate positions.

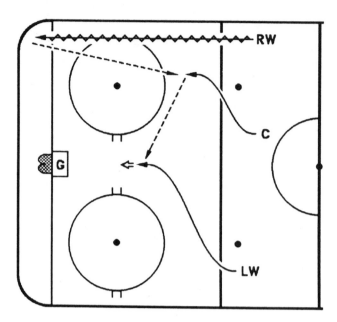

14. Cycling

A forward, X2, carries the puck from the corner and makes a board pass back into the corner as he skates out of the corner. X3 picks up the puck and can repeat the same backboard pass. This offensive play can be used with two or three players.

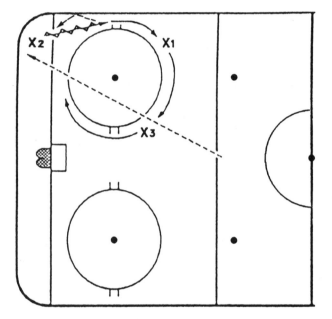

DRILLS FOR SHOOTING THE PUCK IN
1. Off the End Boards

This play is used when the wingers are covered and a play cannot be made or if one offensive player is breaking quickly and can beat the defenseman to the puck. It is imperative to gain control of the puck after it has been shot into the offensive end.

The center or winger shoots the puck off the end boards. The center and the winger on the puck side go for the rebound off the boards. The offside winger trails the play and moves into the high slot area.

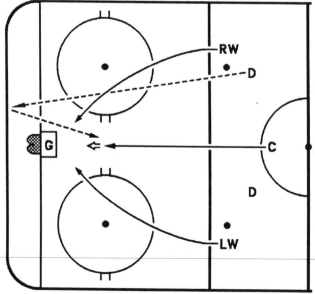

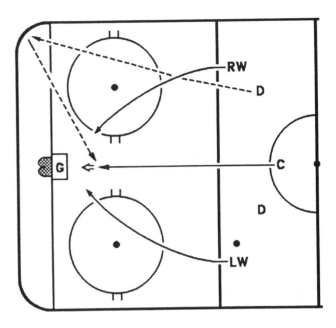

2. Puck Shot in the Corner

The center or winger shoots the puck into the corner at such an angle that the puck will come out in front of the net. The center goes for the slot area. The offside winger cuts to the front of the net.

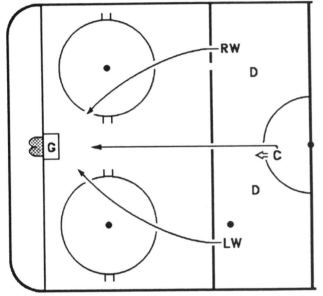

3. Puck Shot at the Net

The center or winger shoots the puck at the goaltender, using preferably a bounce shot, to allow the forwards time to move in. The center moves straight in. The wingers cut in for the goalposts looking for a rebound.

4. Rim the Boards

The forward gets over the offensive blue line near the boards and shoots the puck around the rim of the boards to the far corner. The forward on the far side moves directly to the corner to pick up the puck. The puck should be shot hard and about one foot off the ice to prevent the opposition goaltender from stopping it behind the net.

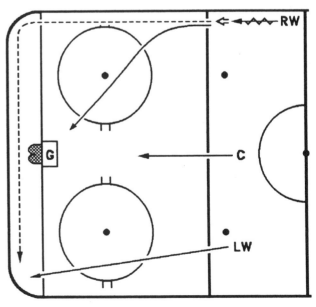

OTHER OFFENSIVE PLAYS

1. One-on-One

The offensive player should attempt to pull the defenseman away from the slot area. Having done this, the offensive player will try to move into the slot area using a shift on the defenseman. He should use the defenseman as a screen and shoot if the defenseman does not move from the slot area.

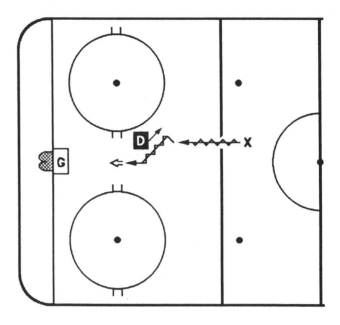

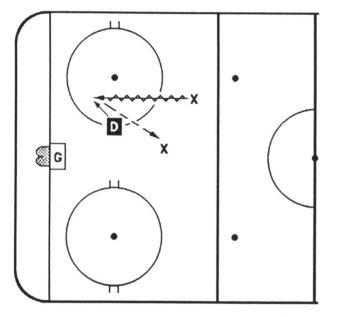

2. Two-on-One Trailer

The offensive player with the puck attempts to draw the defenseman over and away from the slot area. The player with the puck drops the puck back to the other, trailing, offensive player.

3. Behind the Defenseman

The offensive player with the puck cuts wide. The other offensive player cuts behind the defenseman and receives the pass.

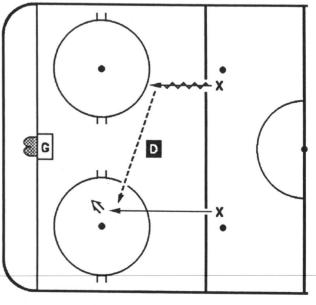

4. Drop Pass

The offensive player with the puck moves directly at the defenseman. The player with the puck drops a pass to the other trailing forward. After dropping the pass, the offensive player takes out (picks) the defenseman long enough for the other forward to skate to the goal.

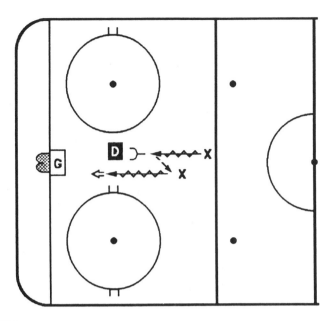

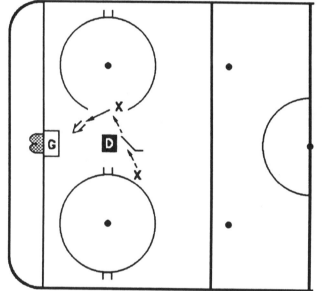

5. Through the Stick

The forwards are abreast with the defenseman between. The forward with the puck passes over the defenseman's stick or between his stick and skates to the other forward.

6. Two-on-One Crossing

The forward with the puck cuts across in front of the defenseman, with the other forward cutting behind him. The pass is usually across, or a drop pass may be used.

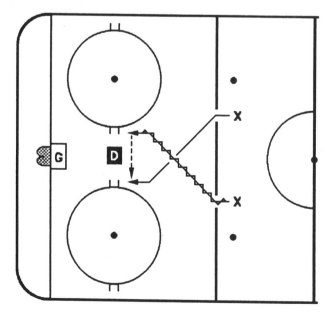

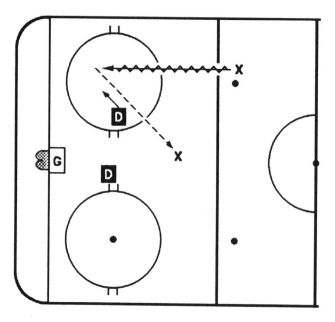

7. Pass Back

Players attempt to isolate one defenseman, making a two-on-one situation. The offensive player with the puck moves wide and draws one defenseman over. The offensive player passes the puck back to the other forward and moves to the net for a rebound.

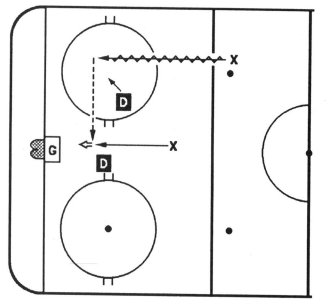

8. Two-on-One to the Net

The offensive player with the puck moves wide and draws the defenseman over. The other forward slips through the defense and receives a pass.

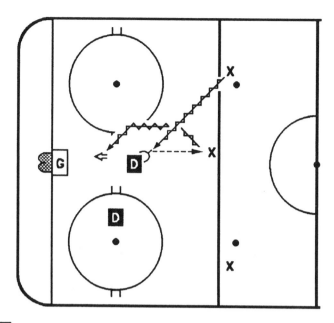

9. Drop Pass

The offensive player with the puck skates directly at the defenseman and then drop passes the puck to the other forward. After the drop pass, the offensive player moves into the defenseman to act as a screen. The forward receiving the drop pass either shoots or goes around the defenseman.

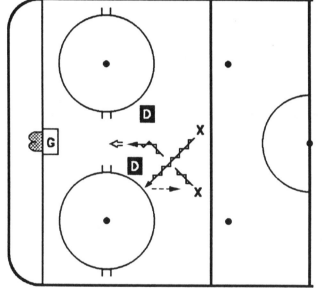

10. Cross-and-Drop Pass

The forwards cross in front of one defenseman, and the pass is dropped with the man receiving the pass cutting to the inside or outside.

DRILLS FOR OFFENSIVE PLAY

1. One-Two-Three Principle—One Player

The player receives a cross-ice pass, drives around the pylon, and takes a shot on goal. After shooting, the player stays at that end on the same side of the rink. Players alternate sides.

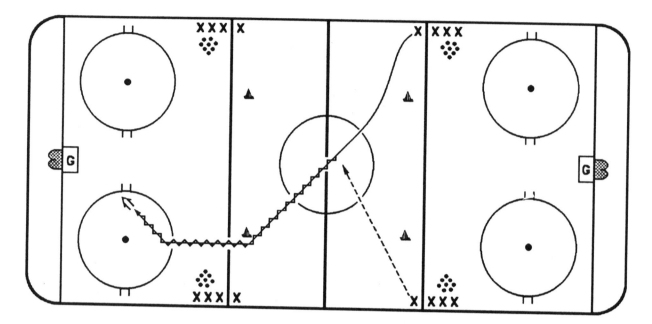

2. One-Two-Three Principle—Two Players

In this variation on 1, two players leave at the same time from the same side. The first player takes a cross-ice pass, drives around the pylon, and takes a shot on goal. The second player drives for the net. Players alternate sides.

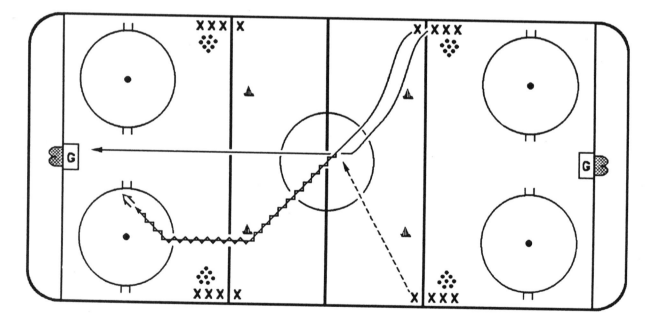

3. One-Two-Three Principle—Three Players
In this variation on 1, the players leave at the same time. The third player cuts around the opposite pylon and trails the play. The second man drives for the net. The puck carrier passes to the trailer.

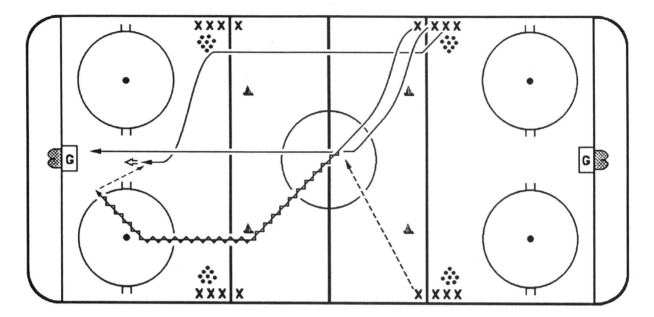

4. One-on-One (not shown)
Drills 1 and 2 on page 78, in chapter 8, "Stickhandling and Puck Control," can be used to drill players on the one-on-one situation.

5. One-on-One from Both Directions
The defenseman skates behind the net, turns up ice, and passes to a forward coming off the boards. Another defenseman stands on the blue line and begins skating backward for a one-on-one. The defenseman passing the puck follows the play up to the far blue line and stops. The drill is repeated from the other end with the defenseman who passed the puck from the one end acting as the defensive man coming in the opposite direction. The defensemen, after passing and working defensively, return to the end of the ice they started at. The forwards take the pass and then work offensively and stay at the opposite end on the opposite side of the boards.

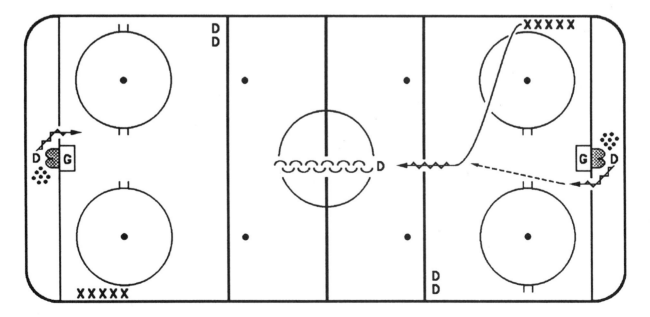

6. Two-on-One Drill

Players work on two-on-one drills in both directions. The defensemen stay on the same side of the ice. The forwards work in both directions. Defensemen work both sides by changing sides halfway through the drill.

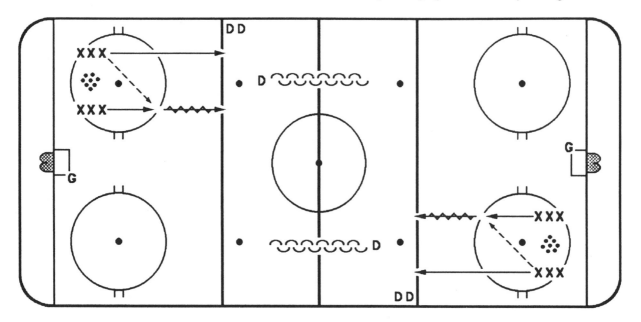

7. Two-on-One Variation

This drill uses the full ice surface. The forwards work from the corners with rink-wide passes. The defensemen work the same end, and the forwards work in both directions. The forwards working in the opposite direction do not start until a play has been completed on the net.

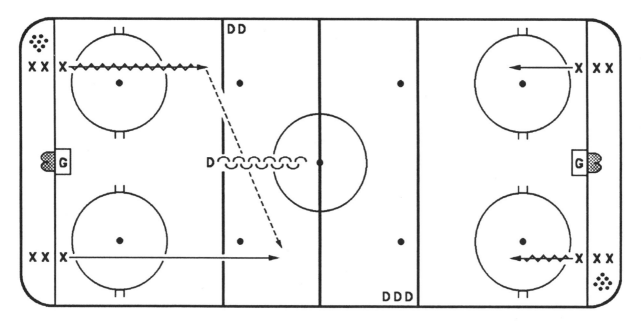

8. Defensemen Behind the Net

In this variation on 7, defensemen at both ends pass the puck to the forward by circling the net. The drill works in both directions.

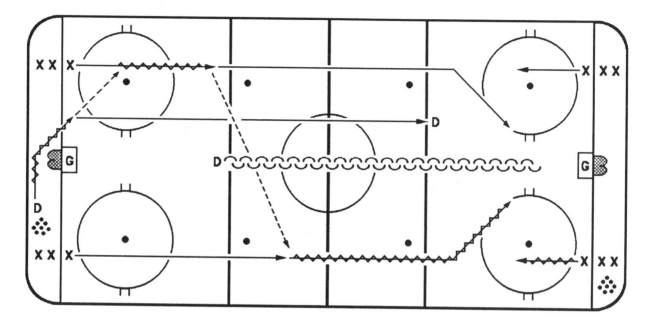

9. One Way

In this two-on-one drill the forwards start from the two corners. The defenseman starts the play by circling the net and passing to either forward. Another defenseman is standing at the blue line and takes the two-on-one.

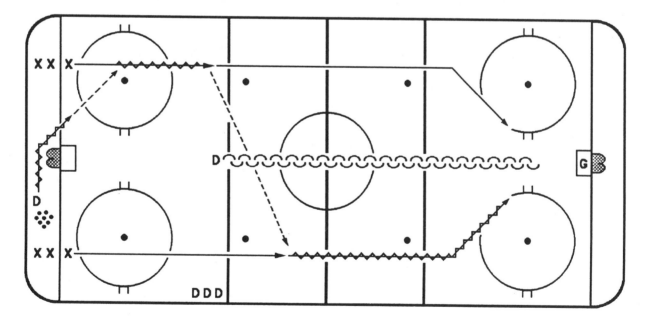

10. Half-Ice In One Direction

This two-on-one drill simulates a three-on-two situation in which a center and one winger are working on one defenseman. The other winger and defenseman are eliminated, but the play is made on only one side of the ice as if it were a three-on-two.

The center stays on the same side of the ice as the winger. The first center goes with the right winger. The next center goes with the left winger. The center starts with the puck.

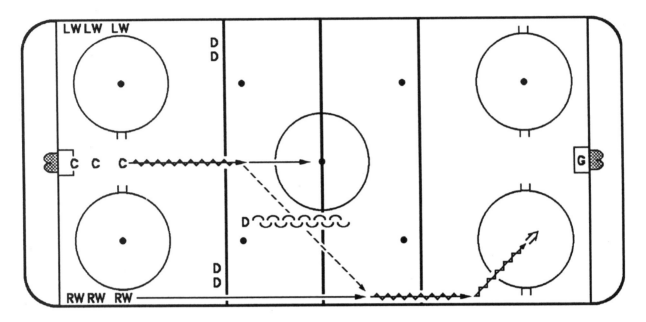

11. Half-Ice in Both Directions

In this variation on 10, also a two-on-one drill, players switch sides halfway through the drill. The centers start with the puck.

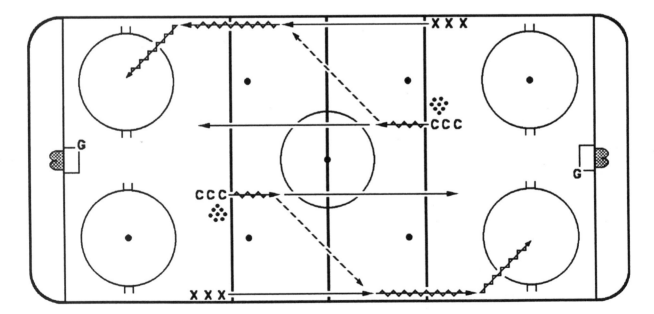

12. Two-on-One Swing Drill

Two forwards skate over the far blue line and receive a pass from a defenseman in that end. D1 starts at the same end as the forwards, skates around the center circle, turns backward, and defends against the attacking forwards. Once D2 has made the pass to one of the swinging forwards, the first two forwards and D2 start doing the drill the same way but coming from the opposite direction. Players return to the lines they came from.

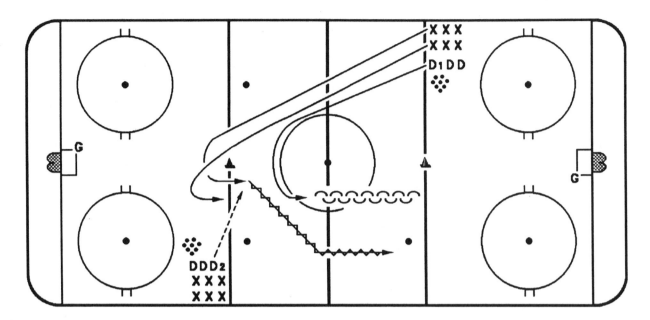

13. Three-on-Two in One Direction

The defenseman behind the net starts the passing for the three-on-two. The defense pairs take turns passing the puck up and working defensively.

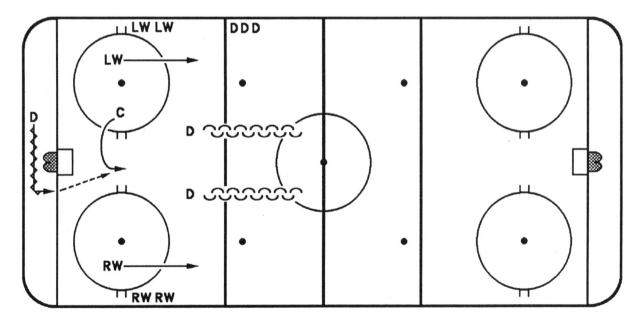

14. Three-on-Two in Both Directions

There must be a minimum of three forward lines and four defensemen for this drill. If six defensemen are available, have one at each end to start the play. Two forward lines must be at the end at which the drill starts. The forward lines stay at the opposite end after completing the rush and return in the opposite direction when their turn comes again.

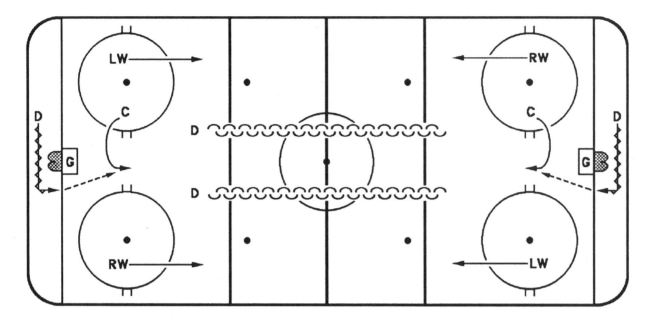

15. Three-on-Two in Both Directions with One Line in Succession

In this variation of 14, the forward line, after making a play in one direction, immediately moves back in the other direction against another defense pair.

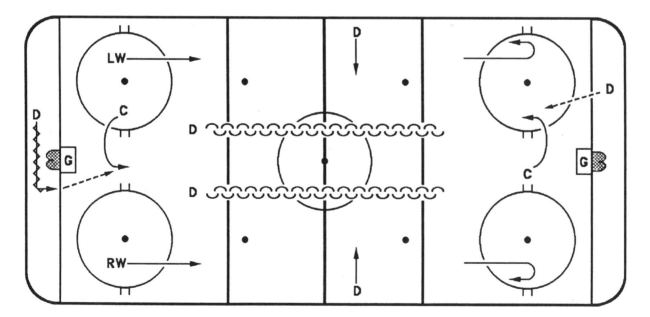

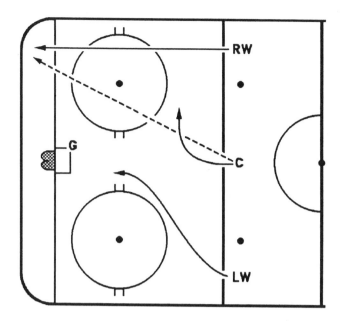

16. Offensive Triangle Drill
The forwards line up on the blue line and the puck is shot into the corner. The forwards work the various options of the offensive triangle. They shoot the puck into both corners.

17. Offensive Triangle Drill Against Defensemen
The defenseman on the side the puck is shot into goes to the corner for the puck. The other defenseman goes for the front of the net.

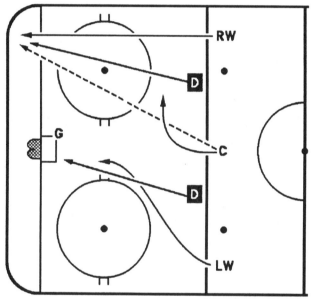

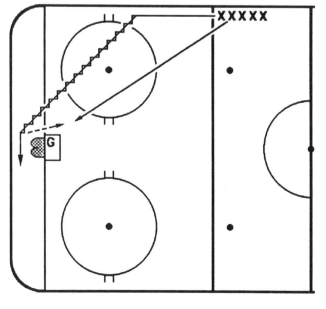

18. Pass Back Drill
The first forward with the puck goes behind the net and passes the puck back on the same side to the trailing forward.

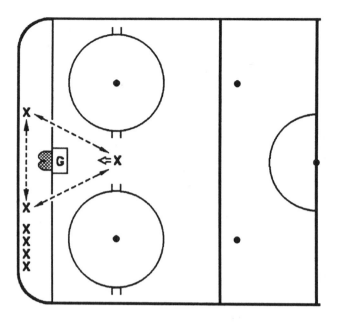

19. Offensive Triangle Around the Net
Three forwards pass the puck quickly around in the triangle, and the forward in the slot takes a shot on goal. Rotate the players in and out.

20. Five-on-Five
Have players execute 13 when moving out of their own end.

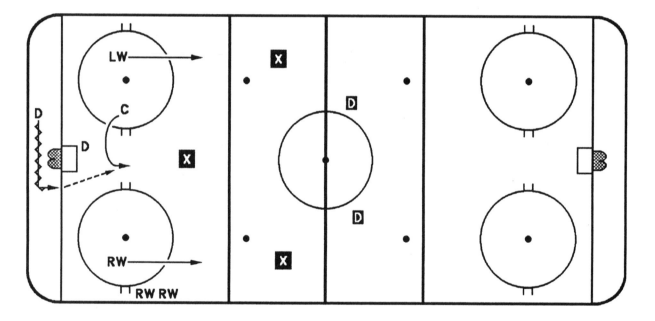

11. DEFENSIVE TEAM PLAY

"Defense is dull, boring, commonplace. It is unimaginative plodding attention to duty. It is grit and determination and perseverance. It requires simply an act of will. There is never a day you can't play defense. All you need is the decision to put out, to give one hundred percent."

George Sheehan • *Running and Being: The Total Experience*

Defense is the basic phase of the game during which the team is not in possession of the puck. The purpose is to recover possession of the puck and/or prevent the opposition from scoring. One of the most important jobs of the coach is to teach defensive play and sell the importance of it to his team. Most teams that are successful are the ones that play well defensively.

Defensive team play has two basic objectives:
1. Deny or restrict the use of time and space by the offensive team.
2. Regain possession of the puck or at least limit puck possession by the opponent.

The Canadian Hockey Association lists four basic principles and tactics to succeed defensively.

Principle #1	**Pressure**
Principle #2	**Stall/Contain**
Principle #3	**Support**
Principle #4	**Transition**

Principle #1   Pressure
Pressure reduces time and space. Pressure is accomplished by:
    (a) Speed—quickness to defend—limit offensive option—force errors
    (b) Pursuit—involves immediate and correct angling to limit opponent's options
    (c) Concentration—grouping of defensive players to restrict space
    (d) Commit—determines whether the defensive player commits or contains the offensive player with the puck

Principle #2   Stall/Contain
Force the opponent to stop or slow down the speed of the attack. Allow time for better defensive coverage. The defensive player pressures directly or steers the opponent to the outside lane. This is accomplished by holding the ice (as in a two-on-one), keeping on the defensive side of the opponent and forcing to the outside.

Principle #3   Support
Support means that the defensive player must be active away from the puck by reducing the passing options and reading and reacting to the movement of the offensive players. This is usually accomplished by man to man or zone coverage. It also requires that the defensive team is not outnumbered in the defensive zone of the ice.

Principle #4   Transition
The defensive team must be alert to change quickly from defense to offense when possession of the puck is gained from the offensive team.

Qualities of a Good Defensive Player

Most players can become adept at defensive play if they have a positive attitude; have a sound defensive system; are in excellent physical condition; and are able to read and react. Some specific skills involved include:

1. Checking ability—Forwards
   - knowing when to pressure and when to contain
   - knowing how to take a player out without getting a penalty
   - forwards knowing how to backcheck—covering a player, what to do if the player cuts to the middle of the ice
   - how to pick up the trailing forward

   Defensemen
   - when to pinch
   - closing the gap
   - when to face the play, e.g. the trap
   - take a player out in front of the net

2. When to have a sense of danger on offense
   - unsafe stickhandling
   - last man
   - high forward in offensive zone with the puck
   - getting the puck past the man along the boards

3. Dangerous passing
   - up the middle
   - point to point
   - blind pass outs
   - drop passes
   - diagonal passes (either end)

4. Defensive anticipation
   - point man backing up when partner is shooting
   - picking up the right man when backchecking
   - not getting blocked or picked out of the play
   - when to block shots
   - playing three-on-two and two-on-one correctly

Defensive play is initiated in the opposition's end of the rink by a forechecking pattern. It continues through the neutral zone and becomes extremely important in the defensive zone. The object of defensive play is to gain possession of the puck from the opposition and therefore prevent a score and initiate the offense.

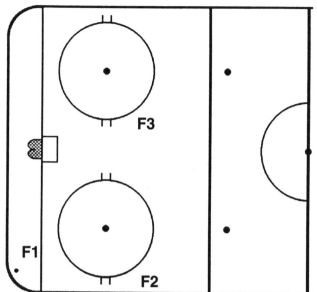

FORECHECKING WHEN THE PUCK IS IN THE CORNER

1. One Man In (1-2-2)

In this system, only one forechecker moves in, and the other two forwards pick up the opposition's wingers. The forechecker can be either the winger or center, depending on which man is in first.

2. Center In (1-2-2)

This system is similar to 1 except the center is always the first man in. F1 and F2 pull up on the boards, covering the opposition's wingers.

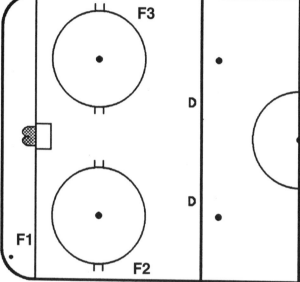

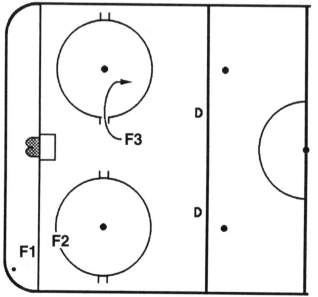

3. Two Men In (2-1-2)

The first forechecker takes the man out of the play, with the second picking up the puck. The third offensive man stations himself in the high slot. If the opposition gains possession of the puck, F3 in front of the net skates back with the opposition's winger.

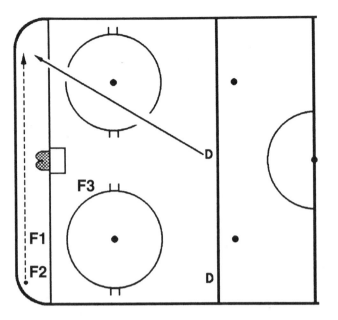

4. Three Men In

This is an all-out pressing type of forechecking system that could be used when a team is behind in a game by one or more goals. If the puck moves to the far-side corner, the offside defenseman moves in.

5. One-Two-Two or One-Four

In this type of forechecking, one forward forechecks, while the other two forwards pick up the wings and pull back as the opposition breaks out. The defense also pulls back. This is used to protect a lead or to forecheck a superior team in a defensive manner.

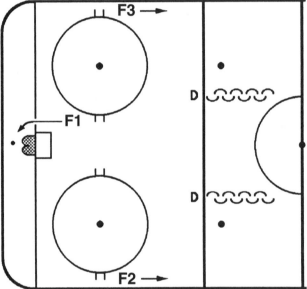

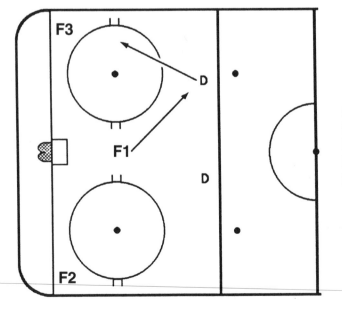

6. Two-One-Two

F1 and F2 forecheck and F1 (third man) plays high in the slot area in this system. If the defenseman pinches in on the puck side, F1 takes the defense position.

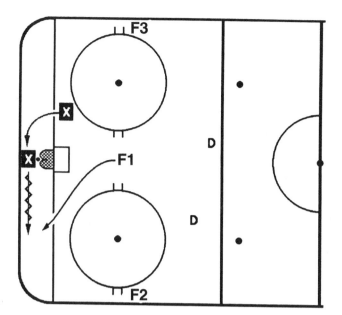

FORECHECKING PUCK BEHIND THE NET
1. Moving Puck Carrier
One man cuts off the puck carrier. The forechecker cuts across the front of the net to ride the man out. F2 and F3 pick up the opposition forwards on the boards.

2. Two Men Cut Off the Puck Carrier
This is the same as 1 except F2 on the puck side moves in to help cut off the puck carrier. The defenseman on the puck side moves in to take the opposition wingers.

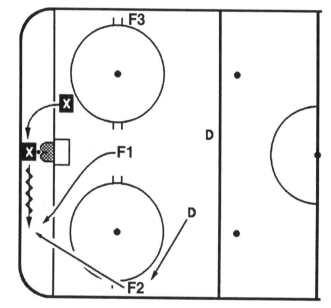

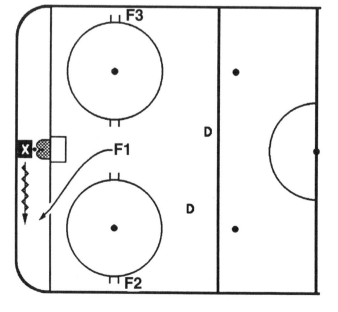

3. Puck Carrier Stops Behind the Net
The forechecker who stops in front of the net is the first man in, usually the center or the forwards. The other two forecheckers cover the opposition forwards on the boards. When the puck carrier moves, F1 moves with him. F2 and F3 stay at the boards.

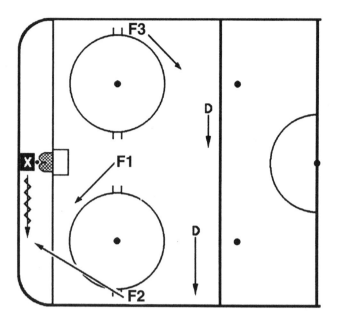

4. Two Men Cut Off the Puck Carrier Variation

In this variation of 2, when the puck carrier moves, F1 moves with the man and F2 moves in. The defenseman on the puck carrier's side moves in to take the forward to the boards.

5. Puck Carrier Is Chased Behind the Net

This system sacrifices a forechecker in order to inhibit the opposition from setting up a breakout pattern. F2 on the puck carrier's side moves in to check him. The defenseman on the puck side moves in to cover the winger.

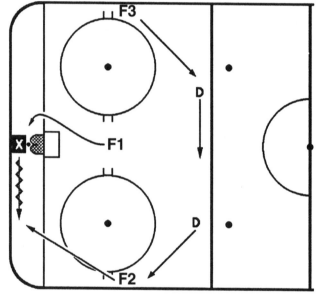

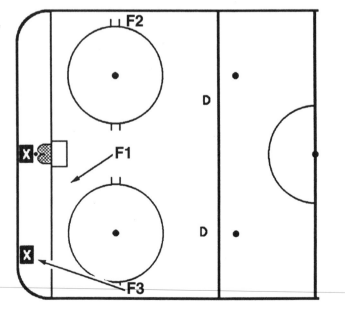

FORECHECKING DEFENSEMAN IN THE CORNER

The following systems address the situation in which the puck carrier stops behind your net and the opposition defenseman moves to the corner.

1. Forechecker in Front of the Net

F2 and F3 pull back with the wingers on the boards. F3 on the defenseman's side moves in if the pass comes to the defenseman.

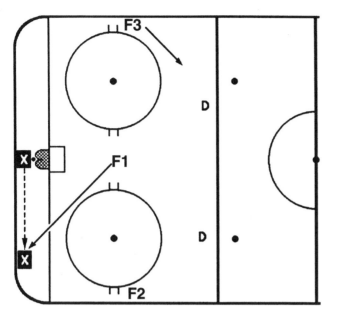

2. Forechecker in Front of the Net Variation
This is another way to defend the net if the forechecker stops in front of the net. F2 and F3 stay on the wingers. F1 follows the pass to the defenseman.

3. Puck Side-to-Side Rotation
The puck moves from one side to the other side. The first man in chases the puck to the net and then swings out to the slot. The second man in moves across to the far side. The man in the slot moves to the corner where the puck has moved.

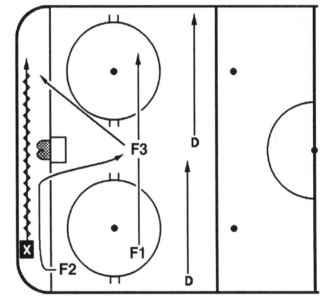

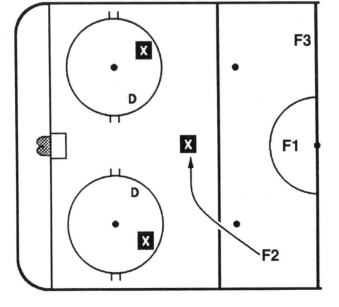

CHECKING SYSTEM FROM THE NEUTRAL ZONE INTO THE DEFENSIVE END
1. Wingers Uncovered
The defenseman must back in but attempt to give as little ice as possible. The first trailing forward (F2) picks up the slot area. The other trailing forwards (F1 and F3) pick up the wingers on the boards.

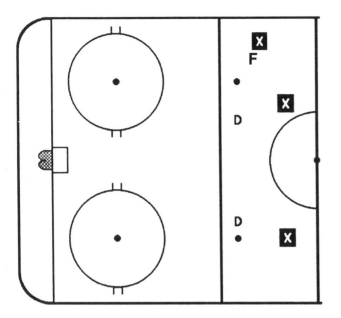

2. Left Wing Lock

One lane covered (left wing lock) or also described as three-on-two with one wing covered.

This system has a high backchecking forward at all times. On some teams it is the left winger that stays high to backcheck, thus the term left wing lock. The backchecker takes a lane and the defense move over. The backchecker is always on the inside of the man. The system has one high man backchecking—a designated forward (eg. left wing) or simply the high forward regardless of position.

3. Three-on-Two with Both Lanes Covered

Both defensemen can stand up over the blue line and force the offensive man to make a play before the blue line. If the puck is shot into the defensive zone, the wingers should be the first to pick it up.

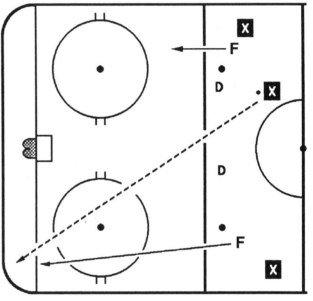

4. Neutral Zone Trap

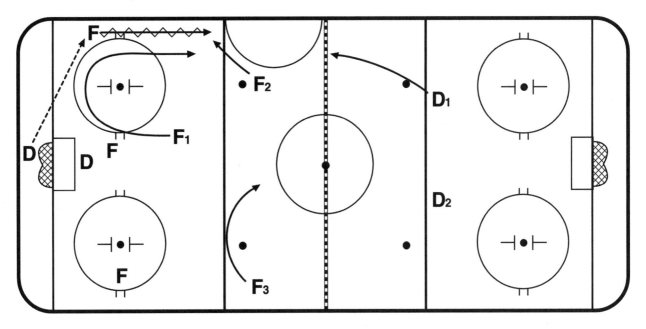

F1 the first forechecker forces the offensive defenseman, D, to pass to the forward on the boards and then angles the forward up the lane on the board side and prevents a pass to the middle. The second forechecker on the puck side moves on the puck carrier when he enters the neutral zone. F3, the third forechecker, moves across and covers the middle of the ice. D1 moves up to cover the area behind F2. D2 cover the weak side.

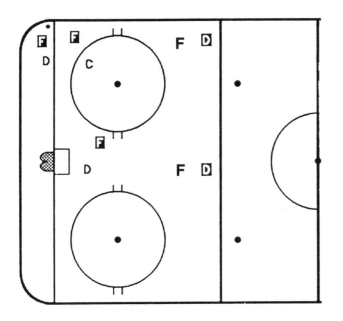

SYSTEMS IN THE DEFENSIVE ZONE
The defensive forwards should stay with the offensive forwards until a play has been made on net. The trailing forward picks up the opposition's next player into the zone, who could be an opposition defenseman. When the play settles into the corner or back to the opposition defenseman at the blue line, the defensive system should go into effect. The systems described are shown with the opposition with the puck in the corner.

1. Wingers on the Points, Center Low
The two wingers are responsible for the opposition defensemen, and the center plays low. The two defensemen cover the opposition forwards.

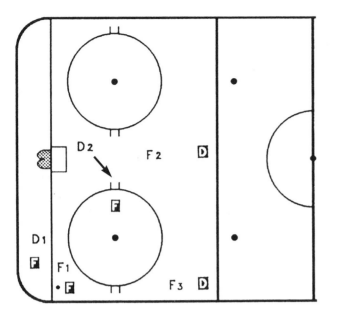

2. Man-on-Man, 1-2-3

The first forward back, F1, goes to the puck. The second forward back, F2, goes to the slot. The third forward back, F3, goes to the puck side, high boards. D1, D2, and F1 play three-on-three low. F1 and F2 cover the opposition defenseman. D2 plays halfway to cover the opposition forward in the slot.

3. Zone

The offside winger covers the high slot and the offside point. The closest winger or center covers the corner, with the other forward covering the near side point. One defenseman covers the corner, with the other defenseman covering the front of the net.

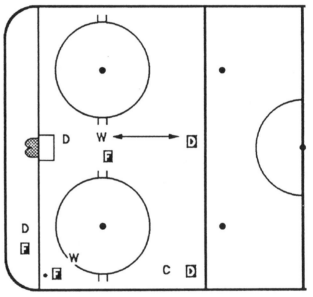

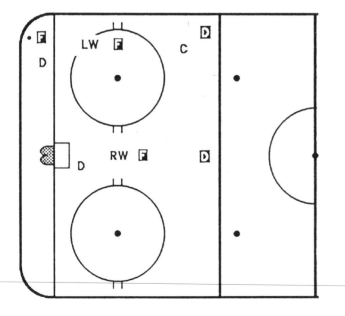

4. Wingers on Wingers, Center on the Points

One defenseman goes to the corner on the puck. The other defenseman stays in front of the net. If the puck is moved quickly to the offside point and the point man moves in, the defenseman in front of the net moves out.

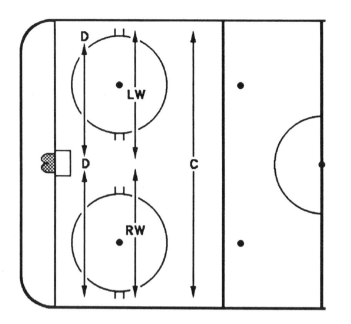

5. Sliding Zone
The center man covers the blue line area. The wingers cover from the board area to the slot. The defensemen cover from the front of the net to the corner.

6. Combination System
The center or the winger is on the puck in the corner. The forward (not in the corner) covers the net side point. The offside winger covers the slot area first and the far side point if the puck comes across to this man. The defensemen cover the front of the net or the corner if the puck is on the other side. A defenseman and a forward are always on the puck in the corners.

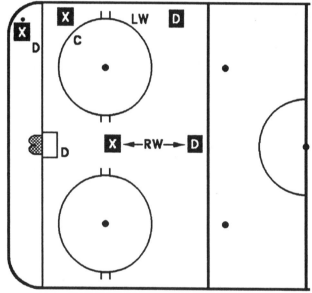

GUIDELINES FOR DEFENDING A LEAD

These are guidelines when defending a lead with five minutes or less to play in a game which guards against making plays which may trap offensive players when there is a quick transition to defense or dangerous plays in the defensive or neutral zone.

DANGEROUS PLAYS

Opposition end
1. Passes back to point
2. Shot from the point
3. Passes point to point
4. Drop passes
5. Blind pass out from the corner or behind the net

Neutral Zone
1. Unsafe stickhandling
2. Long passes
3. Carrying puck back in own zone
4. Stickhandling at the blue line

Defensive Zone
1. Unsafe stickhandling
2. Soft passes
3. Passes up the middle
4. Diagonal passes
5. Shooting around boards without looking
6. Giveaways

Safeguards
1. Avoid penalties
   - no head-on body checks
   - no checking from behind
   - no lazy stick penalties
2. Falling on the puck near the goal—goaltender get out to puck early so referee has an out
3. Forechecking
   - no forward gets caught
   - try to contain rather than set up scoring plays
4. Shoot in—pick open space
5. Never more than two man rush—shoot in more
6. In our end, dump it out more
   - be sure to get the puck past the point man, not to him
   - play off the boards more and deeper as point man often changes
7. The opposition is taking chances at out blue line—no unsafe stickhandling
8. Face-offs—think defensively at all face-offs. Don't get trapped at face-off in their end.
9. Face-offs in opposition end are good when defending a lead
10. Defend against drop man
11. Center ice area—one man checking, wings covered and well ahead of their man, defense standing up at the blue line
12. If opposition has six attackers, try to get over the red line before icing the puck

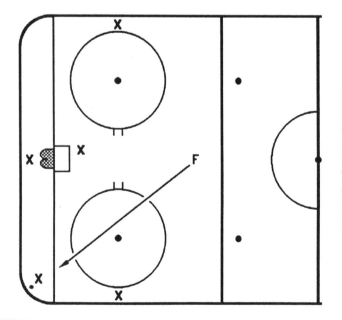

DEFENSIVE TEAM PLAY DRILLS
In addition to the drills that follow, all forechecking drills discussed in chapter 9, "Checking," can be used here.

1. One-on-Five Drill
The puck is shot into the offensive zone, and one forechecker attempts to break up the breakout play. Both ends of the rink can be used for this drill.

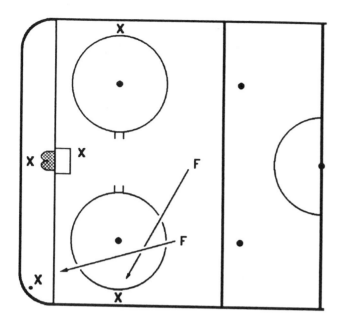

2. Two-on-Five, Three-on-Five, Five-on-Five

In this variation on 1, two forecheckers attempt to break up play, then three forwards and two defensemen. The drill can be executed at both ends of the rink.

3. Without Opposition

Work a defensive system against no opposition. The coach can describe the situation, and the players react by positioning themselves quickly, e.g., puck is in the left corner, the puck moves behind the net, or the puck moves to the far corner. Also drill players on reacting to hand or stick signals by coach. The drill can be run at both ends of the rink as well as in neutral zone if you have three nets.

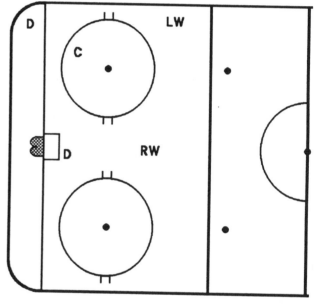

4. Opposition Defensive Team Without Sticks

The offensive team moves the puck around while the defensive team plays without sticks, concentrating on positional play. Both ends of the ice can be used for this drill.

5. Five-on-Five Drill (not shown)

This drill is the same drill as 4 except defensive players have sticks. The drill is worked in the defensive zone, with the offensive team being given the puck in the corner or at the point and worked from that point. The play ends when a goal is scored, the goalie or players hold the puck, or the puck is moved out of the defensive end over the blue line. The drill can be worked at both ends of the rink.

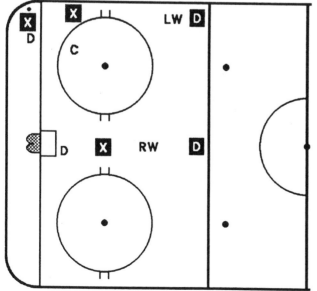

12. PENALTY KILLING

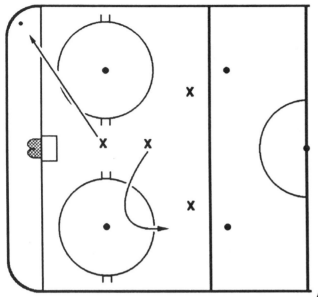

There are a number of penalty killing systems used in hockey.

FORECHECKING PATTERNS IN THE OFFENSIVE ZONE
One Man Short
1. Stacked Formation ("I")

The first forechecker moves to the puck side. The second forechecker swings to the opposite side and picks up the winger on that side.

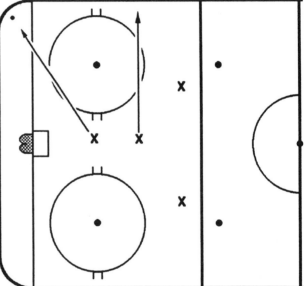

2. Stacked Formation Variation

In this variation of 1, both of the forecheckers move to the same side to attempt to break up the play.

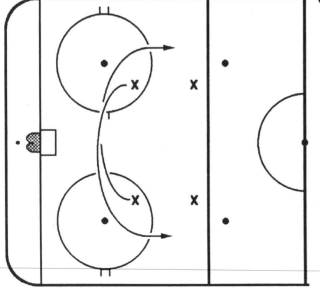

3. Forecheckers Criss-cross

The first forechecker swings across to one side. The second forechecker swings to the opposite side.

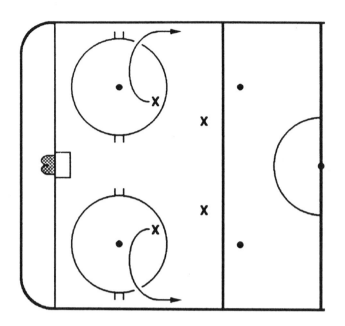

4. Forecheckers Pick Up the Lanes
Both forecheckers pick up the lanes on each side of the ice.

5. Forecheckers Pick Up the Lanes at the Blue Line
In this variation of 4, the forecheckers do not go further than just inside the offensive blue line.

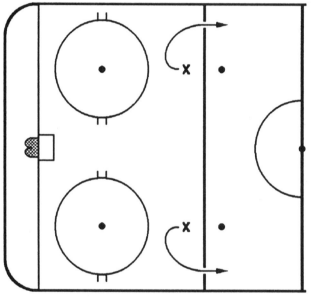

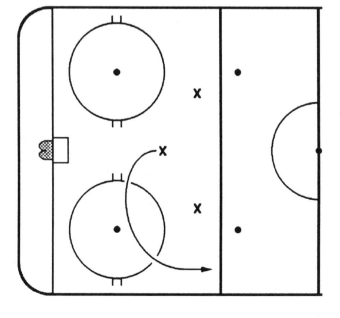

Two Men Short
6. Forechecker Swings
The forechecker moves in and swings with the puck carrier and then picks up the lane.

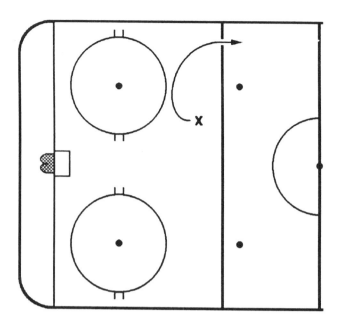

7. No Forecheck
In this variation of 6, the forechecker moves in no further than the blue line and then picks up either lane.

BACKCHECKING PATTERNS IN THE NEUTRAL ZONE
One Man Short
1. Forwards in Lanes
With the lanes covered, the defensemen stand up at the blue line.

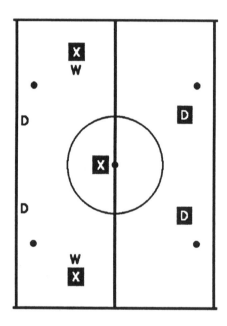

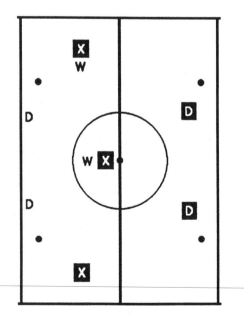

2. One Forward in Lane
In this pattern, one lane is covered, and the other forechecker is in the mid-ice area. The offside defenseman moves over. The forechecker in the mid-ice area moves on the puck carrier.

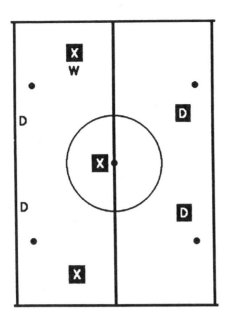

Two Men Short
3. Cover the Lane
The forechecker picks up either lane.

4. Cover the Center Area
The forechecker picks up the center area.

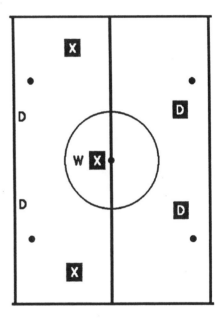

DEFENSIVE ZONE SYSTEMS
One Man Short
1. Standard Box
In the standard box formation, two wingers and two defensemen force the play to the outside. The four defenders move to the outside of the box for the puck only if they have a 90 percent chance of gaining possession.

The puck is behind the net or in the center area.

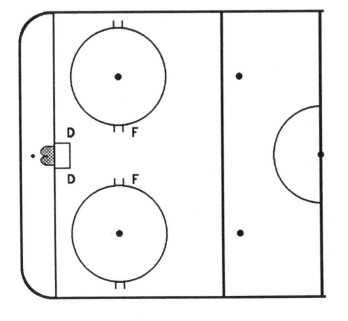

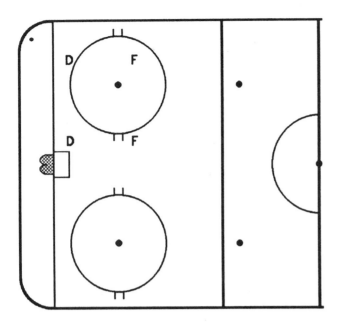

2. Standard Box Variation

In this variation of 1, the puck is in the corner or at the point.

3. Collapsible Box

This pattern is the same as 1 except the box moves to the net area. The box moves out when the puck moves to the corner or back to the point.

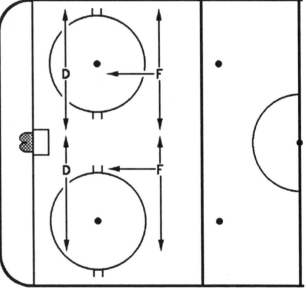

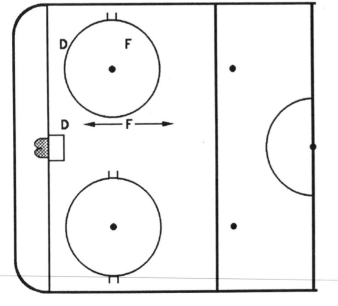

4. Sagging Box

This pattern is the same as 1 except the offside winger to the puck side moves back into the slot area. This man moves out again if the puck is passed to the defenseman on his side.

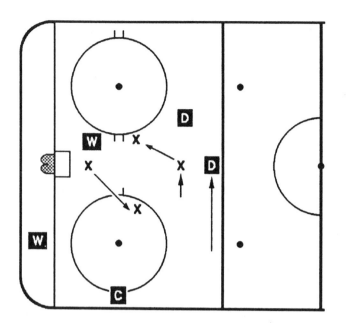

5. The Diamond (Rotating Box)
In this box pattern variation, when the opposition is on the power play, the defenseman moves to the middle of the blue line. The penalty killing forward moves to the middle of the ice with the defenseman. The defenseman on the same side moves out, and the offside defenseman moves to the front of the net. The offside penalty killing forward drops off to form the diamond.

Two Men Short
6. Standard Triangle
The forward at the top of the triangle moves from side to side covering the high slot area and the points.

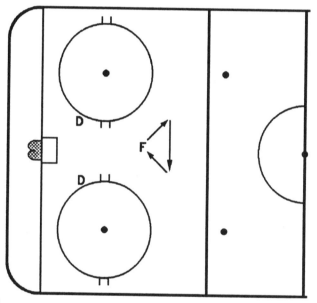

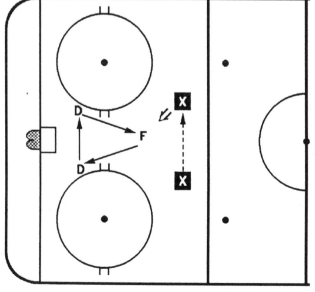

7. Rotating Triangle
This pattern is the same as 6 except the defenseman moves out on the point man if the forward is trapped on the offside. The forward then moves back as a defenseman, and the other defenseman moves to the offside. The defenseman who moves out becomes the top man in the triangle.

8. Sliding Triangle

In this triangle pattern there is one defenseman and two forwards. One defenseman stands in front of the net, moving only from one side of the crease to the other depending upon the side the puck is on. The other two forwards move in and out, eliminating the top man's getting trapped, which is the weakness of the normal triangle formation.

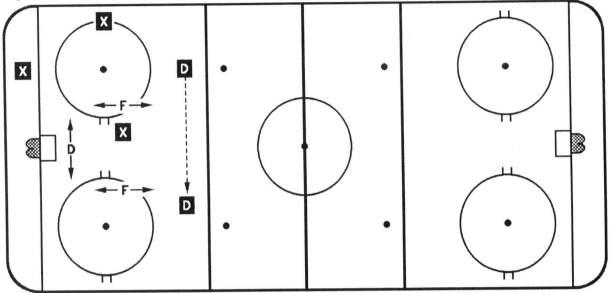

DRILLS FOR PENALTY KILLING

Use the full ice surface to drill players on penalty killing. The puck may be shot into the offensive end by the coach with the offensive team attempting to start the play from there. Time limits for each offensive and defensive unit may be used.

1. No Opposition

Players work the box and triangle patterns without any opposition, reacting to the coach's hand or stick signals.

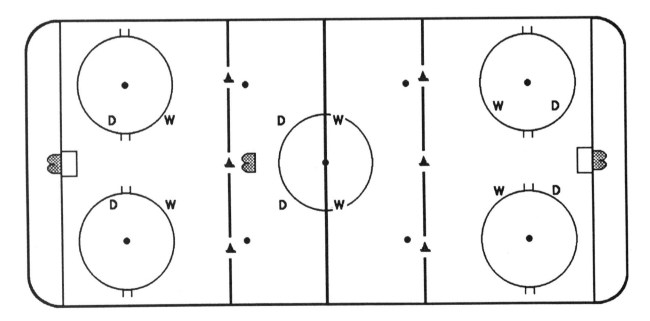

2. With and Without Sticks
Have players work the box and triangle patterns against any offense at each end of the ice, first without sticks and then with sticks.

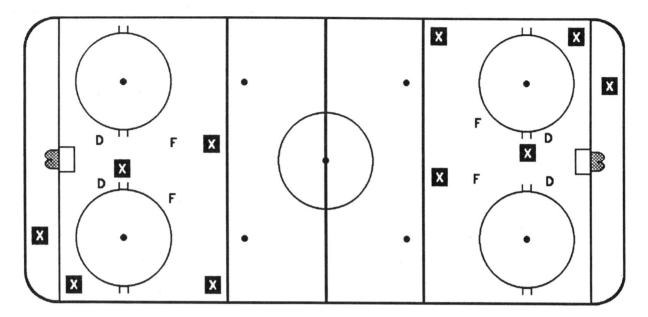

3. Forwards Against Offensive Team
Drill the players on the box and triangle patterns with the forechecking forwards working against the offensive team, bringing the puck out of their own end. This drill can be worked at both ends.

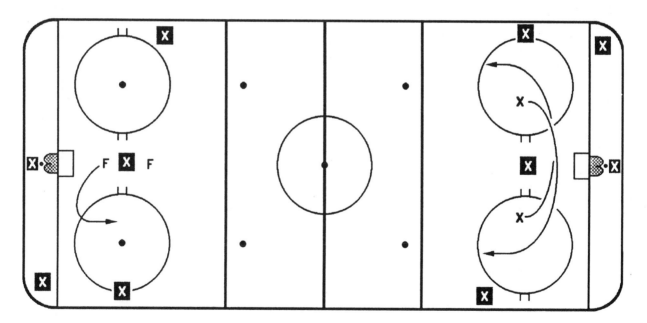

13. POWER PLAY

The objective of the power play is to move the puck into the defensive zone and maintain possession until an excellent scoring opportunity can be set up. The puck should be moved as quickly as possible.

ORGANIZING IN THE DEFENSIVE ZONE—BREAKOUTS

In many instances, the power play is initiated in the defensive zone after the shorthanded team has shot the puck the length of the ice from their defensive zone. There are a number of different methods used to move the puck from the defensive zone of the team with the power play.

BREAKOUTS

1. Behind the Net
The center circles behind the net and takes the puck from the defenseman and moves straight up the center of the ice. The defenseman in front of the net can move to the boards and follow behind the winger to set up a crossing pattern at the far blue line.

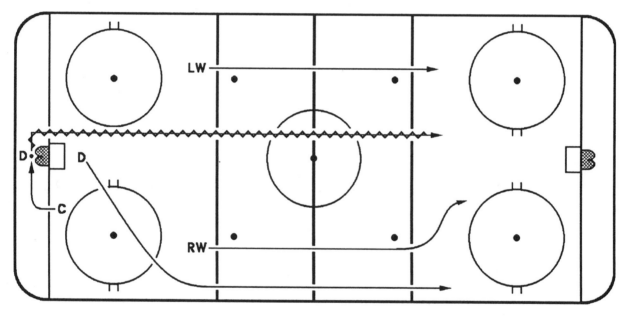

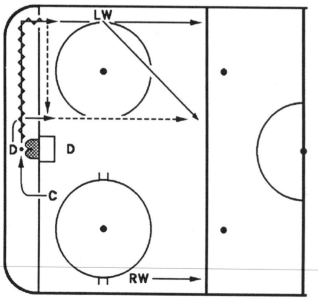

2. Center Behind the Net
The center circles behind the net, takes the puck and moves wide to the corner, and then drops the puck back to the defenseman. The defenseman moves straight up the ice or returns the pass to the center, who has circled back to the center of the ice or to the winger cutting from the boards.

3. Defenseman Behind the Net

The defenseman stops behind the net, and his partner moves to the corner. The center makes a tight turn at the goal line on the opposite side to the defenseman in the corner. The defenseman behind the net gives the puck to the center. The other defenseman in the corner goes straight up the ice to form a four-man attack.

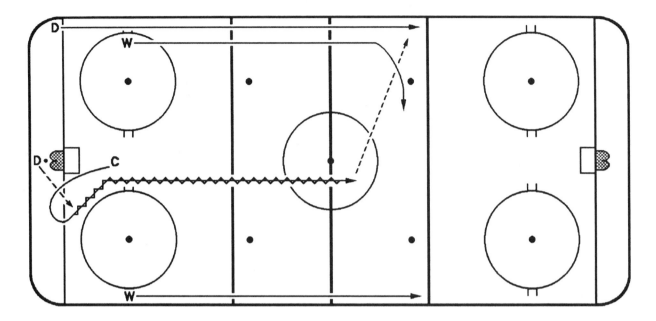

4. Defenseman Behind the Net Variation

The defenseman stops behind the net, and his partner moves to the corner. The center makes a tight turn at the goal line on the opposite side to the defenseman in the corner. The defenseman behind the net gives the puck to the center or the defenseman in the corner. If the puck goes to the defenseman in the corner, he will then take two strides with the puck and pass to the circling center. The defenseman who was in the corner then moves down the boards and becomes the outlet man for the winger cutting across at the blue line.

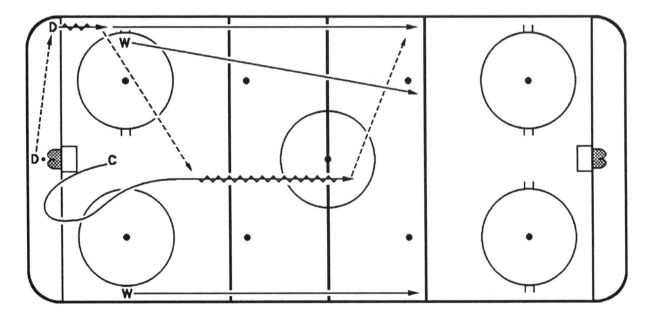

5. Breakout (not shown)
Any standard breakout play can be used in moving the puck from the defensive zone, such as one in which a defenseman is in the corner or one in which a center swings to the corner, such as 21 on page 96.

6. Double Swing with Wingers High at the Blue Line
The defenseman and the center swing to the corner. The wingers are high at the blue line, they cut across, and they are available for a pass from the defenseman or the swing man.

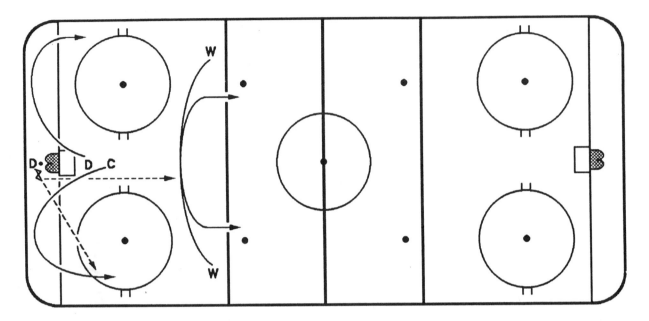

7. Double Swing Variation
In this variation of 6, one winger is at the near blue line, and one winger is at the far blue line. The winger at the near blue line loops in, and the winger at the far blue line cuts across for a pick or a pass as the play moves up the ice.

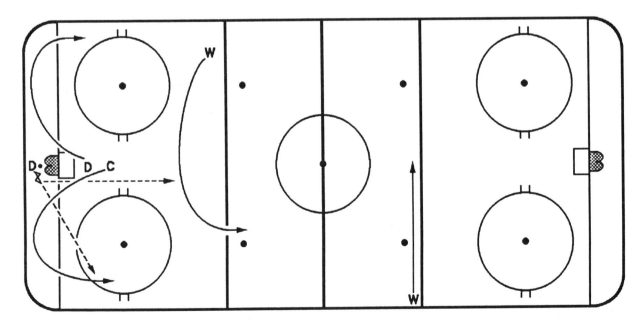

MOVING THROUGH THE NEUTRAL ZONE

In most cases, the team with the power play attempts to have a fourth offensive player involved in the play as the puck is moved across the opposition's blue line.

NEUTRAL ZONE DRILLS
1. Defense Up the Boards
The center carries the puck. The winger cuts in, with the defenseman moving down the boards. One defenseman follows the winger up quickly on either side. The winger cuts to the center area to pull his check with him. The center passes the puck to either the defenseman or the winger.

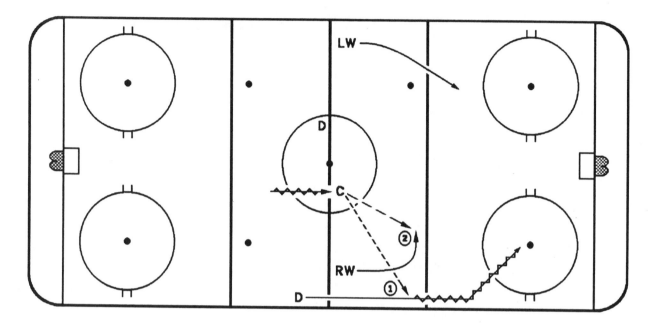

2. Center Up the Boards
The defenseman carries the puck, with the center following the winger up the boards. The play for the winger is the same as in 1 except the defenseman passes to the center or the winger cuts across.

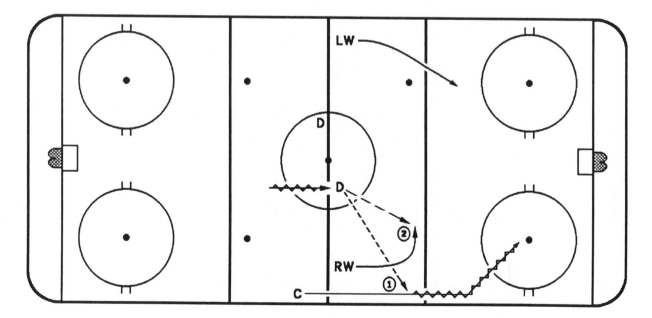

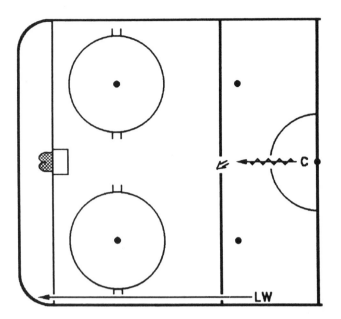

3. Shoot In
The puck carrier shoots the puck into the offensive zone. It is important that the puck is shot into the offensive zone with the wings in full flight. Getting possession of the puck after shooting is extremely important; otherwise, the play is ineffective.

4. Rim the Boards
The puck carrier moves down the ice close to the boards and shoots the puck in to rim the boards. It is picked up by the outside forward. The puck can then be passed quickly back to the defense to set up the power play.

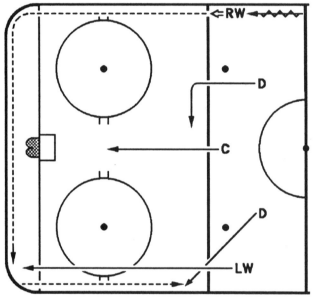

PLAY IN THE OFFENSIVE ZONE

When you're one or two men shorthanded, the object in the offensive zone is for the players to move the puck quickly and for the offensive players to be placed strategically so they can set up in an open area for a scoring opportunity.

DRILLS
1. Forwards in the Corners
The forwards are in the corners, and the center is in the slot area.

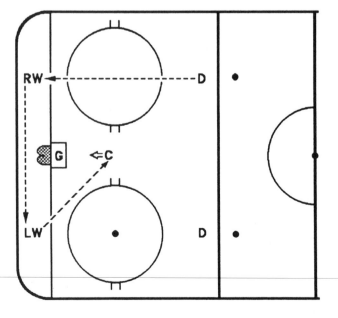

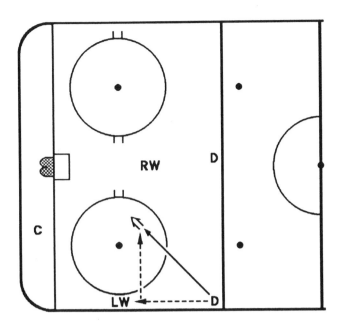

2. Give-and-Go with Defenseman
The defenseman passes to the forward in the corner and then moves to the net for a return pass.

3. Give-and-Go Variation If the defender moves with the defenseman, the forward can pass to another forward in the corner.

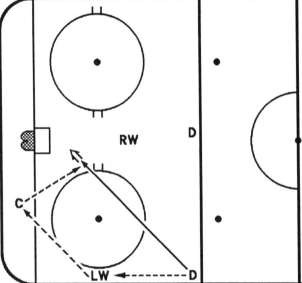

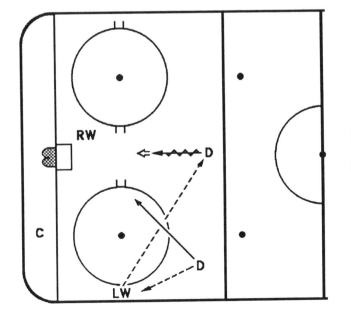

4. Pass to Offside Defenseman
This play is the same as 3 except the forward passes to the offside defenseman.

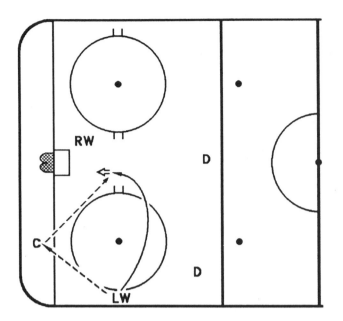

5. Give-and-Go in the Corner
The winger passes to the center and then moves to the net for a return pass on the give-and-go.

6. Two-on-One in the Corner Variation
If the defenseman moves with the winger, the center can pass to the defenseman moving into the high slot.

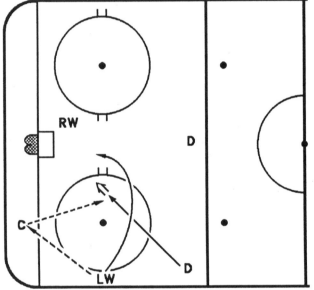

7. Umbrella Power Play (4 options)
    (a) D1 moves to the middle and shoots.
    (b) D2 moves wider across the blue line. D1 moves to the middle and passes back to F1 sho shoots.
    (c) D1 moves to the middle, passes back to F1. F1 passes to F2 who tries for the one-timer.
    (d) D1 moves to the middle and passes to D2 who has moved to the top of the circle. D2 shoots.

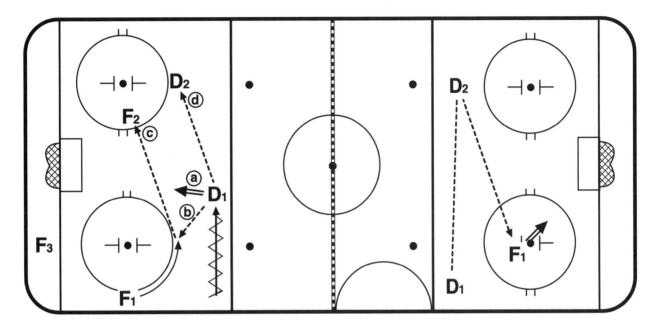

8. Wrist
D1 moves towards the middle and shoots a quick wrist shot. F1 and F2 go to the front of the net.

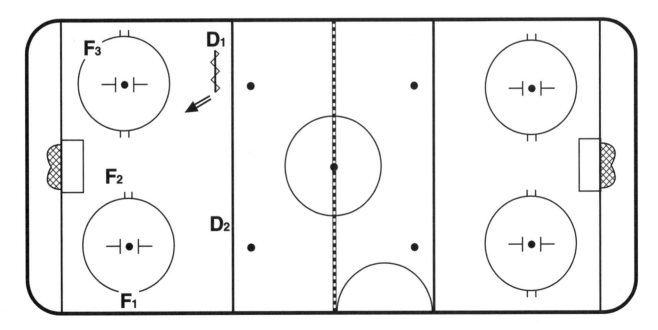

9. Slot

D1 passes to F3. F3 and F1 pass the puck back and forth. F3 passes to F2 (right hand shot) for a one-timer.

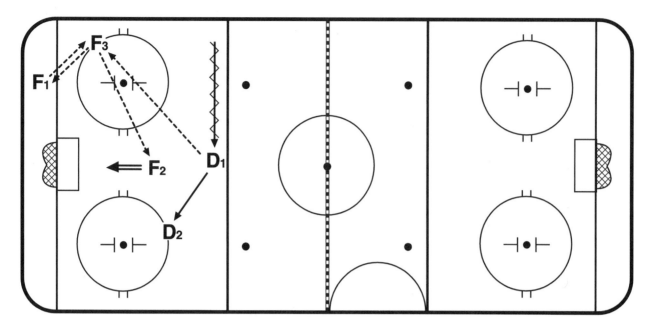

Slot (variation)

Same as above except F3 passes through to D2 who moves in from the top of the far circle.

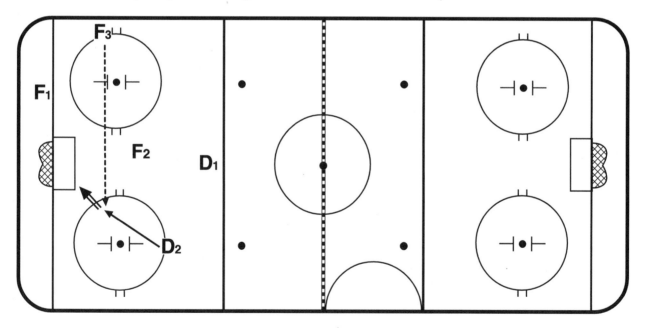

10. Pass Across

The center moves to the front of the net to tie up the defenseman. The winger coming from the corner passes the puck across to the offside winger, who is standing off the far side goalpost.

If the winger coming to the net is covered, the winger should look for the defenseman moving down into the high slot.

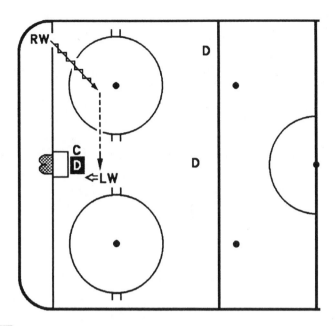

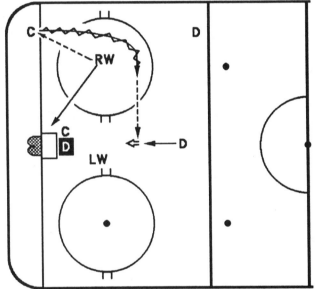

11. Pass to Offside Defenseman

A two-on-one situation is set up in the corner, with the other forward tying up the defenseman in the front of the net. The forward in the corner tries to pass to the offside defenseman moving in from the point.

12. Walk Out with Pick

The center with the puck moves around behind the net and circles in front to pass to the far side winger or shoots. The winger in front of the net picks the opposition defenseman on that side.

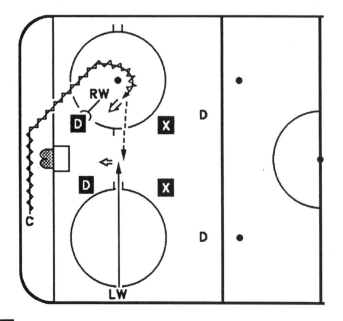

13. High Pick

The center with the puck circles behind the net, continues out near the blue line, and then moves down the middle for a shot. The two wingers pick the opposition defensemen in front of the net. The near side defenseman picks the near opposition forward at the top of the box.

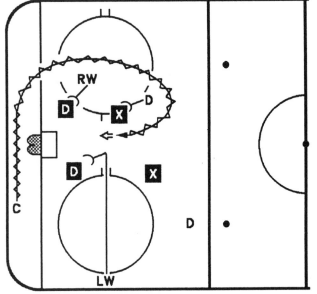

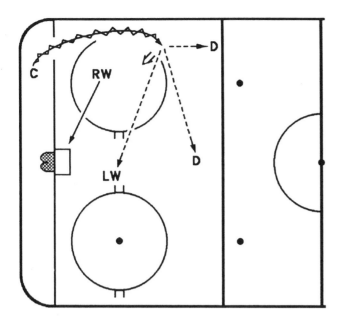

14. Combined System

From a two-on-one situation in the corner, the forward looks for the following possibilities in sequence:

- pass to the give-and-go man
- move out from corner for a possible shot
- pass to the offside winger
- pass the offside point man
- pass to the near side point man

15. Around the Outside

The puck is passed quickly around the outside from the center, left winger, defenseman, defenseman, and right winger and then quickly across to the left winger, who is moving in for a direct shot.

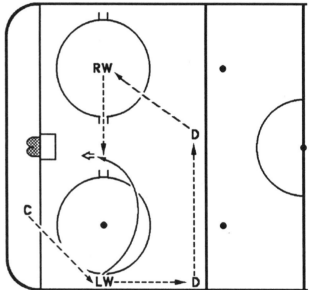

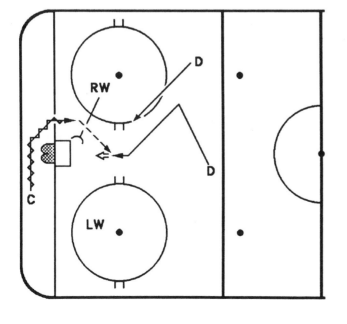

16. Behind the Net

The center moves from behind the net. The right winger picks for the defenseman, the right defenseman moves through the slot, and the left defenseman moves over, takes a pass from the center, and shoots.

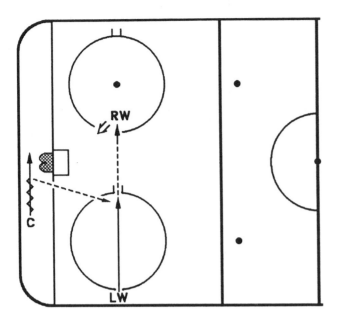

17. Pass Back
The center goes behind the net and passes back on the same side to the winger moving in. The winger either shoots or passes the puck across to the offside forward.

18. Defense Moves to the Boards
The defenseman takes a pass from the other defenseman in the middle of the ice. The defenseman receiving the pass then skates toward the boards and passes the puck back to the offside defenseman, who has moved to the middle of the ice. The defenseman shoots, and the other forwards go to the front of the net.

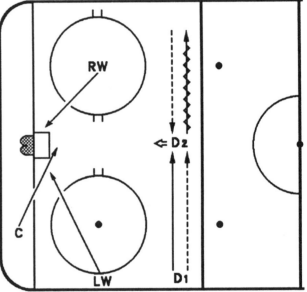

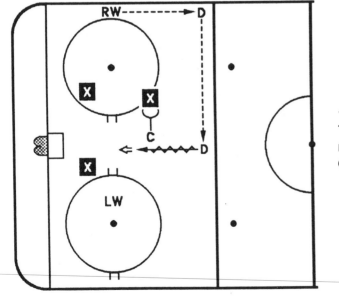

19. Two Men Short
The puck is passed from defenseman to defenseman, and the center picks off the top man in the defensive triangle.

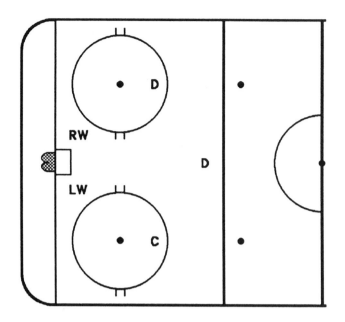

20. Defenseman to Middle with Two Men Short
The defenseman moves to the middle part of the ice, the offside defenseman and another forward form an umbrella (or outlets), and the other two forwards go to the front of the net.

DRILLS FOR THE POWER PLAY
1. Passing Warm-up
One touch, circle, circle man in the middle, circle follow the pass

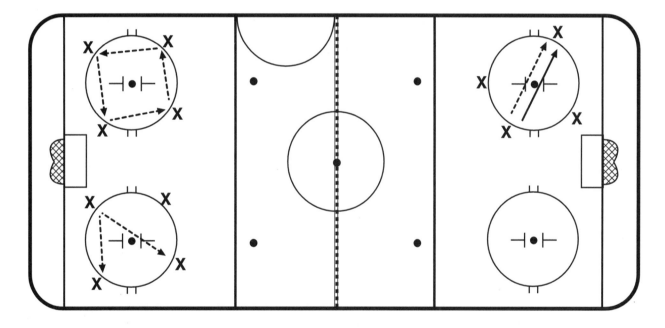

2. Defense and Forward Lead-up Drills

Forwards
– pass across, move to the slot, return pass for one-timer off boards—pivot and shoot off the pass—one-timer

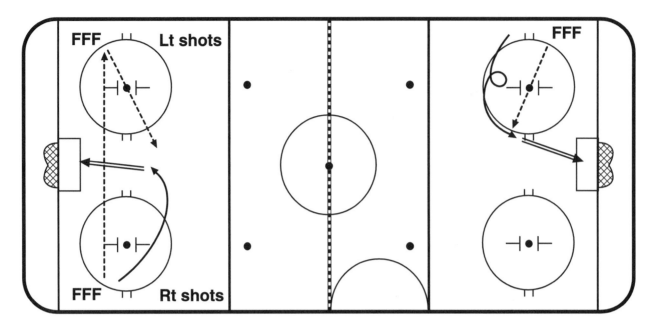

Defense

– take a pass move along the blue line and shoot—slap shot and wrist shot—add man in front
– take a pass, move along the blue line, pass to the other D at the top of the circle—one-timer

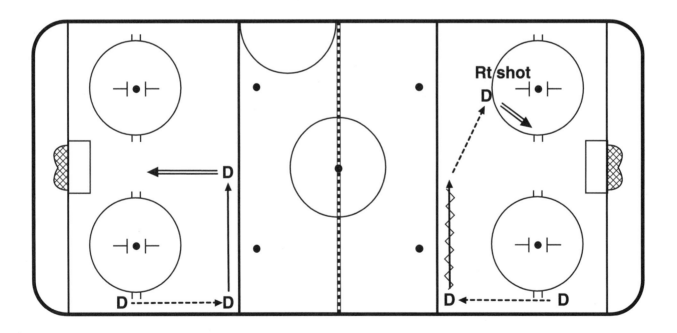

D moves across to the middle, the other D moves along the blue line to the boards, D passes to the boards, takes a return pass and shoots.

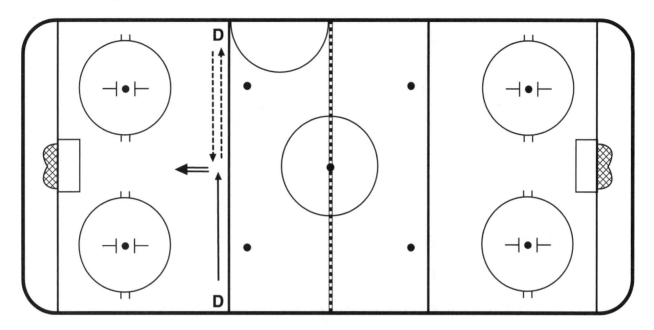

3. One Defence and One Forward Drill
D pass to the forward coming off the boards (use the face-off circle for the path of the forward).
Right shot D to right shot forward
Left shot D to left shot forward
Change D left shot to right forward

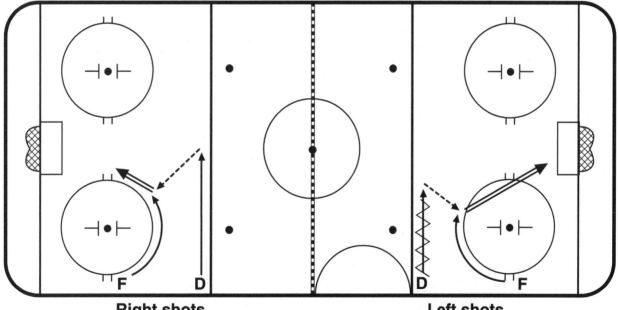

Right shots   **Left shots**

4. One Defense and Two Forwards Drill
D to F coming from boards to forward in the slot—one-timer

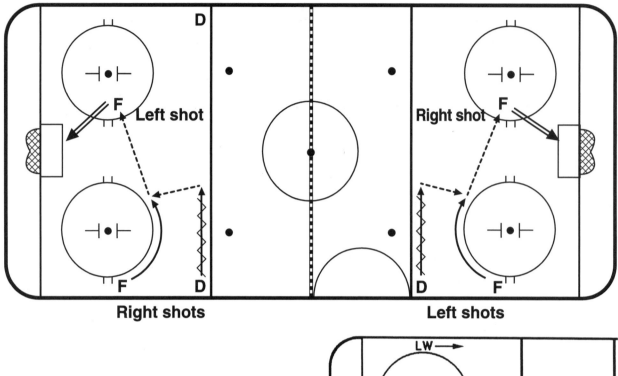

Right shots
Left shots

5. BREAKOUTS
(i) No Opposition
Work breakout patterns and neutral zone plays with no opposition. The drill can be worked at both ends, with the groups not passing the red line. Plays worked between the red line and offensive blue line can work between the defensive blue line and center red line.

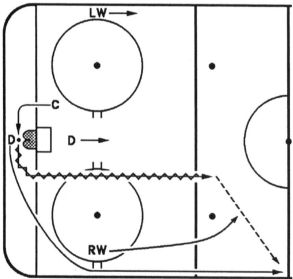

(ii) Two Forecheckers
In this variation of i, two forecheckers attempt to break up the play.

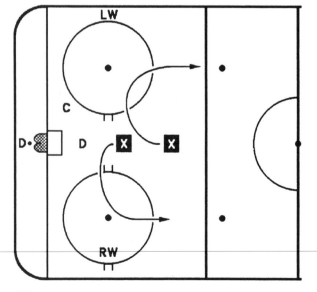

6. No Opposition

Drill players on offensive patterns against no opposition. Three areas of the ice can be used.

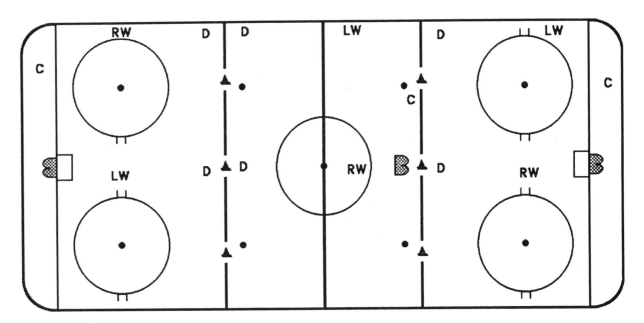

7. Defenders Without Sticks (not shown)

Drill players on offensive patterns against defenders without sticks. Both ends of the rink or three areas can be used.

8. Defenders With Sticks

Drill players on offensive patterns against defenders with sticks.

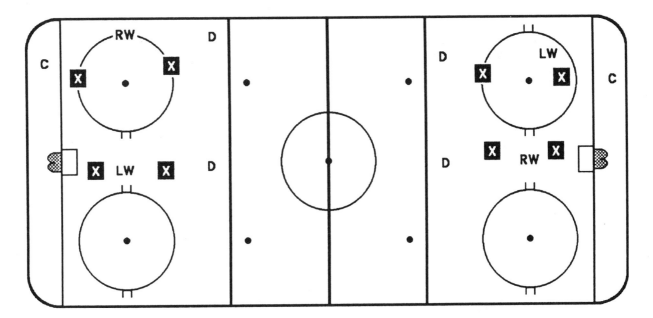

9. Power-Play Scrimmage (not shown)

(vs. three first, then vs. four)

If the penalty killers get the puck, ice it immediately in the initial stages of these drills. Give each power play unit a total of two minutes. Keep number of goals scored.

10. Practice Offensive Zone Face-Offs

D2 moves in to the hash marks. F1 draws directly to D1.

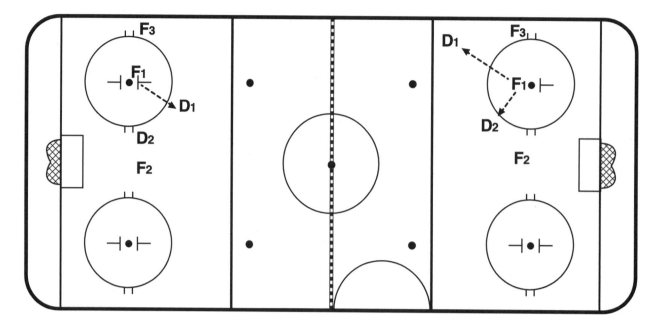

14. FACE-OFF ALIGNMENTS

FACE-OFF TECHNIQUES

The man taking the face-off should make sure that all players are in position before taking the face-off.

The player taking the face-off should be able to watch the puck in the referee's hand and the opponent's stick at the same time by using peripheral vision. Quick reaction time is essential in this skill.

Players taking the face-off should have many methods of winning:

BACKHAND

This is the most common method. The player draws the puck at an angle or, in some instances, directly back on the backhand side.

FOREHAND

The player anticipates the dropping of the puck. He rotates his body by a quarter turn. He comes in front of, behind, or under an opponent's stick.

ANTICIPATE THE DROPPING OF THE PUCK

The player anticipates the dropping of the puck. As soon as the puck leaves the official's hand, he hits the blade of the opponent's stick and then draws the puck back.

HOLD AND DRAW

The player holds the opponent's stick with the blade of his own stick until the puck has made contact with the ice. Then he draws the puck back.

LIFT AND DRAW

If the opponent is attempting to slash the blade of the stick and is not going for the puck, the player taking the face-off lifts the blade of the stick and then goes for the puck.

SHOOT

The puck is shot directly from the face-off.

SKATE THROUGH AND SHOOT

The face-off man pushes the opponent's stick upward, skates through the face-off dot, and kicks the puck to the stick.

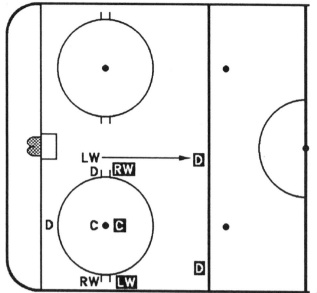

Note that all face-offs are reversed for the opposite side of the ice.

DEFENSIVE ZONE FACE-OFFS
1. Full Strength
Assignments:

(LW) Takes right defenseman
(RW) Takes left winger
(C) Takes draw and center
(LD) Takes right winger
(RD) Takes puck drawn back or center moving to net

2. Full Strength

Assignments:
(LW) Takes right defenseman
(RW) Takes left winger and then left defenseman
(C) Takes center
(LD) Takes right winger
(RD) Takes puck drawn back or center

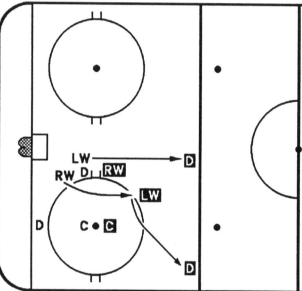

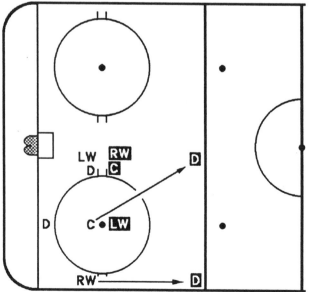

3. Full Strength

Assignments:
(LW) Takes right winger
(RW) Takes left defenseman
(C) Takes left wing then right defenseman
(LD) Takes center
(RD) Takes puck drawn back or center moving to net

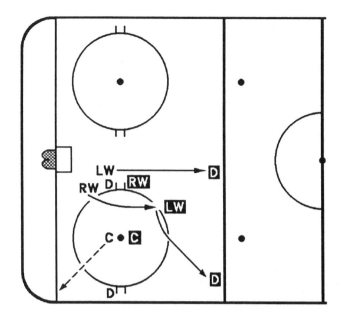

4. Full Strength
Assignments:

(LW)   Takes right defenseman
(RW)   Takes left winger then near side point
(C)   Takes draw and center
(LD)   Takes right winger or goes to net
(RD)   Takes puck drawn back or moves to net

5. Face-off Inside Blue line
F1 draws the puck back to D1, who passes to D2. D2 passes through to F3 who has skated in front of the net (high shot).

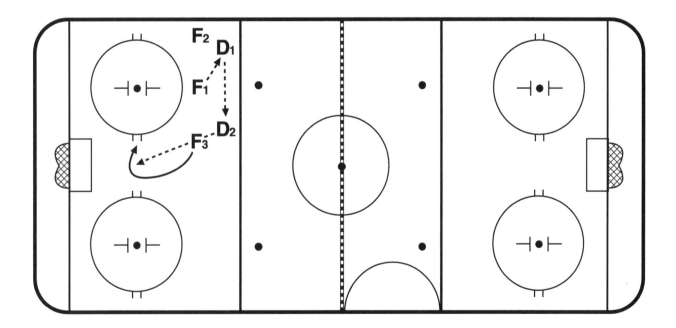

6. Face-off Inside Blue Line Variation

F2 draws the puck back to D1. D1 passes wide to D2. F3 blocks and D2 moves in and shoots.

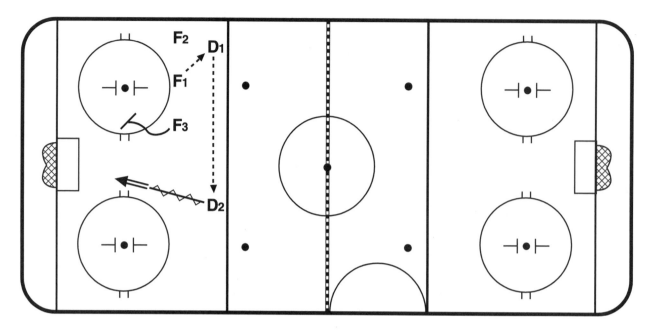

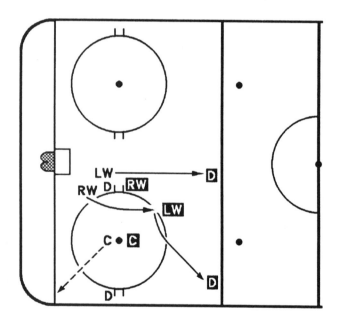

7. One Man Short

Assignments:

(W)	Takes right defenseman
(C)	Takes center and left defense
(LD)	Takes right winger
(RD)	Takes puck drawn back or center moving to net

8. One Man Short
Assignments:

(W)   Takes left winger and then left defense
(C)   Takes center
(LD)   Takes right winger
(RD)   Takes puck drawn back or center moving to net

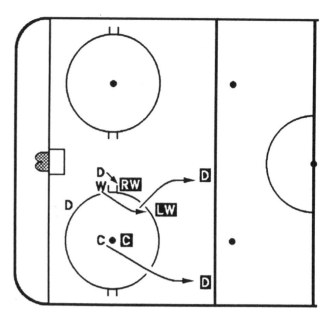

9. One Man Short
Assignments:

(W)   Takes right winger then right defenseman
(C)   Takes left winger then left defenseman
(LD)   Takes center
(RD)   Takes draw and left winger moving to net

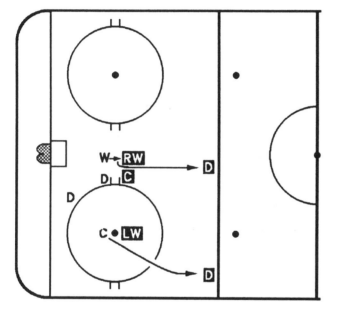

10. Two Men Short
Assignments:

(C)   Takes center then left winger
(LD)   Takes right winger
(RD)   Takes puck drawn back or center moving to net

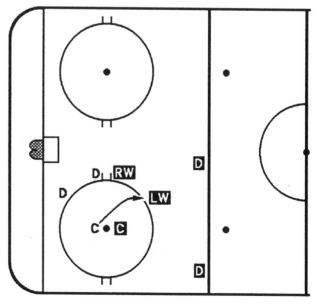

11. Two Men Short
Assignments:

(C) Takes left winger
(LD) Takes right winger
(RD) Takes center

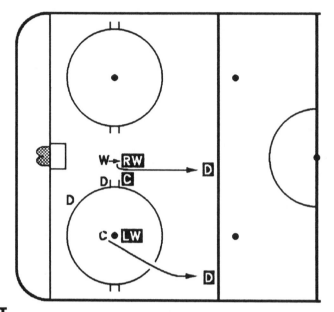

12. Two Men Short
Assignments:

(C) Takes center
(LD) Takes right winger
(RD) Takes left winger

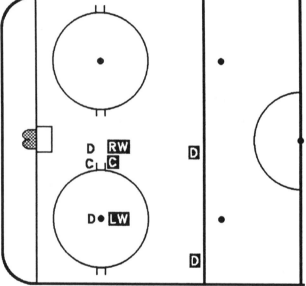

NEUTRAL ZONE FACE-OFFS OUTSIDE OWN BLUE LINE
1. Full Strength
Assignments:

(C) Pushes puck straight forward or to either wing
(LW) Takes right winger or goes for puck
(RW) Takes left winger or goes for puck

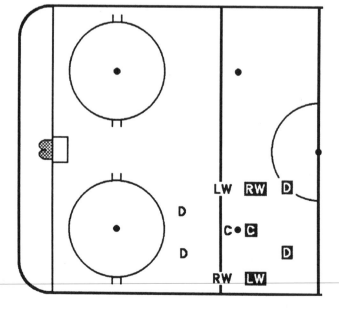

2. Full Strength
Assignments:

(C) Pushes puck forward to the left side
(LW) Goes for the puck
(LD) Moves to cut off right winger
(RW) Covers left winger
(RD) Backs up play

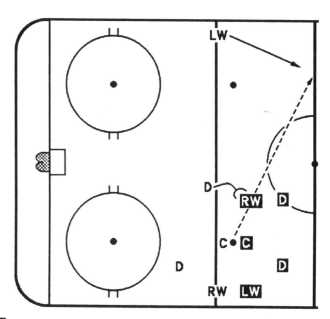

3. Full Strength
Assignments:

(LW) Goes for puck
(C) Cuts off right winger
(RW) Shoots puck to the left side
(LD) Backs up play
(RD) Covers left winger

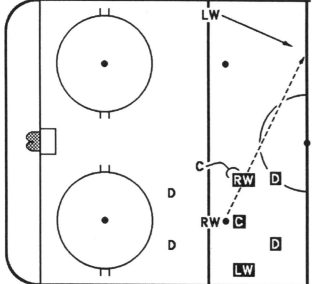

4. One Man Short
Assignments:

(W) Takes right winger
(C) Takes center
(LD) Backs up the play
(RD) Takes left winger

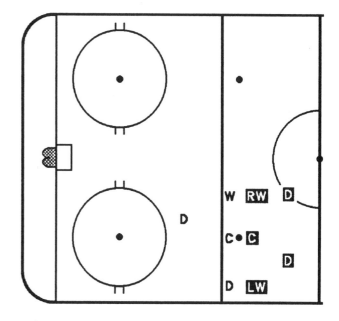

171

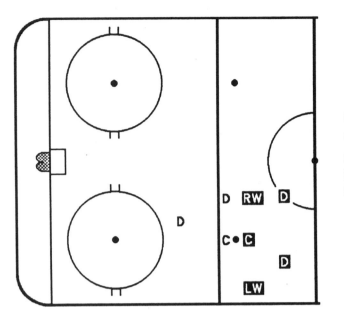

5. Two Men Short
Assignments:

(LD)	Takes right winger
(C)	Takes center
(RD)	Backs up play and watches left winger

NEUTRAL ZONE FACE-OFFS AT CENTER ICE
1. Full Strength
Assignments:

(C)	Shoots puck forward to left or right winger
(LD)	Backs up play
(RD)	Backs up play
(LW)	Goes for puck
(RW)	Goes for forwards

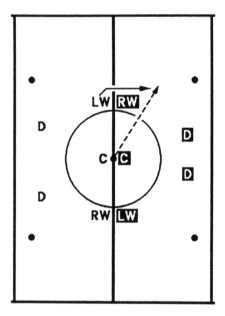

2. Neutral Zone

F1 draws the puck back to D1. F1 loops as shown. D1 passes to D2 who passes to F1. F3 and F2 cross as shown.

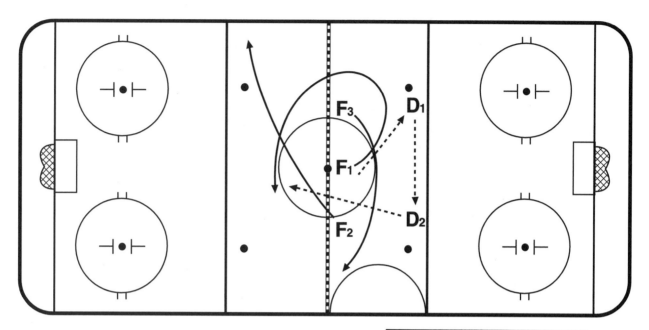

3. Full Strength

Assignments:

(C) Draws puck back to left defenseman and gets in position to receive puck from right defenseman

(LD) Receives puck and passes to right defenseman

(RD) Passes puck to center

(LW) Covers right winger

(RW) Covers left winger

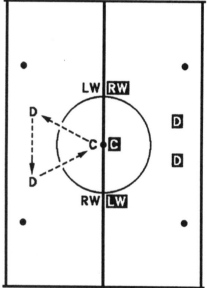

4. Full Strength

Assignments:

(LW) Takes right winger
(C) Shoots puck to right winger
(RD) Cuts off left winger
(RW) Goes for the puck
(LD) Backs up the play

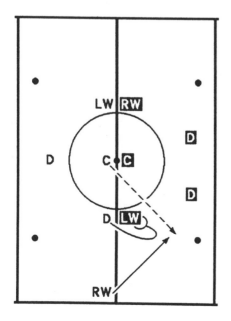

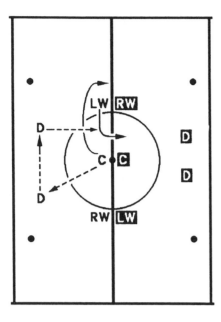

5. Full Strength
Assignments:

(C)	Draws puck back to right defenseman and crosses with center
(RD)	Passes to left defenseman
(LW)	Crosses with center
(LD)	Passes puck to crossing left winger

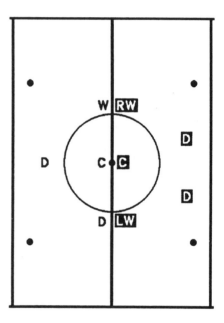

6. One Man Short
Assignments:

(W)	Takes right winger
(C)	Takes center
(RD)	Takes left winger
(LD)	Backs up the play

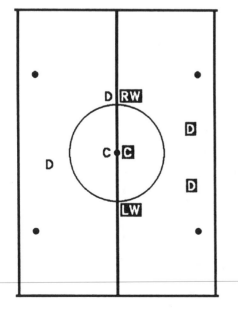

7. Two Men Short
Assignments:

(LD)	Takes right winger
(C)	Takes center
(RD)	Backs up the play and watches left winger or lines up opposite the left winger

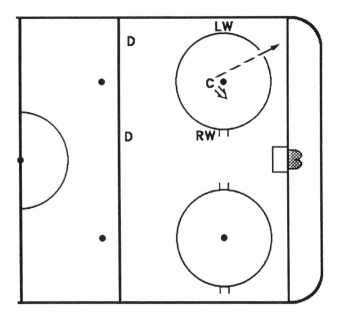

OFFENSIVE ZONE FACE-OFFS
1. Full Strength
Assignments:

(C)   Shoots for net or draws to the left side
(LW)   Goes for the puck in the corner
(RW)   Goes for the net

2. Full Strength
Assignments:

(C)   Draws the puck back to the left winger
(RW)   Prevents opposition from reaching left winger and then goes for the net
(LW)   Takes the draw from center and shoots for the net

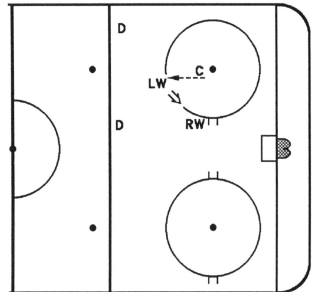

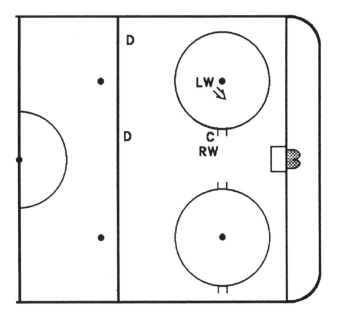

3. Full Strength
Assignments:

(LW)   Shoots for the net
(C)   Goes for the net
(RW)   Goes for the net

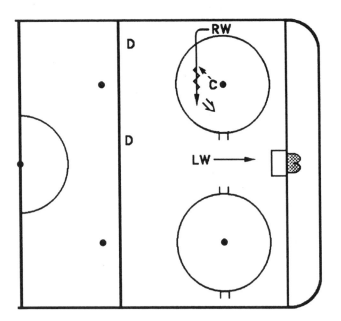

4. Full Strength

Wingers with right-hand shot switch to the left side. Right winger moves across circle and shoots. Left winger blocks defensive player.

5. Full Strength

Assignments:

(C)   Draws the puck back to the left defense-man

(LW) Goes for the net

(RW) Goes for the net

(LD) Shoots

(RD) Backs up the play

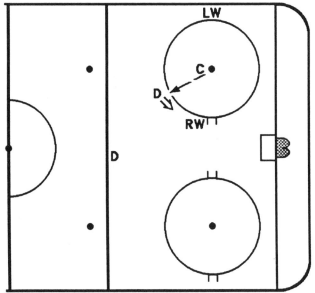

6. Offensive Zone

The puck is drawn directly back to the D1. D1 moves across to the middle, moves in and shoots. The D2 and F2 in front of the net block or screen.

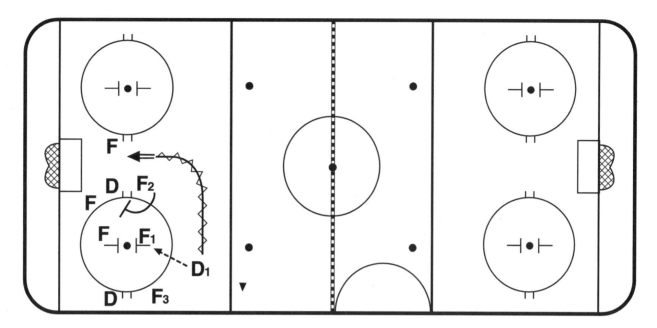

7. Offensive Zone Variation

F1 draws direct to D2 who shoots.

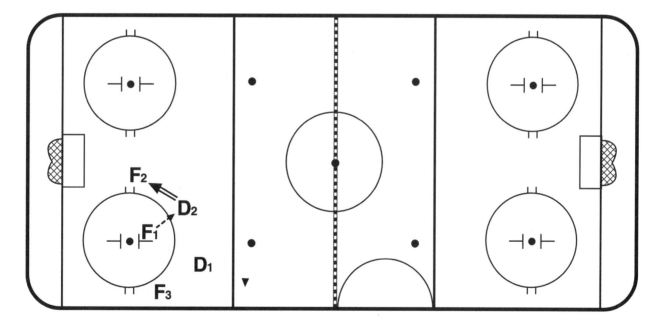

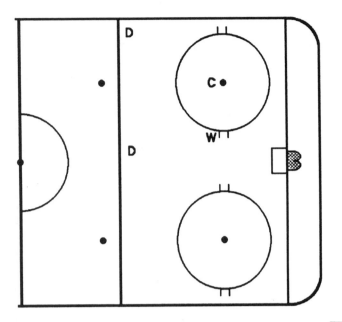

8. One Man Short
Assignments:

(C)	Takes center
(W)	Takes left winger or goes for the net
(LD)	Backs up the play
(RD)	Backs up the play

9. Two Men Short
Assignments:

(C)	Takes face-off
(LD)	Backs up the play and is in position to receive draw
(RD)	Backs up the play and watches for a quick break

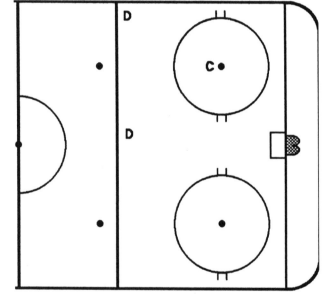

10. 6 vs. 5 Goalie Out
F1 draws directly to D1 (left shot). D1 one touch passes to D2 (right shot). D2 shoots a one-timer (quick shot.)

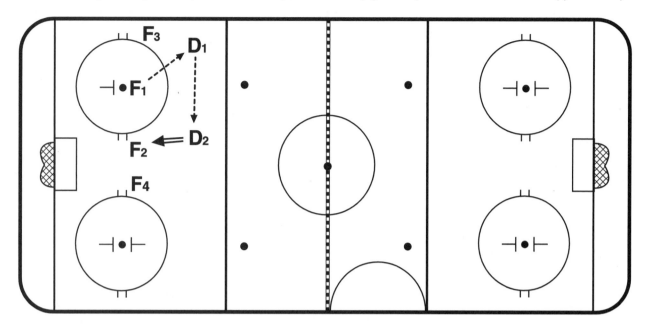

11. 6 vs. 5 Goalie Out
F1 pushes the puck forward from the face-off. F4 retrieves the puck and passes to F3 behind the net. F3 passes to F2 in front of the net who then shoots quickly.

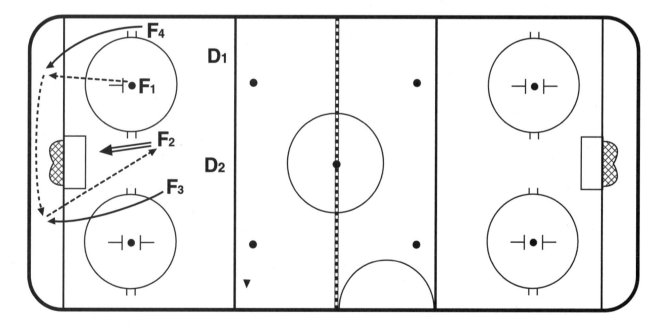

15. GOALTENDING

Most hockey experts believe that the goaltender is the most important player on a hockey team. An excellent goaltender can make the difference on any team and be instrumental in improving the team's chances for success.

QUALITIES OF A GOOD GOALTENDER

SKATING ABILITY
Many think that the goaltender should be the best skater on the team. He is required to complete many quick skating movements. All good goaltenders master the fundamentals of skating, such as starting and stopping, skating backward and forward, moving side to side, dropping to the knees and returning to a standing position, dropping on the side and back and returning to a standing position, pivoting, and making quick turns.

REACTION TIME
The goaltender must be able to react quickly to the movement of the puck and to move the whole body, catching glove, stick glove, or leg to stop the puck, skills that can be improved through constant practice.

PLAYING ANGLES
As the goaltending position is studied further, it becomes increasingly apparent that in certain situations the puck shot is faster than the body can react to stop the puck. Positioning the body at the optimal angle to reduce the openings in the net is one of the key objectives for successful goaltending. It is important that the goaltender play the angles evenly and not overcover or undercover the short or far side. Experienced goaltenders stop many shots by body position alone.

GOALTENDING STANCES

BASIC STANCE
In the basic stance the feet are shoulder-width apart, the knees and trunk are flexed, and the head is up. The catching glove is open at the side and slightly in front of the knee. The stick is held firmly about 1 to $1^{1}/_{2}$ inches in front of the skates to cushion the shots and prevent rebounds.

CROUCH
The crouch differs from the stand-up style in that the upper body is bent well forward at the waist. The legs are farther apart and the knees are in a half-squat position. The stick is held on the thin shaft next to the wide part of the stick, and the catching glove is only slightly to the side of and halfway down the pad.

BUTTERFLY OR "V"
The legs are well apart, and the feet are more than shoulder-width apart. The catching glove is usually only slightly below the waist and out from the pad. The stick is held in front of the opening between the pads, and usually out from the pads and tilting slightly backward.

GOALTENDING SKILLS

MOVING SIDE TO SIDE
Good lateral movement is essential for a goaltender. There are two common methods that the goaltender uses to move side to side:

a) **Shuffle**

   With short lateral shuffles the goaltender can move across the net following the puck. To move right to left, point both skates forward, with the left skate unweighted slightly. Use the right leg to push off with the inside edge. The goaltender uses a number of short (1 to $1^{1}/_{2}$ inches) shuffles to move laterally.

b) **T Push**

   The T push is used to move quickly from one side of the net to the other. To move right to left, rotate the left leg outward and parallel to the goal line. With the left leg, push off the ball of the foot on the inside edge, using a quick thrusting action.

MOVING IN AND OUT

Moving in an out of the crease is essential for the goaltender. When the puck carrier is farther out, the goaltender must move out to cut down the shooting angle. When the puck carrier moves closer to the goal, the goaltender moves back towards the crease.

There are two methods a goaltender uses to move in and out of the net.

a) **Sculling**

Sculling is a skating movement used with one skate, usually the one farthest from the puck. The other leg is used as the glide leg. To move forward, point the toe of the skate slightly outward, and use a quick heel push on the inside edge to propel the foot forward. To move backward, point the toe of the skate inward, and use the inside edge at the toe of the skate for the thrust.

b) **Telescoping**

In telescoping, the basic stance is maintained while both skates use short arc-like thrusts to move forward or backward. The skates do not leave the ice during these thrusts, providing a quick technique for moving in and out to challenge the shooters.

DOWN AND UP MOVEMENT

Goaltenders must be able to return to their feet quickly when down on their knees. There are two common methods used for this.

a) **Both Knees and Up**

Move the skates outward, fanning the legs. Press the heels against the ice, and lean the upper body back as the knees lift up. As the knees are lifting, lean the upper body forward, place the weight on the toes of the skates, and bring the feet closer together.

b) **One Knee and Up**

In this method, one knee is left on the ice, the other knee is lifted up, and the skate blade is placed on the ice. This leg is then extended to lift the other knee off the ice.

SKATE SAVE

Rotate the skate in an arc towards the puck. Leave the outside edge on the ice and continue to move the leg sideways to deflect the puck to the corner.

HALF-SPLIT SKATE SAVE

Extend the skate in an arc, with the outside edge on the ice. As the skate-save leg is extended, drop to the opposite knee to support. This allows the maximum extension of the save leg.

FULL-SPLIT SKATE SAVE

This differs from the half-split skate save in that the support leg is fully extended outward and slightly backward, with knee slightly bent. This move allows for a fully extended movement of the skate-save leg but does leave the goalie in a difficult position from which to recover.

STANDING PAD SAVE

Bend the knees forward to absorb the impact of the puck and to direct the puck downwards to prevent rebounds.

BUTTERFLY PAD SAVE

The knees are on the ice, with the ankles flat and the toes extended towards the boards. The pads are parallel to the ice; the stick is in front, with the catching glove and blocker at waist height.

HALF-BUTTERFLY PAD SAVE

This move is similar to the butterfly pad save, with one leg extended with the pad parallel to the ice. However, the other leg acts as the support leg.

DOUBLE LEG SLIDE

This is a last-attempt quick movement to cover the far side of the net with both pads. To move right to left, push the right leg vigorously on the inside edge. The right pad is under the left pad, and both feet quickly thrust out to the left, with the goaltender landing on the right hip. The blocker and the catching glove are both extended, one up and one along the ice, to cover as much area of the net as possible.

BLOCKER SAVE
The block is rotated slightly as the puck hits to deflect the puck to the corner.

CATCHING GLOVE
The glove is open to the side, slightly above and in front of the knee. The puck should be caught from the midline of the body out on the side of the catching glove.

BLOCKING WITH THE BODY
To block with the body, the goaltender brings both arms close to the body and bends the body forward. Moving laterally, he then smothers the puck with his arms.

FREEZING THE PUCK WITH THE GLOVE
To freeze the puck with the glove, the goaltender puts the blade of the stick in front of the glove to protect the hand. The body is directly behind the puck.

STOPPING THE PUCK BEHIND THE NET
The goaltender normally moves around behind the net from the side to which the puck is coming and returns on the same side. The stick is held in one or two hands, with the end of the blade pushed hard against the boards. If the puck is off the ice, the body and the stick are pushed against the boards. If the puck is past the midpoint or there are players in the way, the goaltender may return on the side opposite that from which the puck came. The puck should be left slightly out from the end boards for the teammates to pick up.

POKE CHECK
The poke check is used when the puck carrier is in range of an extended stick from the side or straight in. Push the blade of the stick out quickly, with the blocker glove sliding down the shaft and stopping at the butt end. This move is not advisable unless the puck carrier has his head down or is in close enough for the stick blade to reach the puck with an extended arm.

PASSING OR CLEARING THE PUCK
On the backhand, rotate the lower arm and wrist outward, and place the butt of the shaft under the arm. Grip firmly and shift the weight from the back foot to the front foot.

On the forehand, place the catching glove on the lower end of the shaft, with the blocker glove holding the upper end of the shaft.

BOUNCE SHOT SAVE
Pucks shot at the stick should be steered to a teammate or to the corner by turning the blade to an angle greater than 90 degrees. The blade of the stick should not rest against the skates but should be held in front. Pucks hitting the skates should be steered to the corner. The pads should be bent forward slightly to allow shots to project downward instead of outward. Shots to the body should be controlled by both gloves. Shots to the stick glove should be deflected downward or to the corner or, if possible, controlled by the glove hand. Shots to the glove side should be caught cleanly and quickly thrown to the side or back to a teammate. If time permits, in a glove save the puck should be dropped to the stick and passed forward or to the side to a teammate.

SCREEN SHOTS
The goalie keeps low and moves to try to get a view of the puck. He moves out of the net to cut down the angles. The defenseman can help the goaltender by moving the players from in front of the net.

BREAKAWAY
On a breakaway, the goaltender should stay well out as the player crosses the blue line. He should move back into the crease only as the player moves in closer. He should stay out if the player has his head down.

TWO-ON-ONE
In a two-on-one, the goaltender should play the puck carrier and leave the open man to the defenseman. If the puck carrier moves right to the net, the defenseman must then move to prevent the puck carrier from cutting across in front of the net. The goaltender must play the puck, being aware that the other offensive player may have moved to the slot area. The goaltender must play the puck at all times, in all other three-on-one and three-on-two situations.

CLEARING THE PUCK
The goaltender must be quick to clear any pucks in front of the net to a teammate or to the corner. Either the forehand or the backhand pass with one hand on the stick is the quickest method. If time permits, a two-hand forehand pass can be executed.

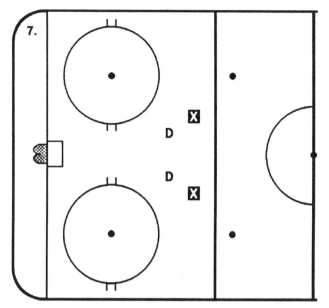

1. Skating (not shown)
Players perform all drills in chapter 5, "Skating."

2. Shooting (not shown)
Players perform all drills in chapter 7, "Shooting."

3. Knees and Up (not shown)
In this agility drill, the goalie goes down on both knees and quickly jumps up to his feet.

4. Side to Side (not shown)
In this agility drill, the goalie moves from post to post as quickly as possible.

5. In and Out, Side to Side (not shown)
In this agility drill, the goalie moves in and out and side to side in his crease.

6. Saves (not shown)
The goalie practices the following movements on both knees: skate saves, full-splits, half-splits, double leg slides, and butterfly pad saves.

7. Movement Drill
Players pass the puck around and the goalie moves with the puck.

8. Pick Up Pucks (not shown)
In this agility drill, goalie, without stick, picks up the puck from a pile on one side, places it in the middle of the crease, moves to the opposite side, and repeats.

9. Movement Drill Variation
Players pass the puck across in a semicircle in front of the net. Goalie moves with the puck.

10. Puck to Corner (not shown)
Players throw or shoot puck at goalie, who steers puck toward corner.

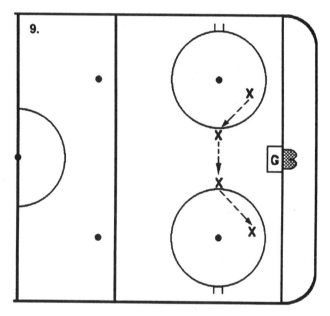

11. Bounce Shots (not shown)
Players throw or shoot bounce shots at goalie.

12. Pass (not shown)
Players shoot on goalie, alternately passing the puck to a breaking forward and to both sides.

13. Behind the Net (not shown)
Players shoot pucks around the boards, and goalie stops them behind the net.

14. Clear (not shown)
Players pass pucks from the corner, and goalie stops the pucks and clears.

15. Angle Drill
Players are stationed at various positions with pucks. Players shoot on command, and goalie covers angle of shooter.

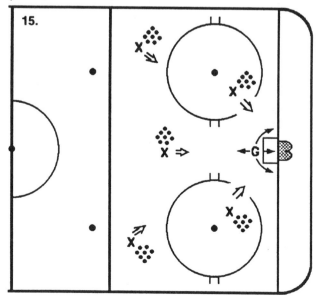

16. Over the Pads (not shown)
Goalie lies on his side. The coach kneels by his side and drops the puck in front of the pads. A player skates in and tries to shoot the puck over the pads.

17. Tight Turn (not shown)
Goalie skates around net with a tight turn.

18. Backward Turn (not shown)
Goalie skates around the net with a tight turn and turns backward.

19. Agility
Goalie jumps over stick, stops, jumps backward, and stops.

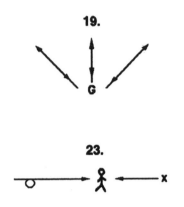

20. In and Out (not shown)
Goalie makes a poke check at puck.

21. Jump (not shown)
Goalie jumps over stick waved two feet off the ice.

22. Screen (not shown)
Goalie rebounds and screens shots from in close.

23. Agility
Goalie does a front roll and then stops a shot.

24. Shots from Coach (not shown)
Goalie lies on his side parallel to front of net or on his stomach perpendicular to front of net. Coach has pucks in a semicircle in front. On command, goalie gets to his feet as quickly as possible and stops shot by coach. This is repeated.

25. Agility (not shown)
Goalie moves on coach's signal all ways.

26. Agility (not shown)
Goalie goes across ice with short side steps.

27. Agility (not shown)
Goalie moves across ice with leg-crossing side steps.

28. Angle Drill (not shown)
Coach moves to various positions, and goalie moves with him to cover angle for shot from that position. Coach advises goalie if angle is correct.

29. Off the Backboards (not shown)
Players shoot pucks off the backboards so that they end up in front of the net, and goalie clears the pucks either to the corner or to a player.

OFF-ICE GOALTENDING DRILLS
Off-ice training for goalies should emphasize flexibility, agility, speed, and strength training. Head and leg movements similar to those used in a game may also be simulated in off-ice training. Remind players to do all exercises slowly.

Flexibility
  1. **Alternate Toe Touch**
  2. **Double-Leg Toe Touch**
  3. **Hurdler's Stretch**
     Goalie touches forehead to alternate knees and then forehead to knees held together.
  4. **Backward Bend**
     In a kneeling position, goalie grasps the ankles and bends backward.
  5. **"V" Sit**
  6. **Bent-Knee Sit-Ups**
  7. **Crouch and Jump**
     Goalie crouches and jumps as high as possible with arms stretched.

Agility
  1. **Jump**
     Goalie jumps back and forth with two feet at once, holding the arms in goaltending position.
  2. **Jump**
     Goalie jumps back and forth going from one to two feet.
  3. **Jump**
     Goalie jumps sideways from one foot to the other.
  4. **Butterfly Position and Up**
  5. **Forward, Backward, and Sideways Running**
  6. **Front Roll to Fast Stop**
     From initial stance, goalie performs front roll quick start and fast stop and then moves sideways and sits down on chair.
  7. **Front Roll and Fast Stop Variation**
     From initial stance, goalie performs front roll quick start and fast stop and then moves sideways and sits down on chair. Coach hits tennis ball at goalie after front roll and fast stop.
  8. **Dive to Crouch**
     Goalie dives forward and then comes back to a crouched position.
  9. **Kip Up**
     Goalie does a front kip up and then a back kip up.
  10. **Front Roll to Half-Splits Position**
  11. **Cartwheel**
  12. **Trampoline Work**
     Goalie does jumps, spins, forward and backward somersaults, and jumps with knees up.

Specific Catching Drills
  1. **Catch Tennis Balls**
     Standing five feet from the wall with a tennis ball in each hand, goalie throws the balls alternately and together against the wall and catches them on the rebound.
  2. **Throw Tennis Balls**
     Working in a pair, two goalies throw two tennis balls back and forth.
  3. **Juggle**
     Goalie juggles two tennis balls.
  4. **Hit the Tennis Ball**
     Goalie hits the tennis ball at the glove side and stick side.
  5. **Medicine Ball**
     Working in a pair, two goalies throw a medicine ball or volleyball back and forth.
  6. **Butterfly Catch**
     Two goalies face each other in a butterfly position. A tennis ball is dropped between them, and the two players attempt to catch the ball.
  7. **Racket**
     The goalie stands in front of a piece of plywood the size of a net with both stick and catching glove. The instructor stands 15 feet away and hits tennis balls with a racket high and low, trying to hit the plywood.
  8. **High and Low**
     The goalie stands in front of a piece of plywood the size of a net with both stick and catching glove. A screening player stands in front of goalie. The instructor stands 15 feet away and hits tennis balls with a racket high and low, trying to hit the plywood.

16. PLAY OF THE DEFENSEMEN

The play of defensemen is an important topic when discussing the requirements for a successful team in today's style of hockey. Defensemen have to be as skilled as anyone on the team. Their traditional defensive role is still important, but their offensive involvement is of increasing value. The good defenseman is expected to:

- work the defense
- be big and strong to move people away from the front of the net
- be quick and agile in moving the puck to initiate the play in the defensive zone

In order to control the middle of the ice you need to have your most skilled players on the defense and at center. If you don't have defensemen who can handle the puck well you may have to think about converting a forward. This is the type of player teams are looking for. Few teams win without them.
Prepare defensemen for this style of play by:

- knowing the skills required for being a successful defenseman
- using drills appropriate for teaching the specific skills
- being able to evaluate the learning efforts of the player and offering feedback

TECHNICAL SKILLS REQUIRED FOR PLAYING DEFENSE

Some say that you only need to teach the technical skills to the young players, but this is not so. All age groups can benefit from technical improvement. Contrary to the way many coaches feel, even the 16 to 20 age group can make great progress if taught properly.

SKATING
In hockey, defensemen have to perform all the skating skills—not just tight turns and quick starts, but backward skating, pivoting, and all the other skating skills. The skating skills that are particularly important for defensemen are:

- backward crossovers, so that skaters can accelerate while skating backward in order to keep in front of the puck carrier
- turning—especially from backward to forward, as it means moving laterally to stop someone from going wide around defensemen
- backward stop and start
- tight turn and moving forward with quick acceleration
- quick start

PASSING
If the defenseman can't pass the puck, none of the basic ideas for breakouts are going to work. Good passing is essential for getting organized in your own end and for performing the re-grouping plays in the neutral zone. All passing skills should be constantly reviewed, with players using both the backhand and the forehand. Some of the more important skills include:

- a sweep and snap pass while skating backward and forward
- a sweep and snap pass coming out of a tight turn
- "one touch" passing
- a clearing flip pass

CHECKING
The defensemen are expected to be good checkers, but often they are not taught the details of performing the various checks. The basic checking skills used by the defensemen are:

- poke check
- shoulder check

- hip check. In the past there have been some real masters of this check, but it is seldom practiced today. Interestingly, there are some coaches who feel that the hip check shouldn't be used at all, especially along the boards, because if the defenseman misses, the opponent is home free. They would rather have the defenseman turn outside and face the man than go in with the rear and risk missing him. The hip check, if executed properly, is really effective in the neutral zone.
- controlling the man along the boards
- controlling the man in front of the net
- a diving poke check. If a defenseman gets caught in a one-on-none and has been beaten, this check can be used in a last effort.

PUCKHANDLING
- skating backward with the puck and then passing it, which often occurs in the neutral zone
- making a pivot and then accelerating forward
- stickhandling through tight turns

SHOOTING
- quick releasing the puck
- slap and snap shots, especially with low follow-throughs for a low shot
- wrist shot
- one-timing the shots

INDIVIDUAL TACTICAL SKILLS

There are players who have reasonable technical skills but lack the ability to fully utilize them in games. Helping players use their skills effectively in a game requires constant work. Do not assume that a defenseman will know how to defend against a one-on-one unless it is practiced. The tactical skills that a defenseman should have are discussed below.

DEFENSIVE ZONE
Defensive Skills
- making a diving poke check in a one-on-none when a defenseman is beaten and is the last man
- making a poke check with head up, stick in one hand, and elbow bent when in range on a one-on-one, while keeping the head up and continuing to take the man
- defending on a two-on-one. The last defender should imagine a line running the length of the ice between the goalposts and play the opponents there. Also, he might think of the situation as a two-on-two in which the goalie has the outside shots and the defenseman has the middle. When the puck gets within 15 feet of the net, the defenseman should go for the puck carrier because the goalie can then move out to play the shooter. It is preferable that the defenseman use the marking on the ice as reference points when out to challenge the puck carrier.
- (most coaches would advocate) staying on your own side and not crossing until there is a threat of scoring on a two-on-two
- playing half-ice on a three-on-two
- closing the gap, and with winger covered, moving toward the middle of the ice on a three-on-two (with one backchecker)
- standing up over the blue line in a three-on-two (with two backcheckers)
- going into the corner to control the opponent
- covering the front of the net
- avoiding and fighting off screens
- intercepting passes and blocking shots, making sure that the blocker is close to the shooter before going down whether with a slide, one knee, or two knees

Offensive Skills

Emphasize the importance of moving the puck quickly, particularly in the defensive zone. In almost all instances this will mean the player makes the pass while moving. Besides getting more power behind the passes, movement also means a greater threat to a forechecker or a defenseman, who will often pull back when a puck carrier is moving toward him.

- retrieving the puck off the end boards at high speed
- feigning moves to get the forechecker off the defenseman as he retrieves the puck off the boards
- being able to pass quickly and accurately coming out of sharp turns
- knowing how to support the play as the last man
- knowing when to pass cross-ice in the defensive zone (a very dangerous play!)

NEUTRAL ZONE
Defensive Skills

- knowing how to look for the opponent who may have cut behind
- knowing how much room to give on attacking situations, e.g., on a two-on-one or a three-on-two with one backchecker, the defender should start from the far blue line and maintain fast backward skating to be able to react to any situation
- knowing how to read the attack
- being able to force the attacker to play to the defenseman's strength

Offensive Skills

- puckhandling skills to set up the re-grouping plays: passing laterally to the other defenseman and making a pass to a curling forward
- moving up to support the forwards in carrying the puck over the opponent's blue line, the "second wave"

OFFENSIVE ZONE
Defensive Skills

- reading when to hold the blue line and when to retreat
- knowing when and how to "pinch"
- knowing how to play the offensive man one-on-one on the blue line
- knowing how to provide support for the other defenseman
- being able to identify and cover the quick counterattack

Offensive Skills

- skating well enough to carry the puck in
- puckhandling and shooting well enough to move in as a scoring threat
- knowing when and where to shoot from the blue line. It is preferable to make most of the shots from mid-ice. When a shot has to be made from the boards, it should be kept low and on the goal so it can be deflected.
- one-timing the shot from the blue line
- making passes to open up the middle for the slot man

TACTICS FOR PLAYING THE FOLLOWING SITUATIONS
1. One-on-One
Defenseman closes the gap, keeps head up with eyes on the opponent's chest; holds the stick with a bent elbow in order to poke check.

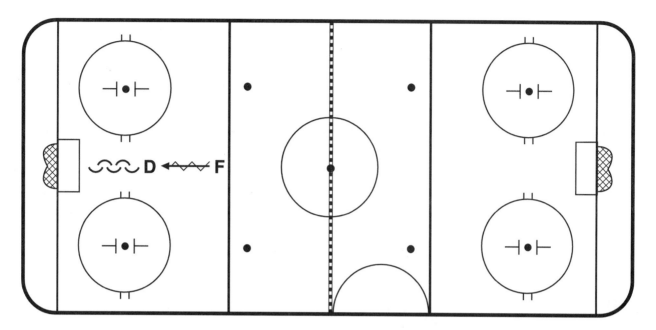

2. Two-on-One
Defenseman stays in the middle of ice, moving to one side or the other only to an imaginary line between goal posts. The defenseman only moves to puck carrier when the forward moves in close on the goalie.

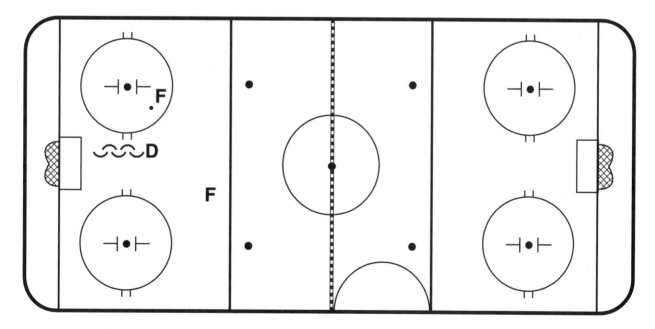

3. Three-on-One
The defenseman plays this situation the same as a two-on-one, staying in the middle of the ice.

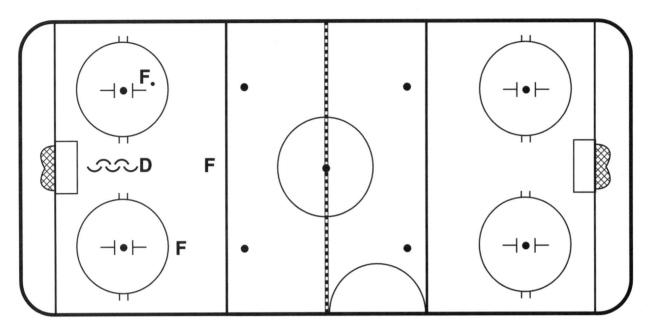

4. Two-on-Two (to the top of the defensive face-off circles)
The defenseman stay in their lanes (same side of the ice) if the forwards cross.

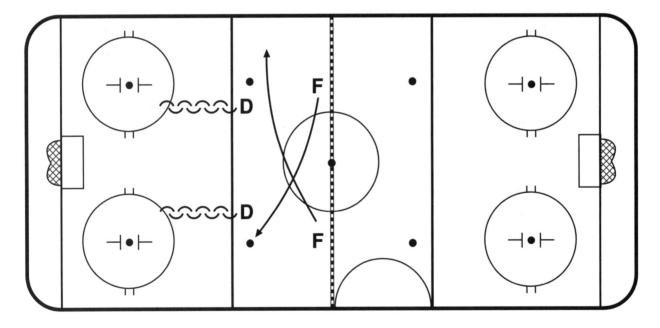

5. Two-on-Two (to the top of the defensive circles in)

If the forwards cross, the defensemen stay with their man.

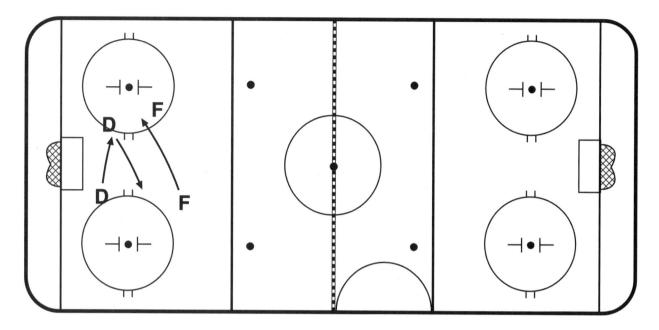

6. Three-on-Two

Defensemen play between the two forwards on their side. The other defenseman covers the other side.

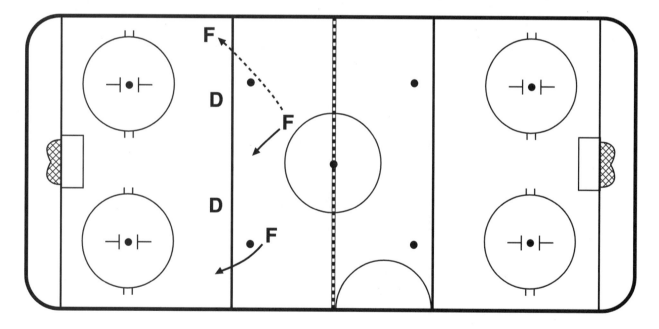

7. Three-on-Two (with one backchecker)

Play three-on-three staying in the lanes. Close the gap. The backchecker stays in the lane if the forward cuts in front of the defense. The defense move over with the backchecker taking the far lane.

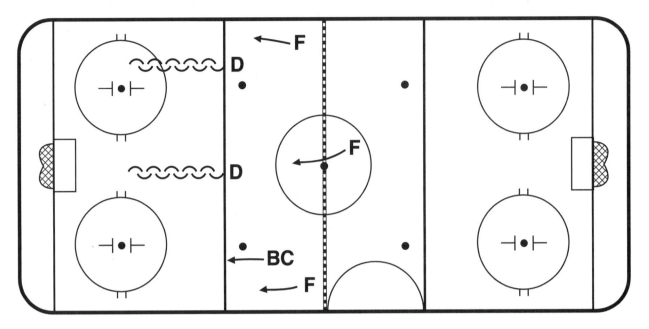

8. Three-on-Three (with two backcheckers)

The defensemen close the gap and try to force the play between the red line and the defensive blue line. The backcheckers take the outside lanes.

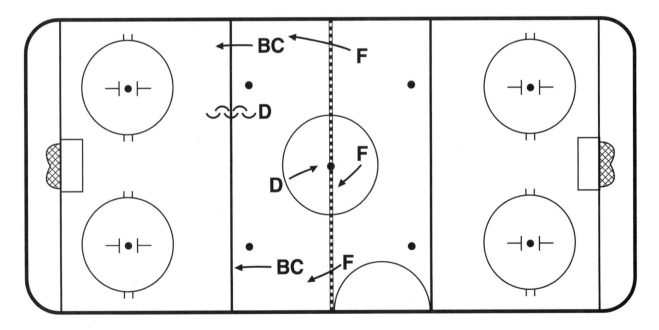

DEVELOPING THE SKILLS

Drills are the means for achieving the desired skills. Being able to show one or two new drills every practice is not as important as using drills that work. Use enough drills to keep things from getting monotonous, but concentrate on ones that emphasize the fundamentals.

The key to using drills properly is knowing what you want to achieve. If there is a particular problem or skill that you feel should be dealt with, then this should be the basis for selecting your drill. If the drill can also be made to simulate game conditions, that will eliminate the further problem of transferring what has been learned to a game situation. When a drill is done with game intensity, it will also add spirit and enthusiasm to your practice that is similar to what is expected during a game.

Besides setting up drills that are skill- and game-specific, note what kind of learning is taking place. The mark of a good coach is knowing the details of what is required and comparing it with what is actually being demonstrated by the players. Evaluating the outcome and offering constructive feedback is essential in the proper use of drills.

How much time should be spent on defensemen-related drills? Certainly there should be a component in every practice, and many of the drills for the forwards could involve the defensemen. If the time is available, consider having a special practice once a week just for the defensemen.

Start all practices with the simplest drill, to build up players' success rates and confidence. Gradually add to the complexity and get closer to game conditions.

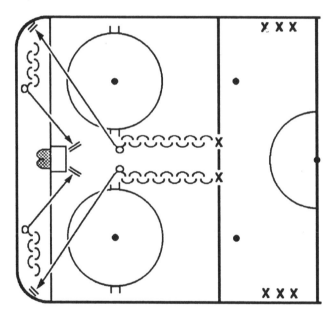

DEFENSEMEN DRILLS
1. Backward Turning, Both Sides
When the offensive team brings the puck into the defensive zone, the defensemen usually have to play their man by pivoting to the inside or outside.

Players skate backward from the blue line and, at an ice marking or signal, turn to the outside, skate forward into the corner, and stop. They then skate backward a few strides, turn in an opposite direction to their first turn, and skate to the net and stop. Have them switch sides after each time through.

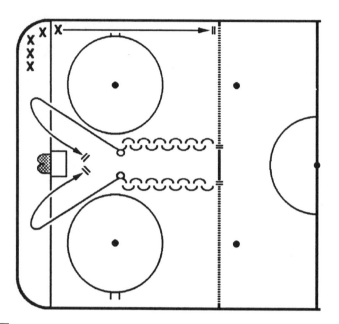

2. Agility

During the game, the defensemen must be able to move quickly in a confined area, e.g., playing the box against a power play.

Players skate forward from the goal line to the blue line, do stepovers halfway across the blue line, skate backward to the middle of the circle, turn to the outside and skate deep into the corner, and make a sharp turn and return to the front of the net.

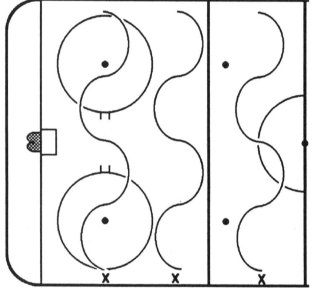

3. Cross-Ice Crossovers

Defensemen are expected to be able to skate backward, accelerating and moving side to side.

Players move as a wave across the ice, making three to four crossovers each way.

Variation: Players execute the same exercise but change direction in response to a signal and do it going lengthwise.

4. One-on-One Cross-Ice

Defensemen must be able to stay face-to-face with an opponent while backing up.

Players are paired off. Attacking players skate forward using three to four crossovers. The defenders skate backward, attempting to stay in front.

Variation: Attackers use a puck, but the defenders do not aggressively attempt to check it away.

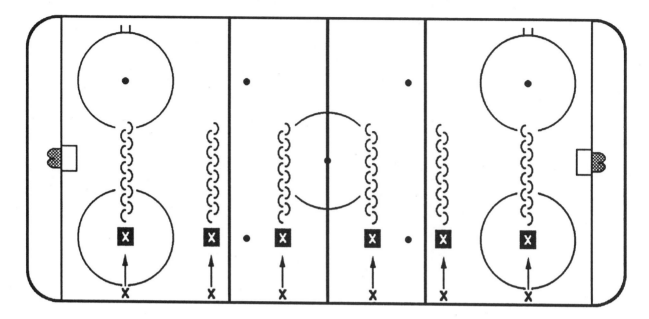

5. Zigzag

Defensemen always have the need for fast backward skating speed plus the ability to quickly transfer to sharp lateral movement to stay with an opponent.

Players skate backward to each of the lines and then cross-step along the length of each line.

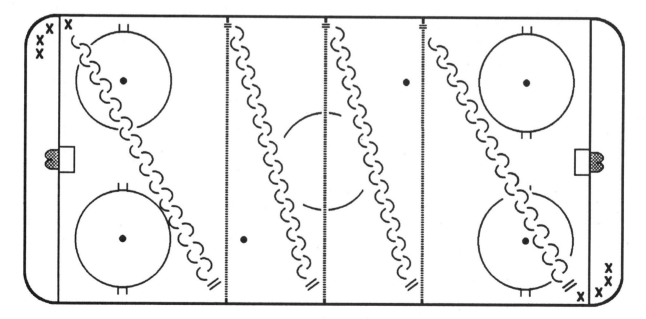

6. Quick Turn

Defensemen must be able to quickly retrieve a puck off the end boards under strong forechecking pressure, make a sharp turn, and move the puck up ice.

Each player dumps the puck in the corner and retrieves it by making a sharp turn and quickly accelerating out with the puck. It is important to pick the puck up using maneuvers that throw off the forechecker, e.g., a head fake or a wave movement of the stick in the opposite direction. Add forecheckers to the drill later.

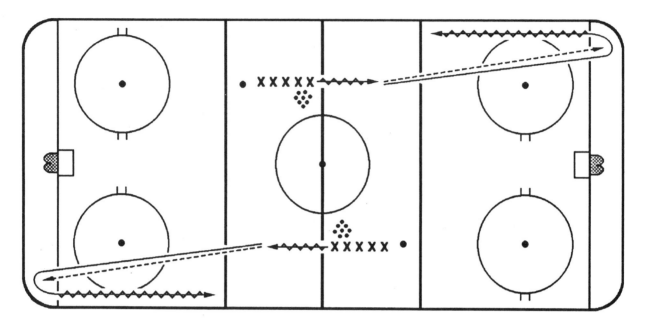

PASSING DRILLS
1. Shuttle Drill

There are a number of occasions during a game when a defenseman has to make passes while skating backward or forward and be able to convert these passes from receptions that vary from a puck sliding along the ice to a puck knocked down by a glove.

One player moves forward, the other moves backward across the ice. The puck is passed back and forth using different skills, e.g., flipping the puck and batting it down with a glove or one touching a return pass.

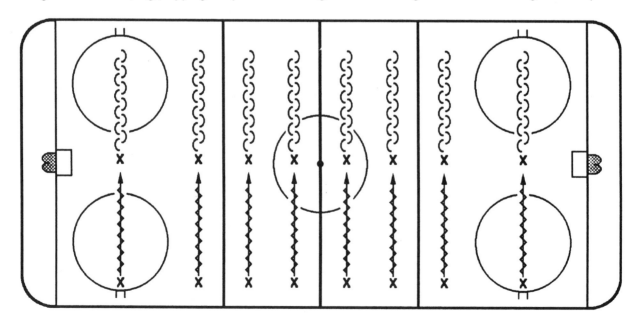

2. Backward Passing

Skating backward with the puck is very important in today's game. Good neutral zone play is difficult if the defensemen can't skate backward with the puck to help spread the forecheckers and give the re-grouping forwards time to find open passing lanes.

The front player in each line (the one with the puck) skates to mid-ice and passes the puck to his partner. Both skate backward to the goal, passing the puck between them.

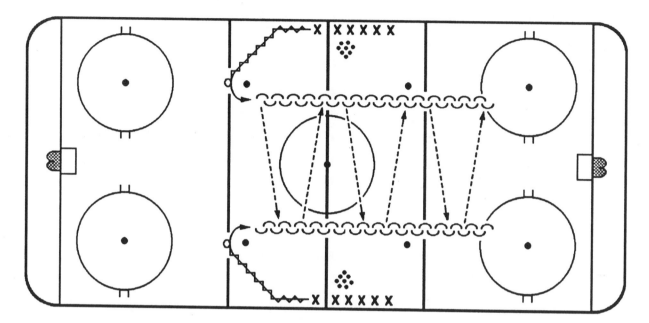

3. Defenseman-to-Defenseman Passing

In neutral zone re-grouping, it is often necessary for one defenseman to pass to the other before moving the puck to a curling forward.

The forward starts out with the puck and passes to the defenseman on his side. The defenseman skates backward with the puck and passes it to his defense partner, who then gives the forward a pass as he curls around center circle.

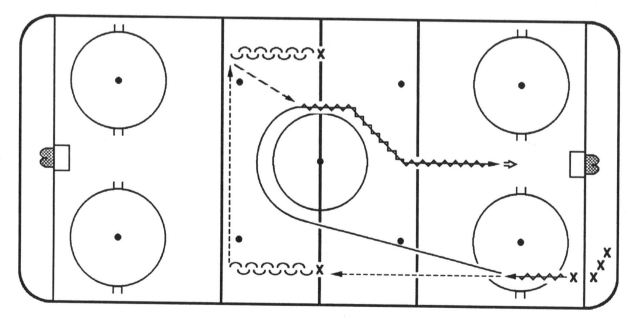

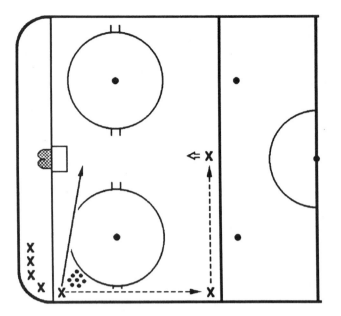

SHOOTING DRILL
Defenseman-to-Defenseman Shooting

Point men often have to make quick decisions on a pass out or when clearing a shot from a corner. To add to the complexity, the puck often arrives in a manner that is difficult to receive.

The player in the corner passes to the defenseman in different ways: off the boards, off the glass, bouncing, and so on. He then goes to the net for deflections. The defenseman learns to play a variety of pass outs. He relays a pass to his defense partner as quickly as possible. He should look toward his partner before passing and not get in the habit of passing blindly. Slow passes likely will have to be returned to a corner man, in which case give-and-go from the corner man can be made.

CHECKING DRILLS

1. Hip Check (not shown)

Defensemen have to have many ways of checking. Sometimes hip checking an opponent is the most effective way. There is a tendency to ignore teaching this type of check, which, if done correctly, can be very effective in taking a man completely out of the play.

The drill begins with the defenseman practicing along the boards. The defenseman goes into the boards with his hip and checks the man. When some success has been attained, the players move out to open ice.

2. Diving Poke Check (not shown)

Sometimes the defenseman is the last man back and is beaten by the puck carrier. A diving poke check is often the only recourse available. Have players experience the different ways of sliding along the ice. Have them slide along the ice trying to touch the puck and the stick of the puck carrier first.

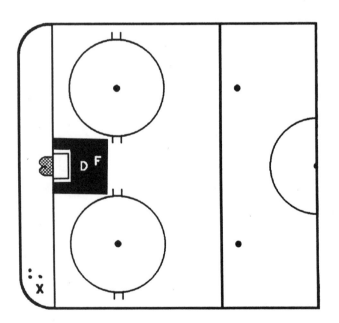

3. Controlling Man in Front of the Net

It is necessary for defensemen to control the area in front of the net. Knowing how to tie up a man is an important part of this play.

The player in the corner has three pucks and passes them out to the forward in the low slot. The forward must move around the low slot area to try to get open for a pass for a shot on goal. The defenseman practices controlling in a legal manner by angling, blocking, pushing, or using his stick.

4. One-on-One

Defensemen should be aware that they can sometimes get beaten on a one-on-one. However, they shouldn't become so obsessed that they are caught leaving the blue line before they have to. The defenseman can keep the puck in if he moves in quickly and challenges the puck carrier before full speed is attained.

The player starts from a corner with the puck. The defenseman should close the gap with the puck carrier by getting within a stick's length before too much speed is built up. The defenseman starts at the blue line and moves at an angle, two strides inside the blue line, to pick up the player coming from the corner. The defenseman now skates backward to play the one-on-one.

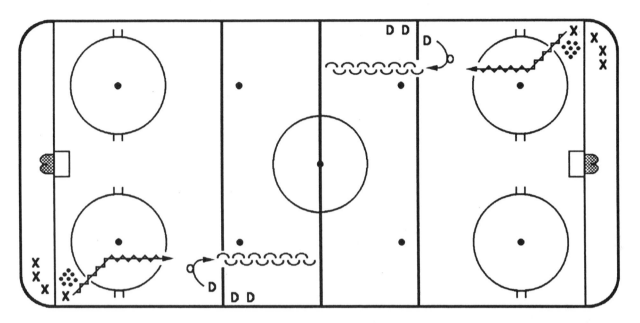

5. One-on-One Swing

Have defensemen execute this drill to improve their backward skating speed.

The player starts the play without a puck and swings around a pylon at the far blue line. He receives a pass from the corner and stickhandles down the ice in a one-on-one. When the original player who started the drill leaves, a player from the inside line leaves and swings around center circle, pivots, and plays the one-on-one. Defensemen rotate lines each time they come back.

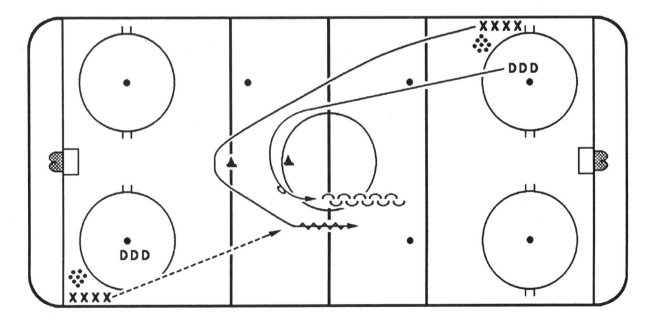

6. One-on-One Swing

This drill forces the defenseman to stretch his backward skating speed to its maximum level. The player starts from the corner without the puck and receives a pass from the defenseman, who swings around the pylon at the blue line. The puck carrier goes for the far net with game intensity. The defenseman skates around the pylon, pivots, and plays the man one-on-one so that it will require all-out backward skating.

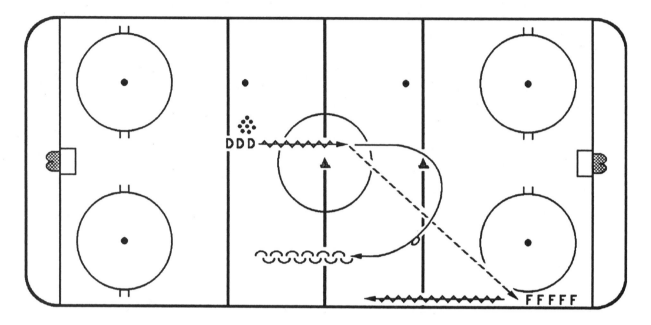

BLOCKING SHOTS

Defensemen sometimes go down to block shots in the high slot, and if they miss, they give the puck carrier an open road to the net.

Set up a drill in the low slot where you want a block to occur, and if necessary, build up the blocker's confidence by using tennis balls. Have the players practice different styles: the slide and one- and two-knee blocks. Experiment with each one to determine its blocking value and effectiveness in preventing the shooter from avoiding the block.

TEAM PLAY SITUATIONS

Defensemen should be starting all the team drills. The more they do this, the more they will have a chance to practice their passing skills. I'm not a believer in the two-on-nones or three-on-nones. Maybe they are good for a warm-up drill, but not for working on something that you are going to use in a game. Besides, a three-on-none is not a game-like situation. The defensemen should be in drills at all times. They should start the play and be in it all the way because that is what happens in a game.

Too often the defenseman on a two-on-one or three-on-one becomes overanxious and moves out of the mid-ice zone, giving the attacker the inside shot. Preferably, the defenseman should stay in the middle and go no farther than the imaginary line between the posts on either side. When the puck gets back to within 10 to 15 feet of the goal, the defenseman has to play the puck carrier.

TEAM PLAY DRILLS

1. Two-on-One

The defenseman starts the play for two forwards with a breakout pass. The defenseman then skates hard for the far blue line and prepares to defend against a two-on-one on the return rush.

The forwards execute a two-on-one rush. Upon completion of the two-on-one play, the defenseman defending the two-on-one play picks up a puck and starts a rush the other way.

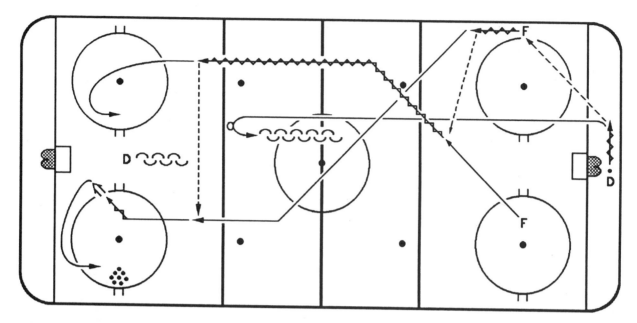

2. Backchecking Drill

In this drill, the coach tries to get the defense to stand up at the blue line. The drill starts with a defenseman-to-defenseman pass, a pass to a forward, and a five-on-four breakout. The two backcheckers pick up the lanes, allow the defensemen to stand up at the blue line, and concentrate on the puck carrier. When the initial rush is completed, the flow is maintained with a five-on-two going the opposite way. This is repeated two or three times.

Variation: Use just one backchecker or one forechecker in the offensive zone and one backchecker in the neutral and defensive zone. Have backcheckers vary their activity by filling lanes, covering a winger, or checking the puck carrier so the defensemen can practice reading and reacting to different situations.

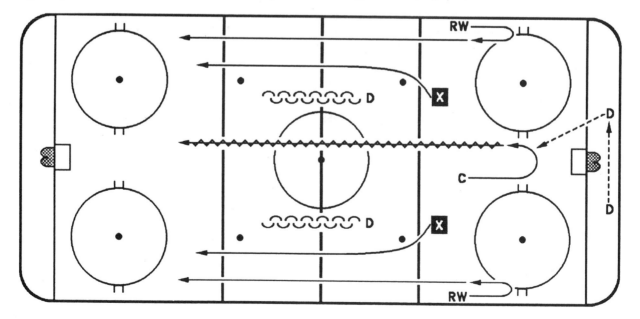

. These backchecking drills should be part of almost every practice. The flow and the variations also make it possible to build up the intensity and simulate game conditions.

17. PLAY OF THE FORWARDS

SPECIFIC ABILITIES OF FORWARDS
A winger needs the ability to

- cut in after taking a pass
- make a quick, hard, accurate shot coming off the wings
- speedskate well
- take and give a pass
- pick up a check

A center needs to

- have good hockey sense
- pass well on forehand and backhand
- stickhandle well
- skate well and quickly and crossover while accelerating
- shoot quickly
- check well
- have better-than-average endurance
- be a good face-off man

POSITIONAL PLAY

DEFENSIVE END
Forwards near the boards should station themselves with the stick in a position to receive and give a pass quickly. The center should be circling with his stick on the ice in a position ready for a pass. The puck should be passed to the head man as quickly as possible.

NEUTRAL ZONE
Forwards skating down by the boards should be looking for an opening to put on a quick acceleration. The stick should be on or near the ice in position for receiving a pass.

OFFENSIVE ZONE
The forwards should use the principle of triangulation when entering the offensive zone. Triangulation means the forwards should form a triangle giving the puck carrier two options.

The forwards should also use the one, two, three principle where the puck carrier attacks with speed, the second forward goes to the net and the third forward remains high for a pass. The puck carrier shoots or passes and the second player goes to the net for a rebound.

DRILLS FOR FORWARDS
All shooting, passing, stickhandling, and checking drills mentioned in chapters 2, 3, 4, and 5 are excellent for forwards. Special emphasis should be placed on the forward's taking a pass in full stride and shooting quickly.

The following drills are used to practice the offensive moves used by the forwards:

1, 2, 3 PRINCIPLE DRILLS

1.

Set up the players as shown. X1 skates through the neutral-zone circle receiving a pass from X3 and drives to the net for a shot on goal. X2 receives a pass from X4, etc. The players stay at the opposite end.
Variation: X1 and X2 start at the same time.

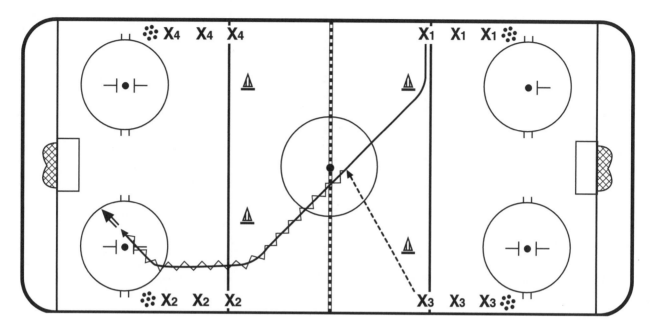

2.

Set the drill up as shown. This drill is the same as the two previous drills but in this drill three players go. The puck carrier goes wide and deep, the second player drives for the net, and the third curls behind the pylon and becomes a trailer (support) for the puck carrier, who passes the puck back to the trailer for the shot on goal.

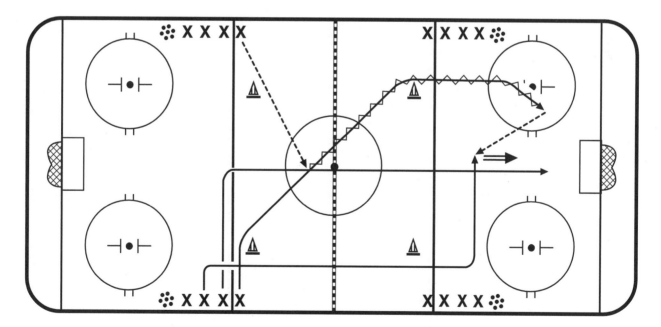

3.

Set up the drill as shown. This is the same as the previous drill except two players go. The puck carrier shoots or passes the puck to this partner driving to the net for a tip-in or rebound. Players change sides after shooting.

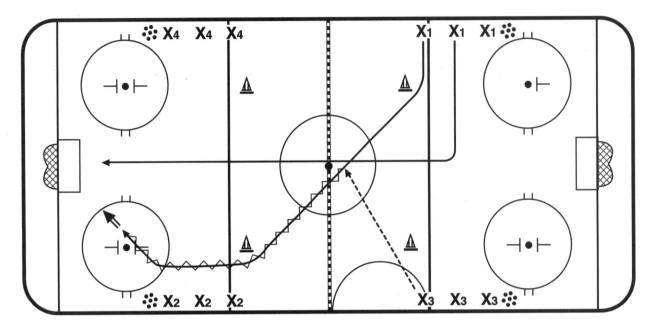

TRIANGULATION DRILLS
4.

X3 carries the puck wide and deep while X1 drives to the far post. X2 supports X3 by coming over to the puck side of center to receive a pass from X3. X2 can shoot, pass back to X3, or pass to X1. The players change lines after each three-on-zero.

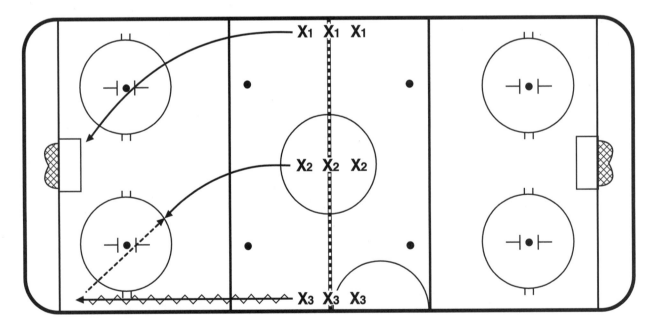

5.

X2 brings the puck over the blue line and stops, or slows, or moves laterally. X1 and X3 drive to the goal for a pass or a rebound if X2 shoots.

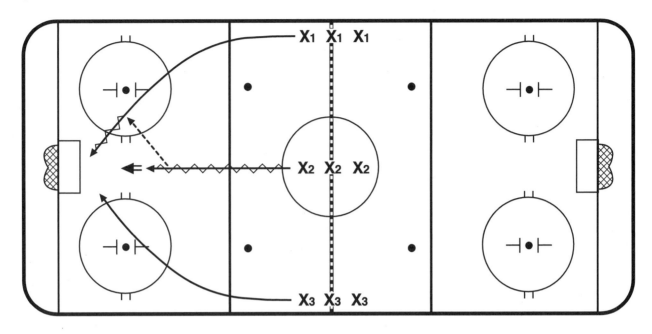

6.

X2 passes to X1 then drives to the goal simulating a pick-off of the off-side defender. X3 comes in late as the high forward for a shot on goal.

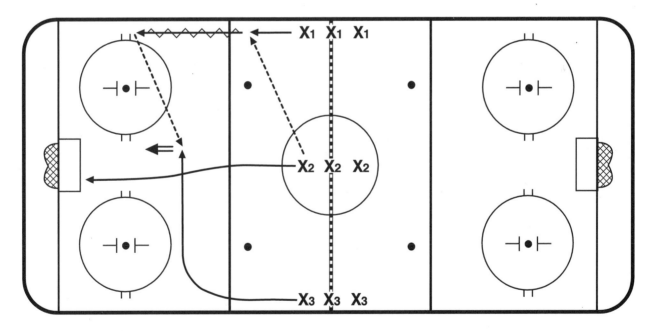

CROSSING, DROP PASS DRILLS

7.

X2 passes to X3, then cuts in behind X3, and drives to the goal. X3 passes to X1 skating down the far side.

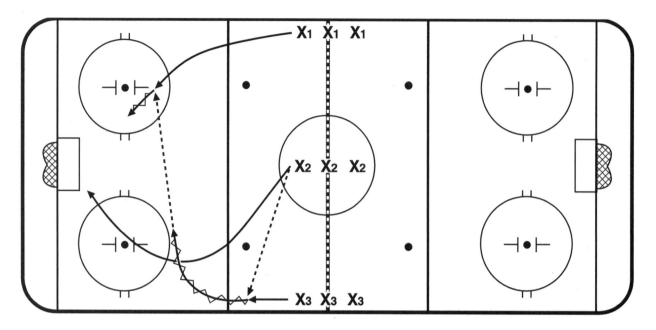

8.

X2 passes the puck to X1 and then cuts across as the trailer. X1 leaves a drop pass for X2. X3 and X1 skate hard to the goal. X2 passes back to X1 for a shot on goal.

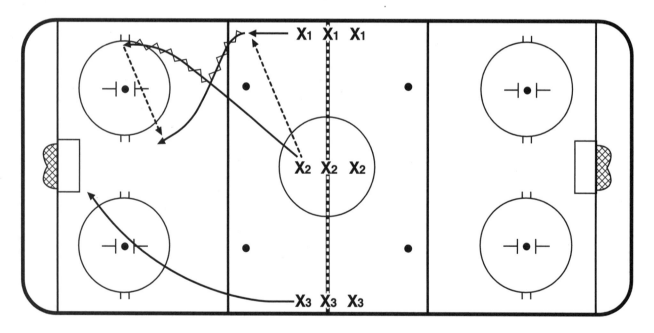

DELAYS

9.

X1 carries the puck into the zone wide and deep and delays by curling. X2 starts as X1 does his delay and drives for the net, taking the pass from X1 and then shooting on goal.

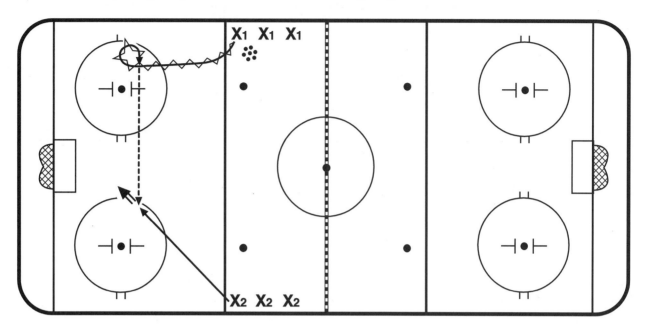

10.

Position players as shown. X1 skates up the boards with a puck and upon reaching the blue line passes rink-wide to X2. X2 skates into the zone, does a delay (curl) at the hash marks, and passes to X1, who has cut across ice and down the slot. Both ends go at the same time.

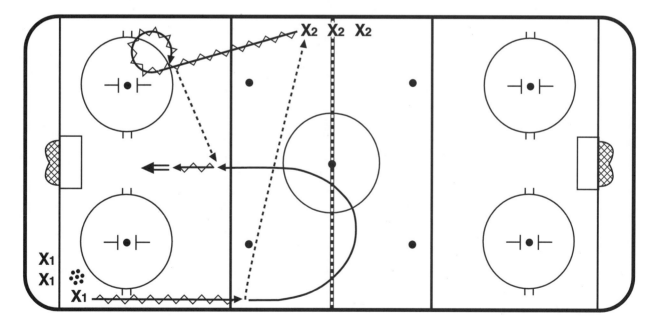

11. Bank Pass

X1 after crossing the blue line bank-passes back to the support trailer X2. X2 retrieves the puck and passes quickly to X3, who is breaking for the net.

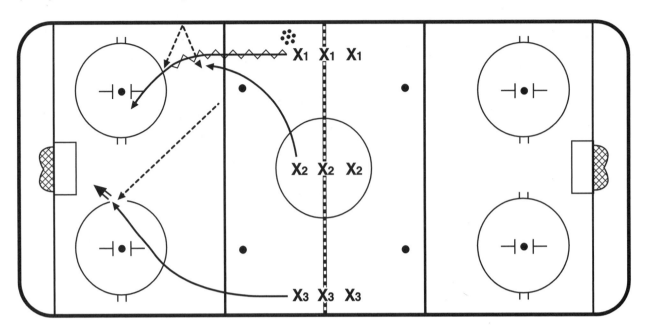

12. Back Door Pass

X1 carries the puck in and does a pass back from behind the net on the same side to X2, who is in a support position. X2 shoots with X3 driving to the net for a rebound.

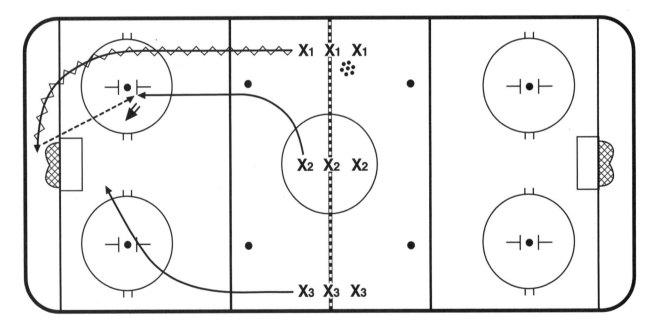

CYCLING

13. (Quiet Zone). The coach shoots the puck into the corner. X1, X2 and X3 skate the circle, back-passing the puck off the boards into the corner. After three back-passes, the low player passes to the player in the slot for a shot on goal.

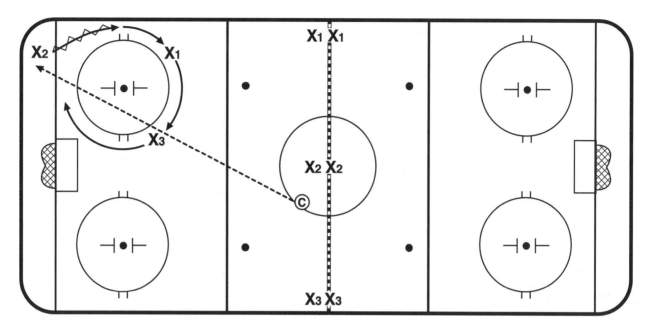

14. (Quiet Zone). X1 starts by making a soft pass to the corner. X1 skates in quickly to retrieve the puck and heads up the ice. X1 board-passes back to X2 who now moves up behind X1. X1 goes to the high slot and receives a pass from X2 for a shot on goal. X2 skates below the goal line for drill on the opposite side.

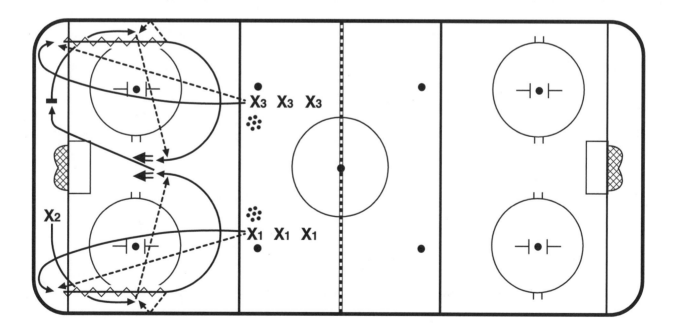

15.

X1, X2 and X3 all go on the whistle. After the shot, X3 receives a pass from the coach and drives wide and deep to the opposite end. X2 follows the play up the ice. X3 delays (curls) and cycles (back-board passes) the puck low. X2 follows up and picks up the puck in the corner. X1 looks for a pass from X2 and takes a shot on goal. At the same time that the X players are going, so do the O players from the other side of the ice.

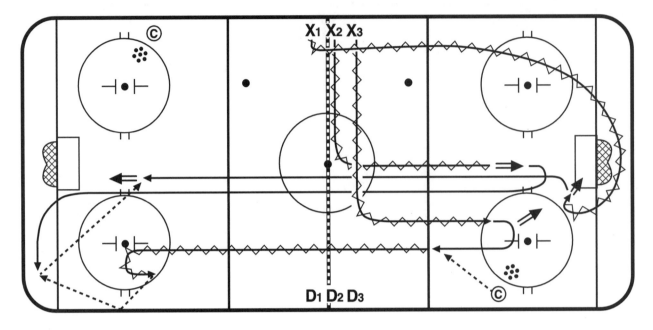

16.

X1 comes into the zone, delays (curls), and passes to the far side D2. D2 shoots with X3 and X2 going to the net.

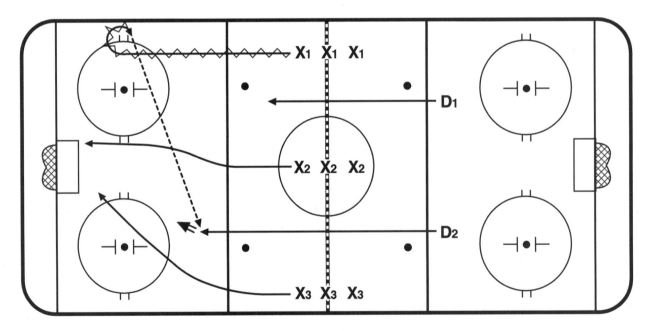

17.
X3 brings the puck in deep and board-passes to X1 supporting behind the goal. X3 and X2 go to the goal for picks, screens, etc. X1 can try to stuff, pass to X2 or X3.

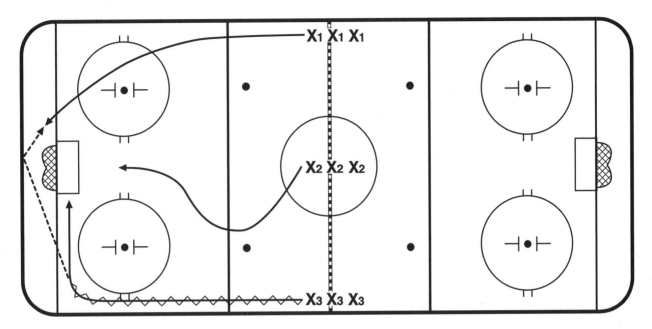

18. Board-Pass Behind Net
X1 from one side skates in behind the goal line and passes the puck behind the net to X3 coming from the other side of the ice. The pass is returned and passed out to X2, who shoots a quick shot from the slot.

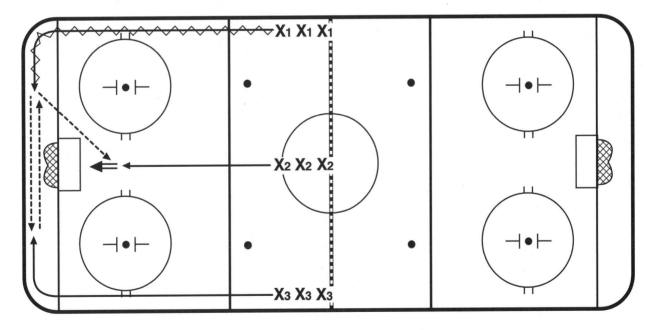

19. Walk Outs

With X1 behind the goal, X2 and X3 are on the face-off dots. If X1 passes to X3, then X2 moves to the slot for a rebound or is support for X3. X1 comes out the opposite side for a shot or rebound.

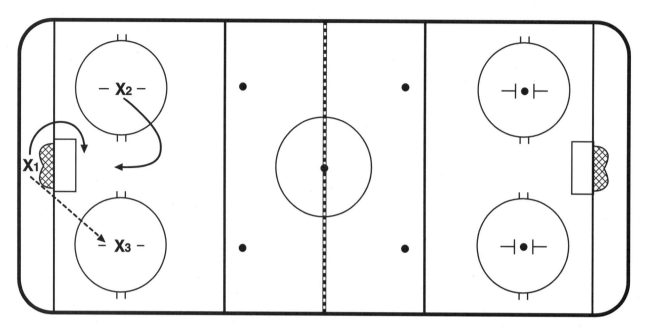

RIMS
20.

X1 shoots the puck in hard around the boards or glass. X3 races to the corner to get the puck and immediately passes back behind the goal to X1. X3 passes to X2 in the high slot for a shot on goal.

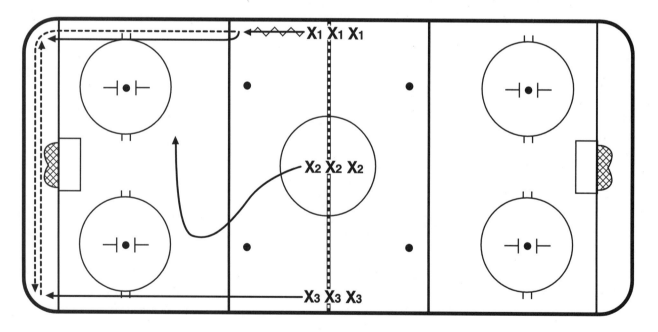

21.

X1 shoots the puck in hard around the boards or glass. X3 skates hard to the corner but lets the puck go to X2 (late forward). X2 can pass to X3 down low or feed a pass to X1.

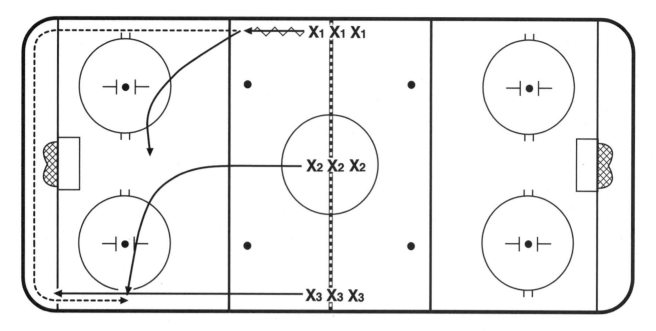

SHOOT-INS
22.

X1 dumps the puck into the opposite corner. X3 board-passes to X1 behind the net. X1 quick passes to X2 in the slot for a shot.

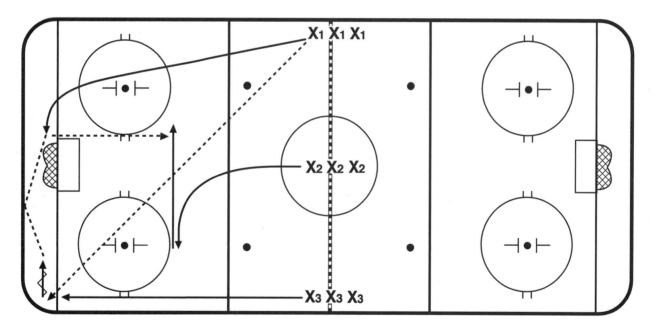

23.
X3 does a diagonal shoot-in. X1 retrieves the puck and turns up the boards but backboard passes (cycles) the puck back to X2, who followed the pass to provide support for the shoot-in.

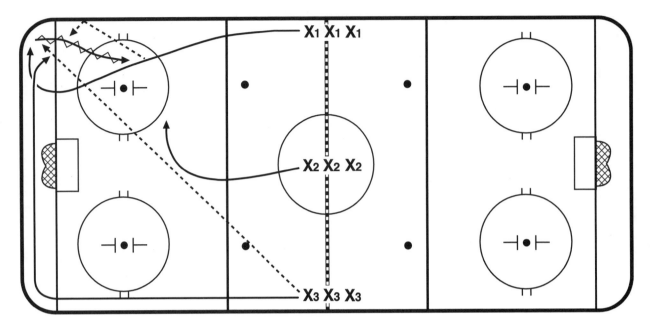

18. SCOUTING, GAME PREPARATION, AND BENCH MANAGEMENT

The saying "Failure to prepare is preparing to fail" is a coaching truism. Careful planning and preparation for games give the athletes and coaches a sense that they are ready for the contest. A well-prepared team knows what to expect from the other team, and this gives the players a feeling of confidence.

Game preparation can be divided into five areas: scouting the opposition, practice utilization for the opposition, pregame meeting, bench management during the game, and between-period adjustments.

SCOUTING

Scouting the opposition should be done as close to the game date as possible. Trends, new personnel, changes in tactics, and so on, are reasons why the latest game of the opposition team should be viewed. Usually one or two members of the staff and the team should scout the game. The scouting report on pages 216-17 can be used to critique and analyze the opposition.

GAME PREPARATION

PREGAME MEETING
It is useful to have a meeting to discuss the opposition's strengths and weaknesses. Such topics as playing style, power play, penalty killing, breakouts, forward lines, defense pairings, goaltending style, outstanding players, and so on, can be discussed during this meeting. The scouting report can be used to discuss the opposition, and if short video segments are available on power play, breakouts, penalty killing, and so on, they can be used at this time.

The pregame meeting should be no longer than 20 to 30 minutes. This should be more than enough time to highlight the opposition. Each player should be aware of such details as arrival time at the arena, the proper time to be in the dressing room, and game and warm-up times.

PREGAME PRACTICE
The practice prior to the next game may also be used to prepare a team for the opposition. Practicing against the opposition's style of forechecking, penalty killing, power play, and breakouts is a way to prepare your team against certain systems.

A pregame meeting may occur before the practice or could be conducted on game day. Skate sharpening and preparation of sticks and equipment should be done after the last practice and before the game, as the players' focus should be totally on the game when they arrive at the arena.

ARRIVAL AT THE ARENA
Coaches and players need information about such details as the size of the ice surface, shape of the corners, height of the glass around the rink (for pucks shot above the board level), type of ice (fast or slow, especially near the end of a period), lighting, and size and location of the entry gates to the bench.

Home Games
Most coaches have a set time at which the players must be in the dressing room. In most situations, players should be there a minimum of 45 minutes before the scheduled warm-up. If dressing room stretching exercises are part of the routine, the players should be prepared for this one hour before the warm-up. A good working relationship with the arena personnel is important in gaining their cooperation in flooding the ice and cleaning the dressing rooms, and so on.

Away Games
That the players have thorough knowledge of all details such as location of arena, parking, entrance doors, and so on, is important for the smooth preparation of a game. The location and size of dressing rooms and information on the availability of a blackboard and chalk or rink diagram board is important information for the coach to know.

OPPOSITION SCOUTING

_____   _____   _____   _____
Score   Team Scouted   vs.   Opposition   Score

_____   _____   _____
Scouted by   Date   Place

Forward Lines	Order of Lines			Defensive Pairs
	1st	2nd	3rd	
___ ___ ___	___ ___ ___			___ ___
___ ___ ___	___ ___ ___			___ ___
___ ___ ___	___ ___ ___			___ ___
___ ___ ___	___ ___ ___			___ ___

Own End with Puck How puck is brought out How they set up center circles Pass up the middle Defensemen carry	
Opposition End with Puck Shoot or carry puck across the blue line Position of center (net or slot) Good shooters Special plays	
Power Play How puck is brought out Center come behind net Center pick up or leave for defenseman How they bring puck in over the blue line Special plays Shoot or carry across blue line Special plays in opposition end Position of center in relation to box	

Penalty Killing	
Force play, how Pick up wings Defense up at the center for rush (at blue line or back in) Any forechecking pattern Box tight or loose Do they cover slot well Special face-off plays Two men short	
Own End (Defensively)	
Who covers points Wingers up, center back; or reverse Defense rough in front Weaknesses Face-off plays	
Opposition End (Checking)	
Who forechecks Position of center Do defensemen hang in at blue line Weaknesses	
Goaltending	
Rebounds Clearing puck Glove hand Stick hand Half splits Skate save Long shots Bounce shots Conditioning Other comments	
General Comments	
Roughness How they start the game Face-offs (unusual) and best man Comments on lines Players to watch Unusual plays Other	

BENCH MANAGEMENT

Bench management is very important. The coach has to adjust to the opposition as well as handle the team in an efficient manner during a game. Details such as the location of the gates on the players' bench and the movement of players going on and coming off the ice are very important. In most cases an assistant trainer or other administrative personnel can open the gates. Some coaches prefer the defensemen to sit at the end of the bench, closer to their own end of the rink, with the forwards at the other end. Players usually come in through the gates and go out over the boards (younger age groups should use the door at all times). Another useful idea is to have the players sit together in lines and defense pairs and move toward the middle of the bench. They are then ready to go over the boards when their names are called. This also allows the coach to be aware of those players who have not been on the ice recently or who have been sitting on the bench for some time, as they will be on the middle of the bench. Some players may be on the bench by design of the coach, or they just may have missed shifts due to penalty killing or power play situations.

It is important for a coach to plan before the game. He needs to plan which players he is going to use in certain situations such as power play and penalty killing, how many lines he is going to use, which players will play more when the team is behind or ahead in the game, and which players can be switched in event of injuries. The coach must also decide if he wants to match lines or cover certain players with a defensive-type player.

Having done all this, the coach must be ready to make quick decisions on playing personnel throughout the game and must have a feel for which players are playing well on a certain night.

It is important that your players know who is going on the ice next. There are different systems for calling players, such as by line or defense pairs, but in most cases the individual name of each player should be called for each line or defense pair up for the next shift. Little problems such as players with the same first or last name should be solved in advance by using nicknames. A good idea is to tell the players to turn and ask the coach if no names were called or if the players did not hear the names. The players should also be aware that they are responsible for replacing a player on the ice when he comes to the bench for a change. Therefore, they must be aware of which player on the ice is playing which position. In penalty killing and power play situations the coach may want to designate which position a replacement is filling on the ice. It is also the responsibility of the player on the bench to make sure that player on the ice is actually coming to the bench. Changing "on the fly" is something which should be practiced. Most changes should be made while your team is in possession of the puck and the play is in the neutral or offensive zone. Some coaches time the on-ice shifts using a stopwatch, with the alternate goalie or assistant coach doing the timing. This allows the players to get into a routine of quick changes. They will also be aware that the coach knows the length of each player's shifts.

If a delayed penalty is indicated and an extra man can be put on the ice when the goaltender comes to the bench, the coach should have a system for the player that replaces the goalie. Usually the coach designates one specific player or a specific position, such as the center of the next line up, to take the place of the goaltender.

The coach should be very aware of the momentum of the game. If his team is being outplayed badly, slowing the pace of the game may be a good strategy. Coaches have been known to change the lines and defense pairs more frequently than usual, change goalies, or even call a time-out if this type of strategy is warranted in an attempt to change the momentum of the game.

The coach should also be in total control of the bench and, along with an assistant coach, should not allow negative comments about fellow teammates or yelling at the referee. The coach should be under control behind the bench, but that does not preclude showing emotion or displeasure with a bad call by the referee. It is important that the coach keep control, as emotions can allow him to get carried away and cause him to be unready for the next quick decision. Emotions, when used wisely, can sometimes be a motivational factor for the players.

On most teams the head coach makes the line changes and personnel adjustments, while the assistant coach gives individual feedback to the players. It is important that the head and assistant coaches are coordinated and that each has a definite role behind the bench. A very important job of the coaches is to have the right players out at the right time and give feedback to the players during the game.

BETWEEN PERIODS OF THE GAME

A good practice for coaches is to meet with the assistant coaches before going into the dressing room between periods. At this time, they could discuss the period statistics, such as shots on goal and where they were taken, plus/minus, weaknesses of the team, strengths of the other teams, players playing well and players playing poorly, and general strategy. After this has been done the head coach can go into the dressing room to discuss strategy and possible changes. Depending on the situation and how the team is performing, the coach can be positive or negative. If the team is playing well, very little need be said. If the team is playing poorly, strategy changes, adjustments in style, personnel changes, and so on, can be discussed. If the coach feels that the team is underachieving, it may be a situation in which the coach can be negative or can use anger to motivate. If the coach has been negative, it may be wise to use some positive motivation just before the team returns to the ice to start the next period.

POSTGAME REVIEW

After the game is over, it is usual practice for a coach to enter the dressing room and make some general comments and congratulate the team on a win or make comments on a loss. The coach should let the players have a few minutes to cool down before making any comments. The coach could then review the schedule for the next practice or game. Some situations such as a big loss or poor play may require a team meeting. Some coaches have a team meeting after each game, when the players are dressed and showered. It may also be necessary to meet individually with any players who are having problems or who may have caused a problem during the game.

In many situations, the head coach meets with the assistant coaches to discuss the games, analyze the statistics, and in some cases view the video of the game if this is available. If there are two or three assistant coaches, and if a video of the game is available, the job of breaking down and analyzing is done by the assistant coaches before the next practice or game. In some cases, the head coach may ask for certain video replays, such as defensive breakdowns or power plays. In most cases the assistant coaches and the head coach will meet to discuss and view the video of the game. This can help the coaches to plan the next practice and work on apparent weaknesses.

A good coach is well organized and will have his team as prepared as possible at all times. Remember, success comes more easily to those who are prepared.

19. STATISTICS

Statistics are a very important tool for the coach to use to assess what is happening during a game and to analyze what happened after the game is over. Over a longer period of time, statistics can show trends which will help the coach assess the strengths and weaknesses of individual players and of the team as a whole.

Although statistics may not be as meaningful with young hockey players, with older players and at higher levels of competition, statistics are important in the analysis of the total game or period by period. Strategy can be devised or altered depending on what is happening during the game. After viewing the statistics, a coach may notice tendencies in individuals or in the team as a whole that can be countered by a simple change in strategy.

Statistics point out individual and team errors that provide feedback to the coach. The coach in turn can then provide feedback to his players. In many cases the coach may have already spotted some or all of these errors, but statistics serve to reinforce or change an idea a coach may have from observation. It is important for the coach in most cases to correct errors and use positive reinforcement. Although negative reinforcement can occasionally be used at the higher levels, it is very important that statistics be used wisely by the coach and that the coach does not become negative to the players by continually emphasizing what they are doing wrong. In most cases statistics can be used in a positive way to emphasize what a player is doing right.

After a thorough review of a game, the coach can also use the statistics to help plan his practices by emphasizing the weak areas of individual and team play. The practices may also be based on game strategy for the upcoming opponent, with the statistics of a previous game against the team as a basis for this planning.

Statistics can also be used as a motivational tool. Over a period of time, statistics can measure improvement and provide goals for both the team and the player. A large battery of statistics, rather than just goals and assists, will point out the importance of all aspects of the game and the value of different types of players on the team.

With younger players, analyzing game statistics may not have the same value. Learning the basic fundamentals and having fun should be the most important aspects of the game. Emphasizing wins and losses, goals, and assists may mean that few, if any, statistics are used. Skill testing may be far more useful than spending time on complex statistics. Performance expectations have to be altered with the young hockey player with the major emphasis being skill improvement.

Statistics, however, do not tell the whole story of a game, and it is important that a coach be able to quickly detect team and individual errors that are happening during a game. Statistics may confirm or change an opinion a coach may have reached through observation. It is the combination of an analytical eye and thorough game analysis that makes the complete coach.

The chart on pages 222-24 exemplifies the types of statistics that can be taken, the purpose of the statistics, and how to use them.

The forms on pages 225 and 226 are examples of a statistics sheet and a compilation of statistics for a team.

In conclusion, statistics are an important part of game analysis. They should be used positively to correct individual and team errors as well as to plan and change strategies before and during a game. If compiled properly and accurately, they can be an important aspect in the success of a team and the development of individual players.

USING THE VIDEO FOR EVALUATION AND GAME ANALYSIS

The video is a common evaluation instrument used by today's hockey coach. Video is used extensively in game analysis for games played, prescouting, and training camp evaluation.

Scoring chances, defensive breakdowns, and team and individual errors can be analyzed. Segments of the video can be shown to the team the next day or even between periods if the video viewing equipment is available. The video assists the coaches in giving a thorough evaluation of the game played. When prescouting a team, a short video presentation can help prepare a team for the upcoming opponent. The opposition's breakouts, power play, penalty killing, forechecking, and so on, can be highlighted in this presentation.

The video can also be used by the coach to assist with individual instruction for players. The player's viewing himself on video with the coach showing and correcting errors can assist in the teaching process. It is also important to show the player some good aspects of his game, to use the video as a positive teaching tool.

In training camp it is useful to video scrimmage games for replay, especially if you are undecided on the selection of some players. Similar to a team game analysis, the video can isolate segments of specific players' play.

The video has many uses for hockey coaches. The expense of the video machines, cameras, and television set for viewing must be considered by a team before making a decision to use the video as a coaching tool. It should also be taken into consideration that the video can be overused in coaching. Long video viewing sessions on a regular basis will sometimes make players negative to its use. Highlighting clips of games that show both the positive and negative aspects of the previous game may be a more significant method for use. It is not necessary to have the players watch the video of every game, but it is a tool that the coaches can use extensively for analysis.

The video, like any coaching tool, is only as good or bad as the people using it. Use it wisely.

STATISTIC	PURPOSE OF STATISTIC	YOUR TEAM	OPPOSITION
Shots attempted	To determine the number and location of shots taken by your own team and the opposition. These shots may or may not hit the net.	INDIVIDUAL Not attempting enough shots. Too many bad angles or outside shots. TEAM Not shooting enough. Too many outside shots.	INDIVIDUAL One player taking too many shots and not being checked closely enough. Player getting no or few shots. Reinforces good checking job. TEAM Too many shots from slot area and/or points. Team getting very few shots.
Shots on net Team opponents' totals Location of shots (team and opposition) Location of goals scored (team and opposition)	To determine the accuracy of the shooting. To determine the location of the shooter when the shots are on the net.	INDIVIDUAL Not shooting enough on net. Shooting from too far out. TEAM Very few shots on net. Too many shots from bad angles or from the outside. Not shooting from the slot area.	INDIVIDUAL One player getting too many shots on net. Player getting very few shots on net. Positive reinforcement on checking. TEAM Too many shots on net from the slot. Too many shots on net from the point or one side of the ice (e.g., right wingers or left defenseman getting too many shots).
Scoring changes	To determine how many direct scoring chances an individual or team is getting. Scoring chances are only counted when a shot is taken in from the high slot area and in toward the net.	INDIVIDUAL No chances means a player is not moving to the slot area for a scoring chance or a player is not being passed to in the scoring area. TEAM No chances means the opposition is clearing the slot and checking well or the team generally is not moving to the slot area.	INDIVIDUAL One player may be getting free in the slot area. TEAM Many good scoring chances means that the slot area is not being covered well.

STATISTIC	PURPOSE OF STATISTIC	YOUR TEAM	OPPOSITION
Shooting percentages	To determine the percentages of shots taken on goal and goals scored.	INDIVIDUAL To determine which players are the most proficient in the scoring area. TEAM To determine if the team's shooting accuracy is adequate.	INDIVIDUAL To determine players who must be watched more carefully, as the scoring percentage is high. TEAM Teams that shoot high percentages must be checked more closely.
Scoring statistics Goals	To determine the top goal scorers.	To determine the top goal scorers and get them on the ice at times when goals are needed (e.g., power play, behind one or two goals, pull the goalie, key face-off in opposition zone). Period-by-period breakdown may show a trend.	Check the top scorers more closely. Get checkers out against the top scorers. Period-by-period breakdown may show defensive weakness at certain times in the game.
Scoring statistics Assists	To determine the best play makers.	Should show best play makers and good or poor line combinations.	Top play makers may be the key to a line and should be checked closely.
First goal Tying goals Winning goals	To determine players who tend to get key goals.	To determine which players tend to score key goals. To know what players to use in critical situations in a game.	To determine which players tend to score key goals in games To be able to defend against these players in critical game situations.
Penalties: minor major unsportsmanlike misconduct match/gross misconducts	To determine which players are penalized, what type of penalties they get, and which players are seldom penalized.	To determine which players tend to get more penalties than others. To determine when not to play players who have a high tendency to be penalized.	To determine which players tend to get more penalties than others To try to draw a penalty from the highly penalized players.
Plus/minus (full strength)	To determine the players who are on the ice when a goal is scored for or against while playing full strength.	A trend will develop if a certain defense pair or line is on for an unusual number of goals for or against. The coach may want to split up a weak defense pair or not play them in critical situations.	Detects strengths/weaknesses of defense pairs or forward lines that are high or low in this category. Close checking may be required against a high plus line. A stronger line may be sent out against a high minus line.

STATISTIC	PURPOSE OF STATISTIC	YOUR TEAM	OPPOSITION
Plus/minus (power play and penalty killing)	To determine the players who are on the ice when a power play goal is scored for or against.	A trend will develop to identify best power play and penalty killing players and/or units.	To determine strong or weak penalty killing units of each opposition. Match your strength against strength and weakness against weakness.
Power play success percentage	To determine the overall success of your power play. Thirty percent or better is considered quite good.	To determine the efficiency of your power play in general and against certain teams.	To determine the strength and scoring percentage of the opposition's power play.
Penalty killing percentage	To determine the efficiency of penalty killing. Eighty percent or better is considered quite good.	To determine the efficiency of your penalty killing teams.	To determine the efficiency of the opposition's penalty killing teams.
Giveaways	To determine the number of poor passes in your zone that are intercepted.	To correct errors in thinking and/or execution in your zone. To determine which players have poor passing skills and which players react well or poorly under pressure in your zone.	To determine which players are poor passers or panic under pressure in their defensive zone. To know when and who to pressure in the opposition zone.
Body checks or takeouts (hits)	To determine the number of body contacts made by the individual and team.	To determine which players are on or are not taking the man out and finishing the check To determine the need for more checking drills and correction of errors in skill.	To determine if the opposition is a physical team or not. If a team is not taking the body, more liberties can be taken in the corners, etc.
Face-offs	To determine the number of face-offs won, lost, or tied in the defensive, neutral, or offensive zones.	If done poorly, work on face-off techniques should be increased in practice. Be able to put the best face-off men out in critical situations. Be able to match against opposition face-off men. Be aware of a poor matchup of face-off men as the game progresses. Be aware of the efficiency of face-off men in each zone.	To determine the strong and weak face-off men. To be able to match against strength and weakness.
Length of shifts	To determine the average length of shifts for each player.	To determine if shifts are too long or too short Note if fatigue seems to be a factor.	To determine if the opposition has a marked tendency toward longer or shorter shifts. This will aid in line matching as well.

STATS SHEET

Date: _____
Opposition: _____

☐ 1st period
☐ 2nd period
☐ 3rd period

Shots on net _____
Giveaways _____
Hits _____

Plus

Minus

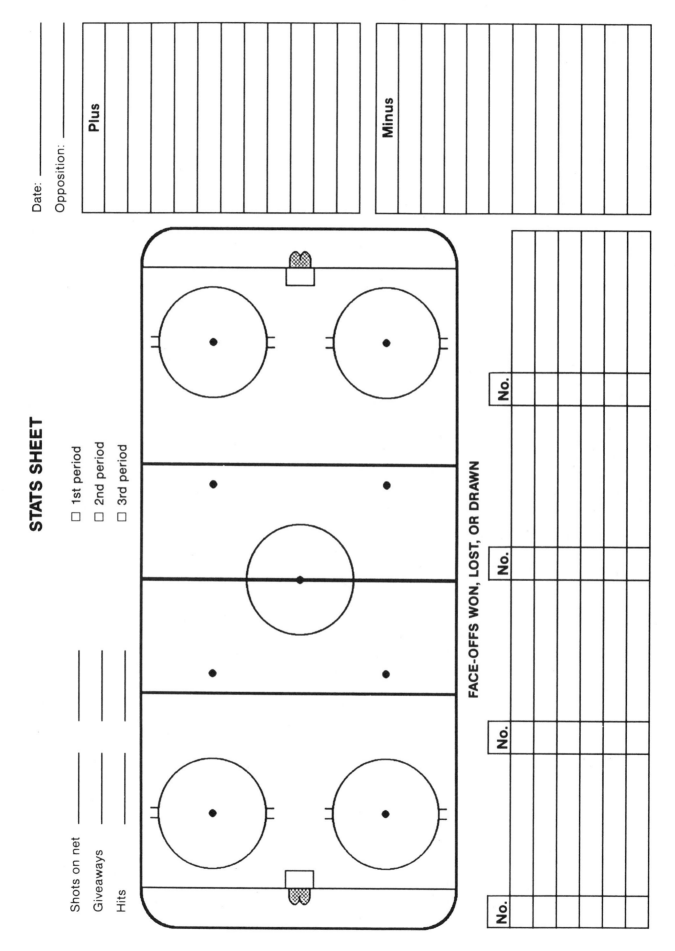

FACE-OFFS WON, LOST, OR DRAWN

No.

No.

No.

No.

225

GAME SUMMARY

No.	Name	Games Played	Hits	Shots	Goals	Assists	Points	Minor Penalties	Major Penalties	Misconduct and GM Penalties	Goals Against, Evenhanded	Goals For, Evenhanded	Plus/Minus	Power Play, Goals For	Penalty Killing, Goals Against, Shorthanded	Goals For Shorthanded,	Bad Pass Giveaways	Face-Offs W	Face-Offs L	Face-Offs %

20. CONDITIONING

Conditioning for ice hockey should be a year-round program to enable the player to reach his full potential. Such a program should test for and improve the physiological factors that relate to ice hockey: strength, power, speed, agility, flexibility, reaction time, and cardiovascular and muscular endurance.

THE 12-MONTH PLAN

To develop a conditioning program for hockey, set up a schedule that divides the year into the following main periods:

- preparation period, general and specific (off-season)
- pre-competition period
- competition period
- taper
- playoffs
- transition period (post-season)

MAY	JUNE	JULY	AUG.	SEPT.	OCT.	NOV.	DEC.	JAN.	FEB.	MAR.	APRIL
Preparation				Pre-com-petition	Competition				Ta-per	Play-offs	Transi-tion
General		Specific									

PREPARATION PERIOD (16 WEEKS)
The preparation period of training is extremely important for the player. During this period the athlete must attempt to raise his level of total conditioning as high as possible. In most cases this level is not improved significantly during the season, and in some component areas of total fitness only a maintenance level is achieved during the competitive season.

The first step in the preparation period should be the compilation of a fitness assessment profile, which measures the athlete's strength, power, flexibility, muscular endurance, agility, fat percentage, and cardiovascular endurance (aerobic and anaerobic).

After the fitness assessment profile has been compiled, the athlete should begin an intensive training program. The preparation period is subdivided into two periods, general (eight weeks) and specific (eight weeks). The general period is devoted to building a solid base of strength and aerobic fitness, along with flexibility. The specific period includes anaerobic work along with more sports-specific training, while continuing strength and aerobic work, and flexibility training.

PRE-COMPETITION PERIOD (TWO TO THREE WEEKS)
The pre-competition period usually lasts two to three weeks. During this period, players are selected for the team, and play a number of exhibition and scrimmage games. Circuit training for general fitness is one of the best methods of conditioning during this period, as it allows a large number of players to work out at the same time.

COMPETITION PERIOD
During the competition period, it is important to improve, or at least maintain, the conditioning level achieved in the preparation period. The competition period should consist of programs for anaerobic and aerobic cardiorespiratory endurance conditioning and a daily flexibility program, as well as strength maintenance.

TAPER
One week to 10 days before the playoffs, workouts should be shortened without a decrease in the intensity. Mental preparation and strategy sessions can be included at this time as well, along with more rest days.

PLAYOFFS
During this period, short training periods should be scheduled, along with strategy sessions and rest periods.

TRANSITION PERIOD (FOUR WEEKS)
During the transition period, the hockey player recuperates from the long season, works on general fitness, and perhaps participates in some different sports such as golf, baseball, tennis, and swimming.

During the first week of the transition period, the player should have rest and relaxation combined with unregulated exercise in an enjoyable sport such as tennis, golf, or swimming, with no set exercise pattern. After the long hockey season, it is important for the athlete to recuperate and take time out from a regimented exercise routine.

The next three weeks of the transition period should be spent on general fitness, including some aerobic work consisting of running, cycling, or swimming distances of a minimum of 3 kilometers three times per week. Flexibility exercises should be done daily, and other enjoyable sports should be played to maintain general fitness.

In summary, the transition period is a time for recuperation and maintenance of good fitness. Although it is a time to rest from hockey and relax, it is also a time for maintaining general fitness through exercise.

IMPORTANT PHYSIOLOGICAL FACTORS IN ICE HOCKEY

Strength, power, speed, muscular and cardiovascular endurance, agility, flexibility, and movement time are important physiological factors for the total development of the ice hockey player.

Strength, power, speed, and muscular endurance are related and are key factors in the performance of a hockey player. The ability to skate and accelerate quickly both backwards and forwards, to shoot, to check, and to win battles for the puck along the boards and in the corners is related to these training factors.

STRENGTH

Strength, the ability to apply a force, should be developed in the upper and lower body and the trunk area. Abdominal strength, particularly rotational abdominal strength, should be emphasized to avoid tearing the abdominal wall. It is believed that overdevelopment of the obliques on the shooting side can cause abdominal problems on the opposite side.

Generally 40 percent of the training time should be spent on the upper body, with the remaining 60 percent devoted to the lower body and trunk.

Strength development uses the principles of overload and progressive resistance. Overload is increasing the muscle load beyond previous requirements. Progressive resistance is a gradually increasing resistance. Strength can be developed through isotonic, isokinetic, and isometric methods.

Isotonic exercises are those in which muscle tension overcomes the resistance, and movement occurs. Training with weights is the most common method of isotonics, but body exercises such as chin-ups and push-ups are also included in this category. Exercises that closely simulate the movements in hockey are the most effective.

Isokinetic exercises are those in which the muscle is maximally loaded throughout its range of motion. Machines such as Cybex, Appolo, and Mini Gym are examples of devices used in this type of training.

Isometrics are exercises in which tension is developed in the muscle but no movement occurs. Pushing against an immoveable object (for example, a wall) or pulling or pushing against your opposite arm is an example of an isometric exercise.

Isotonics and isokinetics are methods favored by most experts, with more emphasis on isotonics since they can be tailored to sport-specific movements.

POWER

Power training occurs after a base of strength has been built. Power is involved with both strength and speed, and the ability to move the body or an object quickly. Power training, then, involves moving weights or the body quickly to simulate or actually execute movements that are used in the sport. Power training involves training with weights, sprinting, and plyometrics. Plyometrics, used by sprinters and gymnasts for more than 30 years, are exercises in which the muscles are first lengthened and then contracted, during hopping and bounding movements.

SPEED

Speed relates to applying a force to a mass quickly; strength, power, and correct technique are key factors. Power and strength training will increase speed. However, technique is also important, and a large number of repetitions of the skill, performed correctly, in addition to power and strength training, is essential for increasing speed.

MUSCULAR ENDURANCE

Muscular endurance, the ability to make repeated contractions and/or movements in a sport, is developed by performing a large number of movements using weights or the body. Repeated contractions with weights—between 20 and 30 repetitions—and body exercises such as push-ups and sit-ups, with a large number of repetitions, are common muscular endurance exercises. Since strength is an important factor in muscular endurance, regular strength training programs will lead to improvement.

CARDIOVASCULAR ENDURANCE

The Energy Systems

Cardiovascular endurance is directly related to the body's ability to supply adenosine triphosphate (ATP), a chemical that, when broken down, supplies the energy for muscle contraction.

ATP is supplied to the muscles by three methods: storage in the muscles (alactate or ATP-PC system), the breakdown of glucose without oxygen (lactic acid system), and the breakdown of carbohydrates and fats in the presence of oxygen (oxygen system). The alactate system and the lactic acid system are without oxygen and are classified as anaerobic. The ATP-PC system resynthesizes ATP from the creatine phosphate (CP) stored in the muscle.

The supply of CP is limited, and in all-out work can last from 10 to 15 seconds. CP is very important in ice hockey for supplying energy for the short-burst sprint. The fact that 50 percent of the creatine phosphate can be restored in approximately 30 seconds, and over 90 percent can be restored in two minutes, is extremely important for ice hockey, as there is usually a stoppage of play every 30 seconds, with two stoppages of play every shift. Training the anaerobic system can increase the levels of ATP and CP stored in the muscle and can also increase the activity of creatine kinase, which facilitates the breakdown of creatine phosphate.

The lactic acid system is also a limited supplier of ATP. The by-product of this system is the build-up of lactic acid, which causes fatigue when it reaches a high level.

Training the lactic acid system increases the amount of PFK (phosphofructokinase), an enzyme that speeds up the rate at which glycogen is broken down. In addition, training allows the muscle to tolerate higher levels of lactate, which eventually causes fatigue.

The oxygen system supplies an unlimited amount of ATP as long as the fuel can be supplied by carbohydrates and fats.

Although ice hockey is considered primarily an anaerobic sport, the aerobic component is important over the two-hour duration of the game. Also, each shift in ice hockey includes various tempos, from all-out effort to periods of stopping and gliding. It appears that by using the oxygen system at certain periods of the game, the player minimizes the involvement of the lactic acid system. Training aerobically increases the myoglobin content (store for O_2) and increases the oxidation of fats and carbohydrates. All three energy systems are important for ice hockey and should be trained for maximum cardiovascular endurance.

FLEXIBILITY

Flexibility exercises are important in ice hockey to ensure a full range of motion in all movements and to prevent injuries. Flexibility exercises also reduce muscle soreness and relieve general aches and pains. Slow stretch and PNF, two common types of flexibility exercises, are discussed and illustrated on pages 241–244.

AGILITY

Agility is the ability to change direction quickly and is a primary skill in ice hockey. Strength, power, and reaction time are important contributors to agility. Agility can best be improved by practicing a movement pattern correctly at increasing speeds.

MOVEMENT TIME

Movement time may be defined as the period from the receipt of a stimulus to the end of the movement. It is essential in most aspects of ice hockey but is especially important in goaltending. Movement time involves reaction and response time. Reaction time begins when a player receives a stimulus and ends at the initiation of the response, while response time spans initiation to the end of the response. Current research supports the fact that reaction time is little affected by practice, but response time is directly affected. Movement time can be improved by repeated practice of the correct movement pattern.

STRENGTH AND POWER TRAINING GUIDELINES

Coaches should review the following general guidelines for strength training with players and be sure they understand them completely.

1. Always have a good warm-up lasting at least 10 to 15 minutes. A light jog or running on a treadmill, or riding a stationary bike for five to six minutes, followed by four to five minutes of flexibility exercises, is a significant warm-up.
2. If you're unfamiliar with an exercise, make sure you are properly instructed on technique and that you work with a partner.
3. Use a light resistance with 10 repetitions before lifting heavier weights.
4. Perform all exercises with a smooth, even rhythm, through a full range of motion.
5. Work out three times per week.
6. Select starting weights by finding a load of one repetition and train at a percentage of maximum: for example, maximum lift, one rep = 50 pounds; % of maximum = 80%; weight used for exercise = 40 pounds.
7. Breathe when lifting weights. Inhale when contracting the muscle; exhale when relaxing the muscle.
8. Rest two to six minutes between sets of exercises, and stretch, massage, or shake the muscle groups being trained.
9. Perform each exercise in the order listed, with the percentage of maximum, repetitions, and sets suggested.
10. Conclude the workout with a cool-down, walking and stretching according to the flexibility program outlined.

STRENGTH EXERCISES

UPPER BODY

Military Press
With hands shoulder-width apart, grip the barbell. With your feet shoulder-width apart, rest the barbell on either the back of your shoulders or the front of your chest. Press the weight upward, fully extending your arms. Lower the weight slowly to the starting position. Repeat.

Supine Bench Press
Lie on the bench on your back, with knees bent at right angles and feet flat on the floor. Hold the barbell flat on your chest, with hands slightly more than shoulder-width apart. Push arms upward until fully extended, then lower the barbell slowly to your chest. Repeat.

Incline Bench Press
Sit on the incline bench with the barbell at chest level, hands shoulder-width apart, knees bent, feet on the floor. Raise the weight to arm's length and lower slowly. Repeat.

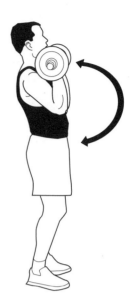

Biceps Curl
Hold the barbell with a wide or narrow grip. Keep the back straight, feet astride, and arms extended. Raise the bar to your chest, and then lower slowly to the starting position. Repeat.

Seated Triceps Extensions
Hold the barbell above your head. Lower the weight behind your head, keeping your elbows close to your ears. Repeat.

Standing Lateral Raise
Hold the dumbbells with arms extended straight at your sides. Keeping your arms straight, raise the weights laterally to shoulder height. Lower slowly and repeat.

Lateral Pulldown

Kneel or sit with your hands holding the bar at the widest points. Pull the bar down behind or in front of your neck, then return the bar slowly to the starting position. Repeat.

Dips

Start with the arms and body straight, then lower your body, keeping your elbows close to your body. Repeat.

Bent-over Rowing

Keep the feet astride and the arms extended downward. Grasp the middle of the bar, with hands 8 inches apart. With head raised and eyes looking forward, pull the bar up to your chest and then lower it. Repeat.

Shrug

Using a shoulder-width grip, with arms locked, raise the shoulders as high as possible. Do not bend your knees. Repeat. This movement is a shoulder exercise only.

TRUNK

Prone Hyperextension

Lie on the bench with your trunk extended. Place your hands behind your head and lower your trunk towards the floor. Raise your body in a straight line. Repeat. A light weight may be placed behind the head.

Crunches

Lying on your back, sit up slowly, raising bent knees and chest at the same time. Lower slowly. Repeat.

Bent Knee Sit-ups

Lie on your back with knees bent and feet flat on the floor. Clasp your hands behind your head and raise your upper body towards your knees. During the movement, rotate your trunk and touch left elbow to right knee. Lower your trunk to the floor slowly and repeat, touching right elbow to left knee. Repeat sequence.

LOWER BODY

Lateral Side Step

Stand with one foot on a box 16 to 18 inches high, with the thigh parallel to the floor. Keeping your back straight and head and chest up, raise and lower your leg. Repeat. A front step up can be done in a similar way.

Lunge

Place the barbell on your shoulders with a wide, shoulder-width grip. Keeping the back arched and the head and chest up, step forward until your back knee touches or almost touches the floor. Repeat. The step forward should be long enough to feel the stretch in the rear leg.

Half Squat

With your feet shoulder-width apart and your head up, place the barbell on the shoulders. Bend slowly to the half-squat position. As the movement is completed, push up onto your toes. Repeat.

Note: Younger, inexperienced athletes should do the half squat. More advanced athletes may do a full squat, as long as the weight used is not excessive.

Reverse Leg Press

Stand to one side of the machine and push back with one leg, using a motion similar to skating.

Hamstring Curl

Lie face down on the bench and place your feet under the roller pads, just above the ankle joint. Grasp the handles to keep your body from moving. Curl your legs by bringing your heels to your buttocks. Pause and slowly lower the resistance. Repeat.

Heel Raise

Standing with your toes on a block about 2 inches high, rest the barbell on your shoulders. Slowly raise up onto your toes, hold, and return to the starting position. Repeat.

UPPER AND LOWER BODY

 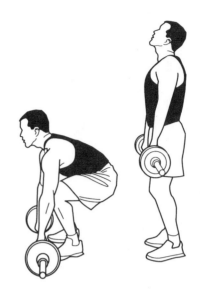

Cleans
Using a palms-down grip, grasp the barbell on the floor, bending your knees and keeping your back straight. Lift the weight in one motion to your shoulders. Use only your arms to lower the weight slowly. Repeat.

Dead Lift
Stand over the bar with your hands 2 feet apart. Making sure that your back is straight, your head is up, and your knees are bent, lift the weight until your body is completely upright. Repeat.

WRIST AND LOWER ARMS

Wrist Curl
Sit and rest your forearms on the bench, with your wrists extended over the end, and hold the bar, palms facing upward. Let the bar roll to the ends of your fingers. Roll your fingers up and grab the bar with the palms of your hands. Flex your wrists as far as possible. Repeat.

Wrist Rolls
Standing with your arms extended at shoulder height, slowly wind the rope until the weight is raised to the handle. Then slowly lower the weight. Repeat.

Forearm Twist
With your elbows bent at right angles, use the wrist to rotate the weight, alternating right and left.

PLYOMETRICS

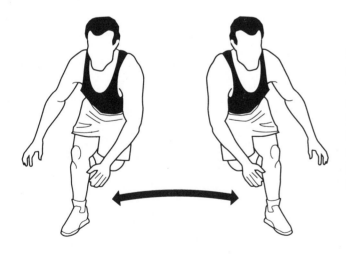

Use of the Slide Board (not illustrated) for Side Steps
The slide board, which is becoming popular for developing speed and power, accurately simulates the skating motion. This board was designed for speedskaters and was popularized by Olympic speedskater Eric Aeiden. Early boards had to be lubricated, but portable, non-lubricated boards, such as the Power Stride Board, are now available.

Side Steps
Starting with your knees bent, step to the side as far as possible, then stride back. Repeat. A slide board can also be used for this exercise.

Continuous Standing Long Jump

Standing with your feet parallel and shoulder-width apart, swing your arms backward, bending your knees and hips, then swing your arms forward, in an explosive upward and forward movement. In midair, pull your knees up to your body. Land, extending your legs forward and bending your knees, to absorb the shock. Continue moving forward with a succession of standing long jumps.

Single Leg Hops

From a standing position, drive one leg up and forward to gain distance. Land on the same foot and continue with the same leg while holding the other leg in a stationary position. Pull your arms in to the sides before landing and swing them upward and forward during takeoff. Repeat with the other leg. The exercise can also be done alternating legs after each hop.

Stride Steps

With your knees bent, take one stride step forward and to the side. Absorb the impact with the ball of the foot, then stride forward with the other leg. Repeat. This exercise is similar to the side steps, except the movement is forward and to the side.

Side Jumps Over the Bench

Stand on one side of a bench or a series of parallel benches, swing your arms, and jump over the bench(es), moving forward. Land and jump again, moving down the length of the bench(es).

Stair Bounding

This exercise is similar to the stride steps except stairs are used. Bound sideways up one or two steps of the stairs each time.

Medicine Ball Rotation

Grasp the medicine ball and rotate right and left, using quick, explosive movements.

THE PHASES OF STRENGTH AND POWER DEVELOPMENT

There are four phases of strength and power development as outlined by Bompa (1994).

1. Anatomical Adaptation
2. Maximum Strength
3. Conversion to Power
4. Maintenance

1. ANATOMICAL ADAPTATION

This is the first phase of the strength and power development and its purpose is to bring about adaptation of tendons, ligaments and muscle tissue to handle progressively increasing loads. This phase features lighter submaximal loads with an emphasis on correct technique and adapting the body to a strength training regime. With younger athletes such as 16 and 17 year olds who are just beginning training, the training period should be six to eight weeks while for an older athlete who has two years of strength training experience, the training period can be four weeks.

2. MAXIMUM STRENGTH PHASE

The objective of this phase is to develop the highest level of force possible. The body adapts the neuromuscular system to heavy loads and the recruitment of as many muscle fibers as possible in a given movement. In hockey it is very important to strengthen the trunk muscles in this phase. For the hockey player this phase is usually done in one eight-week period. For the more experienced athlete this phase can be done in two four-week sessions interspersed with a power conversion phase.

3. POWER CONVERSION PHASE

The main purpose of this phase is to convert or transform gains in maximum strength into power and sport specific movements. Lighter loads are employed with fast contractions where the athlete is exposed to activities in which the nervous system is activated and the speed of contraction is sport specific. Weights and plyometrics are used in this phase along with sport specific movements using resistance with light weights, rubber bands, medicine balls, etc.

Plyometrics are exercises in which the muscle is lengthened (eccentric contraction) followed by a contraction (concentric) movement. Examples of these types of exercises are hopping, bench jumping, medicine ball throws. Plyometrics should only be used with mature athletes as technique and a general strength base are very important to prevent injuries.

4. MAINTENANCE PHASE

This phase continues throughout the competitive season stopping usually one to two weeks before the playoff competition. Without this phase, strength and power gains can be lessened by a detraining effect.

Two to four exercises done one to two times per week are usually sufficient to maintain strength and power gained in the first three phases. The training sessions should be shorter, usually lasting between 30 and 40 minutes.

STRENGTH/POWER PHASES

The following five-phase strength/power program is for hockey players who have had at least two years of general strength training. Individuals who are just beginning a strength/power program should utilize the three-phase program. Strength/power programs usually begin at post-puberty, which is around age 16 or 17.

BEGINNERS (16 weeks)	Phase I	Anatomical Adaptation	8 weeks
	Phase II	Maximum Strength	4 weeks
	Phase III	Conversion to Power	4 weeks
ADVANCED (18 weeks)	Phase I	Anatomical Adaptation	4 weeks
	Phase II	Maximum Strength	4 weeks
	Phase III	Conversion to Power	3 weeks
	Phase IV	Maximum Strength	4 weeks
	Phase V	Conversion to Power	3 weeks

PHASE I ANATOMICAL ADAPTATION

	Percentage of maximum	Reps	Sets
Week 1	50	10	2
Week 2	60	10	2
Week 3	70	10	2
Week 4	60	10	2

Note: Beginners use 8 weeks.
Suggested exercises: Biceps Curl, Bent Knee Sit-ups, Hamstring Curl, Triceps Curl, Prone Hyperextension, Bench Press, Military Press, Bent-over Rowing, Wrist Curls, Upright Rowing

PHASE II MAXIMUM STRENGTH

	Percentage of maximum	Reps	Sets
Week 1	75	6	2
Week 2	80	6	2
Week 3	85	6	2
Week 4	80	6	2

Suggested exercises: Squat, Bench Press, Dead Lift, Hamstring Curl, Bent Knee Sit-ups, Shrugs, Lateral Step-ups

PHASE III CONVERSION TO POWER

	Percentage of maximum	Reps	Sets
Week 1	50	10	3
Week 2	60	10	3
Week 3	70	10	3

Suggested exercises: Power Bench Press, Prone Hyperextension Squats, Wrist Curls, Lat Pulldowns, Sit-ups, Lunges

Plyometrics: Side Steps, Standing Long Jump, Stride Jumps, Trunk Rotation with Medicine Ball

PHASE IV MAXIMUM STRENGTH

	Percentage of maximum	Reps	Sets
Week 1	80	6	2
Week 2	85	6	2
Week 3	90	6	2
Week 4	95	6	2

Suggested exercises: Squat Incline Press, Cleans, Reverse Leg Press, Upright Rowing, Crunches

PHASE V CONVERSION TO POWER

	Percentage of maximum	Reps	Sets
Week 1	50	10	3
Week 2	60	10	3
Week 3	70	10	3

Suggested exercises: Incline Press, Cleans, Reverse Leg Press, Wrist Rolls, Dips, Twisting Sit-up
Plyometrics: Side Steps Up Stairs, Single Leg Hops, Bench Hops, Medicine Ball Trunk Rotation

MAINTENANCE PHASE

This phase is done during the competitive season.

80% of maximum   6 Reps   3 Sets

Suggested exercises: Reverse Leg Press, Bench Press, Curls, Triceps Curls, Squat, Bent-over Rowing

Workouts are usually shorter than those of the preparation phases—about 30 to 40 minutes.

FLEXIBILITY

Flexibility exercises are important in ice hockey to ensure a full range of motion in movement patterns and for the prevention of injuries. Flexibility exercises should be included in all warm-ups for both practices and games. If ice time is limited, these exercises may be performed off the ice.

FLEXIBILITY GUIDELINES

1. Flexibility exercises should be included at the beginning and end of all workouts, on or off the ice.
2. Include a slow jog or skate before commencing the flexibility exercises.
3. In the slow-stretching type exercises, the stretch should be slow and gradual until you feel the muscle pulling. However, the stretch should not be painful.
4. In the slow stretch, hold the stretched position for 10 to 20 seconds. Return to the starting position and repeat five times.
5. Take a deep breath before you stretch, and breathe out as you stretch.
6. Do not use bouncy and jerky movements.

SLOW STRETCH (FLEXIBILITY)

NECK STRETCHES

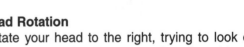

Head Tilt
Tilt your head to the right, bringing your right ear towards your right shoulder. Repeat on the other side.

Head Rotation
Rotate your head to the right, trying to look over your right shoulder. Repeat on the other side.

SHOULDER STRETCHES

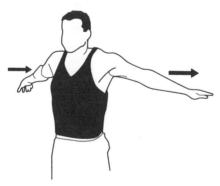

Shoulder Stretch
Keeping your arms straight at shoulder level, try to touch your palms together behind your back. Repeat with both palms facing upward.

Cross-Chest Triceps Stretch
Place your right hand on your left shoulder and with your left hand push your right elbow towards your left shoulder. Repeat on the other side.

TRUNK STRETCHES

Side Stretch
Standing with your left arm above your head, slide your right arm down the right side of the body until the stretch is felt on the left side of the body. Repeat on the other side.

Back Stretch
Lying on your back, bring your bent knees towards your chest. Grasp both knees with your hands and draw them progressively closer to your chest until the stretch is felt in the lower back. Repeat.

LOWER LIMB STRETCHES

Side Groin Stretch
Extend your right leg to the side, keeping your left leg straight. Place your right hand on your right hip. Bend your left knee and move towards your left leg. Repeat on the other side.

Hurdler's Stretch
Extend your left leg straight forward and your right leg back in a bent position. Grasp your left foot with one hand and bring your forehead down to your knee. Repeat with your right leg forward and your left leg back. Then extend both legs forward, grasp both toes, and bring your forehead down to the knees.

Lying Hamstring Stretch

Lie on your back with both knees bent, feet flat on the floor. Grasp the back of your right thigh with your right hand. Straighten your right knee towards your head, until you feel the stretch behind your knee. Repeat with the other leg.

Quad Stretch

Standing with one hand on the wall, hold one leg at the ankle and pull the foot towards your buttocks. Move the leg back until the stretch is felt in the front of the thigh and hip. Repeat with the other leg.

Calf Stretch

With both hands on a wall at shoulder height, place one foot ahead of the other, both feet flat on the floor. Keeping your back straight and feet flat on the floor, bend the front knee and keep the back leg out straight. Lean your body forward until the stretch is felt in the lower leg. Repeat with the other leg.

THE PNF METHOD

The PNF, of 3S, method of flexibility training is now used by many hockey teams. The method is based on research, conducted by Larry Holt at Dalhousie University, and information on the method can be found in his book *Scientific Stretching for Sport*. This method of flexibility training involves a series of isometric contractions (a muscle is under tension but does not move) in the muscle to be stretched, followed by concentric contractions (a muscle moves and shortens) in the opposite muscle group.

The basic steps for this method are as follows. Repeat a total of three to four times.

1. Stretch the muscle to end point without pain.
2. With a partner holding the limb(s) in a stretched position, perform an isometric contraction lasting six seconds.
3. Stretch the muscle further, with light pressure from your partner.

The following flexibility exercises should be done daily. A partner is required for all but one of them.

1. HAMSTRING STRETCH
The athlete lies with one leg straight on the floor and the other straightened and raised as high as possible. The partner holds the leg on the floor and exerts pressure against the raised leg with his shoulder. The athlete attempts to lower the leg with an isometric contraction while the partner exerts the force in the opposite direction. The leg is extended further with light pressure from the partner, and then the isometric contraction is repeated. Repeat the exercise with the other leg.

2. QUADRICEPS STRETCH
The athlete lies on his stomach on the floor with one leg flexed and raised as high as possible. The partner extends pressure with one hand under the knee of the raised leg and the other hand on the back. The athlete attempts to pull the knee downward, with pressure exerted by the partner in the opposite direction. The leg is then raised to a higher position with light pressure from the partner, and another isometric contraction is repeated. Repeat the exercise with the other leg.

3. GROIN STRETCH
The athlete sits with the legs as far apart as possible. The partner holds the legs at the ankles. The athlete then performs an isometric contraction against the pressure of the partner. The legs are then moved farther apart, with light pressure from the partner, and another isometric contraction is performed.

4. TRUNK STRETCH
The athlete sits on the floor with the legs straight and the trunk flexed forward as far as possible. The partner exerts downward pressure on the shoulders. The athlete attempts to raise the trunk with an isometric contraction. He then flexes farther forward, with light pressure from the partner. The isometric contraction is repeated.

5. SHOULDER EXTENSION
The athlete sits with back and legs straight. The arms are extended to the side at shoulder height and moved backward as far as possible. The partner grasps the wrists and exerts pressure backward as the athlete exerts force forward with the arms to execute the isometric contraction. The arms are moved farther backward, with pressure from the partner. The isometric contraction is repeated.

Off-Ice Drills for Quickness and Agility
1. Step Overs (Carioca)
Move laterally, alternately crossing one leg in front and one leg behind.

4.

2. Shake and Bake (fast feet) (not shown)
Short, knees low, running on the spot. Fast movements moving forward.

3. Stride Crossovers (not shown)
Tape a line on the floor. Stand with feet on either side. Touch right toe to left calf. Alternate.

4. Forward Crossovers
Stand with one foot forward and one foot behind. Switch feet back and forth.

6.

5. Lateral Crossovers (not shown)
Stand with feet apart. Jump and cross over feet. Land with ankles crossed. Repeat.

6. Backward Crossovers
Moving left, right leg crosses behind left leg.

7. Within Box Jumps (Single Four) (not shown)
Using one or two feet, jump from square inside a 2 feet x 2 feet box taped to the floor.

8. Within Box Jumps (Double Four) (not shown)
Same as single, but perform the jumps on both feet, in all possible directions.

9. Slalom (not shown)
Use a line on a gymnasium floor or tape a 10 foot line. With feet together, jump in slalom zigzag fashion across the line while moving forward. Move forwards and then backwards.

10. Slalom Jump and Sprint
Use a tape of line on a gym floor, or field (approx. 10 ft). Jump in slalom skiing fashion (zigzag), and at the end of the line, sprint forward for 10–15 m/y.

11. Skipping (not shown)
Skip fast for 30 seconds then rest for 30 seconds.

12. Squat Thrusts (18" bench) (not shown)
Stand, squat, thrust legs backwards. Pull knees into a squat position again. Stand up. Repeat.

13. Side Hops (18" bench) (not shown)
Take off and land on a different foot diagonally and across.

14. Step Hopping (not shown)
Hop up stairs on one foot and then two feet. Hop up one step at a time and then two steps at a time.

15. Split Leg Shuffle (not shown)
Stand with feet together. Jump and land in a wider stance. Jump again and land with feet together. Repeat.

16. Crossovers (not shown)
Similar to No. 1 except there is no lateral movement. Jump in the air and land with legs crossed. Jump in the air again and cross the legs the other way.

17. Hop the Box (not shown)
Stand in the middle of a taped box on the floor with four quadrants. Hop in and out from the center to the eight points, returning to the center each time.

18. Forward Lunges (not shown)
Fall forward with one bent leg forward and the back leg fully extended. Push the front leg and return to the starting position. Repeat with the other leg forward.

19. Depth Jumps (not shown)
Jump off a 16-inch box landing on one or both legs and then jump high in the air fully extending the legs.

20. Depth Jumps—Side Movement (not shown)
Same as No. 19 except on landing take one side step right or left and then spring forward.

21. Single and Double Leg Hops (not shown)
From a standing position, drive one leg up and forward to gain distance. Land on the same foot or alternate foot. Pull the arms to the side before landing and swing them upward and forward during takeoff. Repeat. Vary this by landing on both legs.

22. Side Steps (Slide Board) (not shown)
Using a slide board, step to the side as far as possible and then, stride back.

23. Shuttle Run (not shown)
Run 10 feet and touch the line, run 10 feet back and touch the line. Rest for 30 seconds. Repeat.

CARDIOVASCULAR ENDURANCE

TRAINING THE ENERGY SYSTEMS
As mentioned previously, all three energy systems should be trained for ice hockey. The aerobic system should be trained early in the preparation period (off-season) and then maintained as the start of the competition period approaches. The alactic and lactic anaerobic systems should be trained after the aerobic base is built, and the intensity and duration of this training should increase as the competition period approaches.

GENERAL GUIDELINES FOR TRAINING THE ENERGY SYSTEMS

System	Duration of Exercise	Work-to-Rest Ratio	Percentage of Maximum Heart Rate
Alactic (ATP-PC)	5–10 sec.	1:5 to 1:3	95–100
Lactic	25–60 sec.	1:5 to 1:3	85–95
Aerobic	20–40 min. plus continuous 2–2 1/2 min.	— 1:1.5 to 1:1	70–80 85–90

Interval training is the best method for the systematic training of the energy systems. Although the traditional stops and starts in ice hockey are a form of interval training, a specific system and progression should be devised for their use.

Interval training uses work interspersed with periods of rest to achieve the desired improvement. In intermittent work, the lactic acid accumulation is lower than that occurring during continuous work. The ATP-PC system is used more extensively, and consequently the lactic acid system is not fully depleted. Interval training does the following:

- allows the ATP-PC system to be used over and over
- delays the onset of fatigue by not delving so deeply into the lactic acid system
- allows the system to become more tolerant to lactic acid
- works long enough at sufficient intensity to allow an improvement in the aerobic system

The manipulated variables used in interval training are:

- rate and distance
- repetitions and sets
- duration of the relief interval
- type of activity during relief interval
- frequency of training

Terms	Definitions
Work interval	Portion of interval training program involving high-intensity work bursts
Repetition	One work interval
Relief interval	Time between work interval (can be working, flexing, or light jogging)
Set	Series of work and relief intervals
Training time	Rate at which work is performed

GENERAL GUIDELINES FOR AEROBIC AND ANAEROBIC TRAINING

Aerobic training can include skating, running, rollerblading, or cycling. Aerobic training starts with continuous long-distance work and progresses to interval training.

Anaerobic alactic (ATP-PC) and lactic training can include running, skating, rollerblading, or use of the stationary bicycle.

1. Perform a proper warm-up, including stretching exercises and jogging.
2. Wear proper clothing and footwear.
3. Work out three times per week.
4. Work out on alternate days. Do strength/power training on the other days. Have one rest day after six days of training.
5. Finish the workout with a cool-down. Walk, jog, or rollerblade for one kilometer, and finish with a stretching program.

AEROBIC AND ANAEROBIC OFF-ICE TRAINING—18-WEEK PROGRAM

WEEKS 1 TO 4

Aerobic

- Continuous running or rollerblading
- 70–80 percent of maximum heart rate (approximately 160 beats/minute)
- Start with 20 minutes, and increase to 40 minutes or more
- Train three times per week on alternate days

WEEKS 5 TO 8

Aerobic

- Once per week—continuous running for 40 minutes or more
- Twice per week—aerobic interval training 85–95 percent of maximum
- 3 to 5 heart beats per minute below the maximum
- Follow 2 1/2 minutes work with 2 1/2 minutes rest (1:1 work-to-rest ratio)
- Start with 3 repetitions in 2 sets
- Build to 5 repetitions in 2 sets

WEEKS 9 TO 12

Aerobic
- Once per week, continuous running for 40 minutes or more
- Once per week, aerobic interval training—2 1/2 minutes work and 2 1/2 minutes rest for a total of 30 minutes work and 30 minutes rest

Anaerobic
Lactic
- Once per week
- 30–40 seconds work; work-to-rest ratio 1:5 to 1:3
- 5 repetitions, 2 sets
- Rest for 5 minutes between sets
- 85–90 percent maximum

WEEKS 13 TO 18

Anaerobic
- Twice per week

Alactic
- 5–10 seconds work
- 5 repetitions, 2 sets
- 90–95 percent maximum
- Rest 2 minutes between sets (work-to-rest ratio 1:5 to 1:3)

Lactic
- 30–40 seconds work
- 5 repetitions, 2 sets—build to 6 repetitions in 2 sets
- Rest 5 minutes between sets (work-to-rest ratio 1:3)

Aerobic
- Continuous running for 40 minutes or more once per week

Note: Anaerobic training is emphasized in this training phase. The aerobic training is used for maintaining aerobic fitness and is done once a week.

ON-ICE TRAINING FOR CARDIOVASCULAR ENDURANCE

TRAINING THE ATP-PC SYSTEM (ALACTIC)
The following drills require that you divide your team into three groups.

1. One Width or Two Widths
Have each group skate one or two widths of the rink or from the goal line to the center line in turn. They work for 5 seconds and rest 20 seconds, doing three to four sets of five repetitions each.

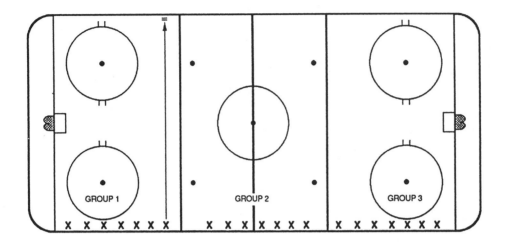

2. Blue Line to Blue Line
Have each group skate blue line to blue line, four times in turn. They work for 12 to 15 seconds and rest 45 seconds, doing two to three sets of four repetitions each.

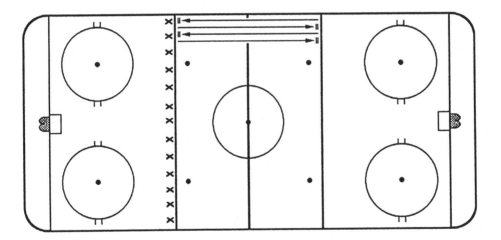

TRAINING THE LACTIC ACID SYSTEM

Drills 1 through 10 require the team be divided into three groups.

1. Dot to Dot

Have each group skate from the defensive face-off dot to the one at the far end four times. They work for 30 seconds and rest for 2 minutes, doing two to three sets of four repetitions each. Allow 4 to 5 minutes' rest between sets.

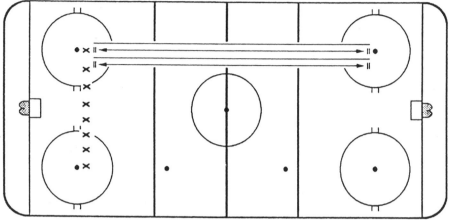

2. Goal Line to Goal Line

Have each group skate from goal line to goal line four times. They work for 40 to 45 seconds and rest for 2 minutes, doing two to three sets of four repetitions each. Allow 4 to 5 minutes' rest between sets.

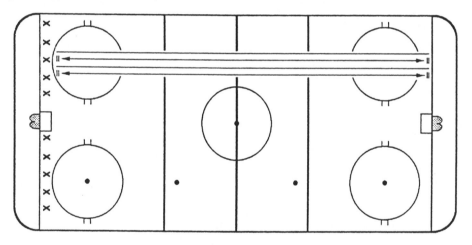

3. Around the Net

Have each group skate around the rink behind the nets for one and one-half laps and then go in the other direction one and one-half laps in turn. They work 40 to 45 seconds and rest for 2 minutes, doing two to three sets of four repetitions each.

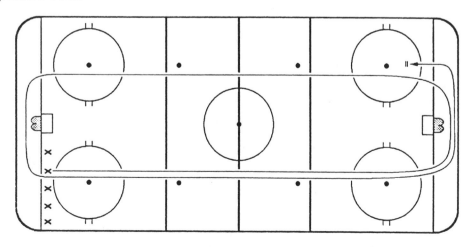

4. Around the Dots

Have each group skate around the defensive zone face-off dots for three laps. They work 40 to 45 seconds and rest for 2 minutes, doing two to three sets of four repetitions each.

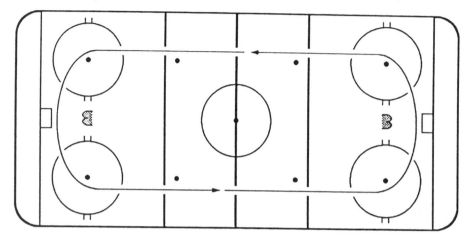

5. Skate the Lines

Have each group skate the different lengths non-stop. They work for 40 to 45 seconds and rest for 2 minutes, doing two to three sets of four repetitions each. Allow 4 to 5 minutes' rest between sets.

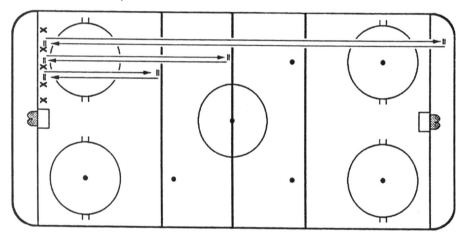

6. Defense, Forwards, Goalies

Defensemen skate forward to the center red line, skate backward back to the blue line, turn, and skate forward to the goal line three times, working on both backward turns. Forwards skate forward across the rink and back three times, touching the boards with their sticks. Goalies skate forward to the red line and drop to both knees with stick and catcher in position, then skate backward to the goal line and do a double leg slide to one side, twice. They work for 30 to 35 seconds and rest for 2 minutes, doing two to three sets of four repetitions each. Allow 4 to 5 minutes' rest between sets.

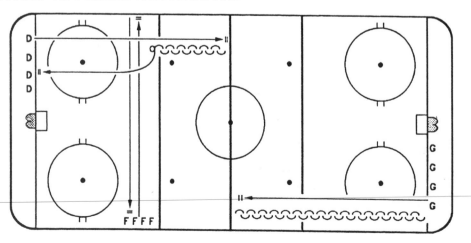

7. Around the Rink

Have each group skate two laps around the rink. They work for 30 to 35 seconds and rest for 2 minutes, doing two to three sets of four repetitions. Allow 4 to 5 minutes' rest between sets.

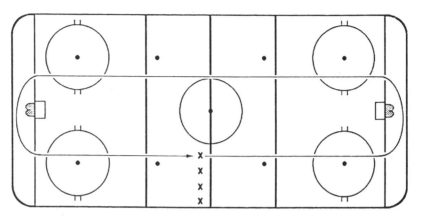

8. Stops and Starts

Have each group do stops and starts using the entire length of the ice, changing direction on the whistle. They work for 30 to 40 seconds and rest for 2 minutes, doing two to three sets of four repetitions each. Allow 4 to 5 minutes' rest between sets.

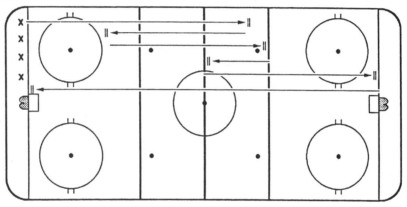

9. Skate the Lines

Have each group skate forward from the goal line to the center red line, back to the near blue line, then to the far blue line, back to the center red line, then to the far goal line, and all the way back. They work for 40 to 50 seconds and rest for 2 minutes, doing two to three sets of four repetitions each. Allow 4 to 5 minutes' rest between sets.

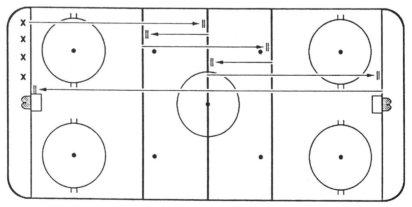

10. Around the Rink

Have each group skate around the rink at 80 to 90 percent maximum speed for 30 to 40 seconds, skate slowly for 30 to 40 seconds, and then repeat. They do two to three sets of five repetitions each. Allow 4 minutes' rest between sets.

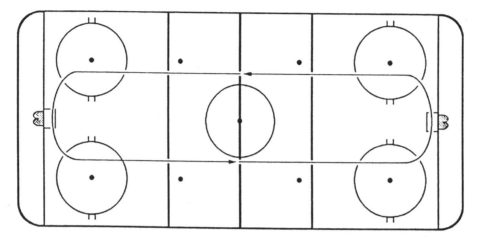

11. Three-on-Three, Four-on-Four

Players scrimmage three-on-three or four-on-four, using the full ice. Players change while the puck is in play. When they change lines, the puck is passed back to the goalie. On off-sides, the puck is passed back to the goalie and the offending team must move outside the blue line. They work for 1 minute and rest for 3 minutes. Change on the whistle.

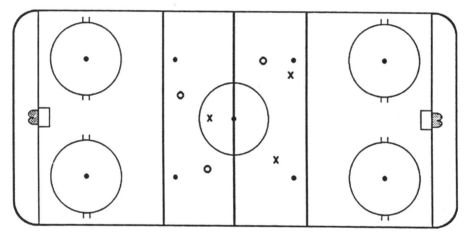

12. Relay Race

Divide the team into four groups and have them run relay races. Each player works for 40 seconds and rests for 2 minutes.

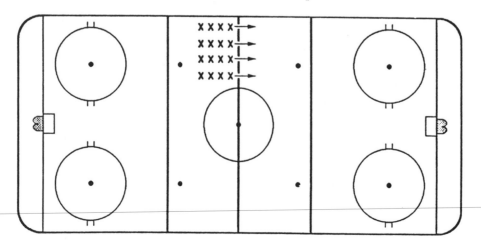

TRAINING THE AEROBIC SYSTEM

1. Change Direction
The entire team skates around the rink, being sure to go behind each net. They skate for 3 minutes and then change direction and skate the other way for an additional 3 minutes.

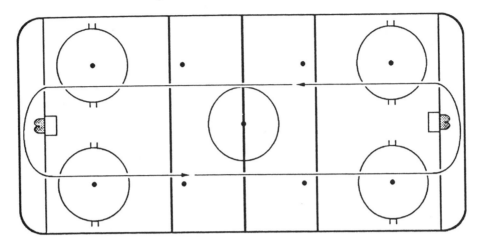

2. Figure Eight
The team repeats 1, but this time skating in a figure eight, crossing at the center-ice face-off dot.

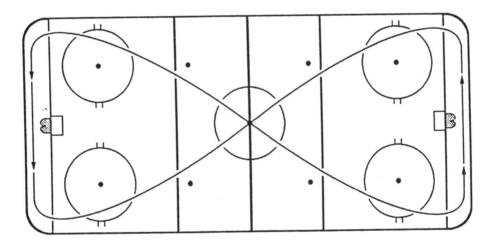

3. The Denver Skate
In this variation on 1, move the nets towards the center with each lap and then back after the first 3 minutes.

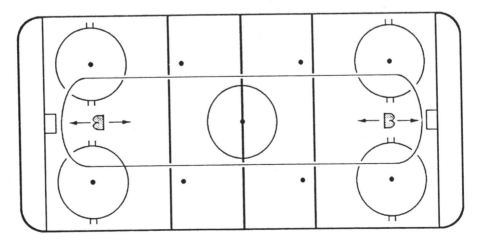

4. Half-ice Scrimmage

Have the team play two five-on-five scrimmages using half-ice. Each game is 10 minutes in length and players change lines after 5 minutes. They work for 5 minutes and rest for 5 minutes.

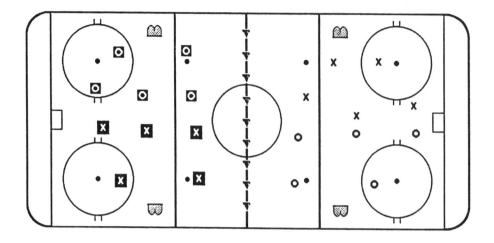

CIRCUIT TRAINING

Circuit training is a general conditioning method in which athletes perform exercises at a number of different exercise stations. Circuit training generally develops muscular strength, muscular and cardiorespiratory endurance, power, and flexibility, and allows a number of people to work out at the same time. Circuits can be set up in many different ways and can be done with or without equipment such as weights.

Circuit training for ice hockey can be used in the following ways:

- directly prior to and/or during the specific preparation period
- throughout the season, two to three times per week, to maintain the fitness level
- two or three times during the season for an intensive 10-day period, to raise the fitness level
- during the off-season, as a general conditioning method

It should be noted that the best method of conditioning for the off-season would be specific training for strength (weight training), cardiovascular endurance (running short sprints and long distances), and flexibility. Circuit training is general training but does not develop as high a level of strength as specific weight training. It will have less effect on cardiorespiratory endurance than a sprint and endurance running program.

The following are examples of three different types of circuits for ice hockey. The first two are designed for an exercise area other than the one at the arena, although some arenas may have a room large enough. The third circuit can be used at the arena, using available space or the ice if enough ice time is available.

Circuits 1 and 2 are intensive and can be used for three 10-day periods during the season, to raise the fitness level, or can be used three to five times per week during the off-season, to improve the fitness level. Circuit 1 is the most demanding and requires equipment. Circuit 2, although still intensive, requires very little equipment. Circuit 3 can be used on the ice daily during the season as a warm-up general conditioning program or once or twice per week, with athletes going through the circuit three times to maintain and improve the fitness level. This circuit requires a minimal amount of equipment.

Each of the three circuits has 10 stations. With a standard hockey team of 20 players, two people work at each circuit for a total of 45 minutes for three complete circuits. An alternative method is for athletes to repeat the same exercise three times before changing to the next station. The exercise would still last 30 seconds, with one minute's rest before athletes start the exercise once more.

Note that all weights listed for circuit 1 are for junior hockey players aged 16 to 19 years. Younger players should use only circuits 2 and 3.

CIRCUIT I

This circuit will help maintain and increase strength, power, and muscular and cardiorespiratory endurance. This circuit is strenuous and can best be used three times a season for 10 days, to increase the strength levels. It is best performed in a small gymnasium or a room of similar size with bleacher seats or stairs. Two athletes work simultaneously at each station for 30 seconds, with one minute allowed for changing stations and rest.

The equipment needed includes two barbells of 65 pounds each, four barbells of 90 pounds each, two barbells of 20 pounds each, two benches, two dumbbells of 15 pounds each, stopwatch, and whistle.

1. Curls
Each athlete grasps a 65-pound barbell, using an underhand grip, with hands shoulder-width apart. With arms extended forward, raise the bar to the chest by bending arms at the elbows, lower the bar to the starting position, and repeat.

2. Bench Leap
Each athlete jumps onto the bench with both feet. Then he jumps back down and repeats.

3. Bench Press
Each athlete lies on a bench holding the 90-pound barbell above with hands shoulder-width apart. He lowers the bar so it touches the chest. Raise the bar back to the starting position and repeat. Inhale at the start of the movement and exhale at the completion of the movement.

4. Stair Running
Each athlete runs up a flight of stairs one step at a time, runs back down, and repeats.

5. Reverse Wrist Curls
In seated position and using a 20-pound barbell, each athlete rests his forearms along the thighs, which are parallel to the floor. The arms and wrists should be extended past the knees. The bar is held with an overhand grip to raise and lower the wrists as far as possible.

6. Bench Hop
Each athlete jumps over a bench with both feet and repeats.

7. Bent Lateral Raise
With a 15-pound dumbbell in each hand, each athlete bends over at the waist until the upper body is parallel to the floor. The dumbbells are raised laterally until they are level with the upper body and the elbows are slightly bent. Lower and repeat.

8. Sit-ups
While lying on the back with knees bent and feet flat on the floor, each athlete clasps the hands behind the head. Start the sit-up with the shoulders flat on the ground and raise the upper body, touching the left elbow to the right knee, and so on, and repeat.

9. Power, Clean, and Press
With knees bent and back straight, the athlete grasps the 90-pound barbell with an overhand or underhand grip. Extend the legs and lift the weight to the chest. Lift the weight up to the shoulders by bending arms. Raise the weight above the head by fully extending the arms. Lower the weight slowly to the floor and repeat.

10. Stair Bounding
Each athlete runs up the stairs two at a time, runs back down, and repeats.

CIRCUIT 2
The purpose of this circuit is to maintain and develop strength, power, and muscular and cardiorespiratory endurance. This circuit can be used in a pre-season training program or during the season in three 10-day cycles. It is best performed in a gymnasium or a large room with a high ceiling. Two athletes work simultaneously at each station for 30 seconds. Allow one minute for rest and changing stations.

Equipment needed includes two long ropes, two chinning bars, two benches, four 15-pound dumbbells, two 20-pound barbells, two wall ladders, stopwatch, and whistle.

1. Rope Climbing
Using the arms only, each athlete climbs the rope to the ceiling.

2. Bench Leap
Each athlete jumps onto the bench with both feet. Jump back down and repeat.

3. Chin-ups
Each athlete performs chin-ups using the underhand grip, completely extending the arms, and without swinging the legs. After raising the chin above the bar, repeat.

4. Squat Jumps
Starting in a crouched position with both hands on the floor, each athlete jumps in the air, completely extending the legs and arms, and repeats.

5. Push-ups
With the back straight, each athlete pushes up, completely extending the arms, lowers the chest to the floor, and repeats.

6. Bench Hop
Each athlete jumps over a bench with both feet and repeats.

7. Ladder
Using arms only, each athlete climbs the wall ladder and repeats.

8. Sit-ups
While lying on his back with knees bent and feet flat on the floor, each athlete clasps his hands behind the head. Start the sit-up with the shoulders flat on the ground and raise the upper body, touching the left elbow to the right knee, and so on, and repeat.

9. Bent Lateral Raise
With a 15-pound dumbbell in each hand, each athlete bends over at the waist until the upper body is parallel to the floor. The dumbbells are raised laterally until they are level with the upper body and the elbows are slightly bent. Lower and repeat.

10. Reverse Wrist Curls
In a seated position and using a 20-pound barbell, each athlete rests his forearms along the thighs, which are parallel to the floor. The arms and wrists should be extended past the knees. The bar is held with an overhand grip to raise and lower the wrists as far as possible.

CIRCUIT 3
The purpose of this circuit is to increase and maintain muscular strength, cardiorespiratory endurance, power, and flexibility. This circuit requires no equipment and can be done off the ice in the space around the arena or on the ice if enough ice time is available. Note that, in this circuit, one person does an exercise for 30 seconds and then his partner does the exercise for 30 seconds. After both have done it, they move to the next station.

The equipment needed includes one wrist roll, two broom handles each two feet long, two ropes, two 15-pound dumbbells, stopwatch, and whistle.

1. Dips
The gate to the benches is opened. The body is raised and lowered, using the arms only.

2. Sit-ups
While lying on his back with knees bent and feet flat on the floor, each athlete clasps his hands behind the head. He starts the sit-up with the shoulders flat on the ground and raises the upper body, touching the left elbow to the right knee, and so on, and repeats.

3. Push-ups
With the back straight, each athlete pushes up, completely extending the arms, lowers the chest to the floor, and repeats.

4. "V" Sits
Each athlete lies flat on the ground. Raise the back and legs at the same time and touches the feet with the hands, keeping the arms and legs straight, and repeat.

5. Arm Circles
With arms extended to the side, each athlete rotates both arms forward in large circles, finishing with small circles, and then rotates backward in a similar fashion.

6. Leg Flexion
One athlete lies on his stomach, while his partner gives resistance on lower legs. The athlete flexes the legs at the knee and hips, moving slowly through the movement with resistance for 10 seconds, and repeats.

7. Leg Extension
Each athlete lies on his stomach with legs flexed. The partner gives resistance while he extends the legs, moving slowly through the movement with resistance for 10 seconds, and repeats.

8. Groin Exercise
Each athlete lies on his back with legs apart and slightly bent. With the partner standing with legs inside the athlete's knees giving resistance, he presses in for 10 seconds. Then, with the partner's legs on the outside, he presses out for 10 seconds.

9. Wrist Roll
Each athlete rolls the weight up by rolling the handle, which has a rope attached to a 20-pound weight. Lower the weight in reverse manner and repeat.

10. Hurdler's Stretch
In a sitting position, the athlete extends the right leg forward and left leg back. Grasp the right ankle with both hands and slowly brings the forehead to the knee. This is repeated with the left leg forward and then with both legs together. Each segment of the exercise is done for 10 seconds.

ON-ICE CIRCUIT
In this circuit, players work two to each station with 30 seconds' work followed by 30 seconds' rest, and then the exercise is repeated. Then the players change stations. Allow one minute for rest and changing stations.

1. Players start at the center line and skate to the blue line and back to the center line four times. Each tries to pick up the hockey stick and push back the other player.
2. Players play keep-away inside the face-off circle.
3. Players practice continuous breakaways from the red line; one man chases the other man, shoots, and changes each time.
4. Without sticks, players try to body check the other man out of the face-off circle.
5. One man skates forward with the puck between the blue lines and passes it to the other man, who is skating backward. The man skating backward then skates forward with the puck and passes to his partner, who is skating forward.
6. Without sticks, players fight for the puck along the boards.
7. Players practice continuous breakaways from the blue line as pucks are picked up at the side of the net.
8. Players do stops and starts between the end boards and the top of the face-off circle.

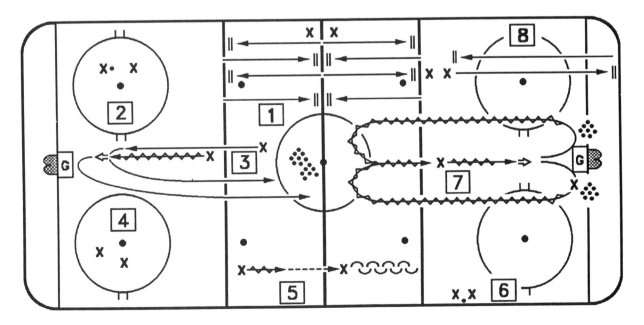

SUMMER TRAINING REPORT

Every four weeks the hockey player sends in a training report showing the progress made.

MAXIMUM STRENGTH TRAINING—MONDAY, WEDNESDAY, FRIDAY

Exercise	Weight	Reps	Sets
1.			
2.			
3.			
4.			
5.			
6.			

PLYOMETRIC EXERCISES

Activity	Reps	Sets
1.		
2.		
3.		
4.		

AEROBIC/ANAEROBIC TRAINING—TUESDAY, THURSDAY, SATURDAY

Day	Activity	Distance	Reps	Sets
Tuesday Interval Exercise				
Thursday Interval Exercise				
Saturday Continuous Exercise				

FITNESS TESTING AT TRAINING CAMP

The following fitness test could be conducted on the first day of training camp.

1. Bench press your body weight 10 times.
2. Squat three-quarters of your body weight 10 times.
3. Perform 55 sit-ups in 60 seconds.
4. Run a distance of 3000 meters (15 laps of a 200-meter track) in 12 minutes.

Note: Exercise 2 is for mature hockey players who have previously strength trained. Substitute the half-squat for players in their first two years of strength training.

21. NUTRITION

The hockey player's diet is an essential link in the physical year-round training program. The energy used to move the muscles and restore energy during recovery is directly related to nutrition, as well as the development of the cardiorespiratory and muscular systems. The hockey player involved in a rigorous training regime has to pay special attention and understand how, what, and when to eat properly.

HOCKEY PLAYERS' DIET

The average person consumes between 1200 and 1500 calories per day from food. The hockey player who trains daily, however, may require between 2000 and 5000 calories per day depending on the training intensity, age, body size, etc.

An optimal diet for an athlete would include approximately 60–65 percent carbohydrates, 25 percent fats, and 15 percent protein.

The four basic food groups supply the carbohydrates, fats, and proteins:

1. Milk and cheese
2. Meat and fish
3. Fruits and vegetables
4. Breads and cereals

Vitamins, minerals, and water are also essential for a well-balanced diet.

The carbohydrates in the diet that are broken down to simple sugars, primarily glucose, are stored in the muscle and liver as glycogen, and are the key to supplying energy for athletic performance. The major problem for today's hockey player is to have a 60–65 percent carbohydrate diet and limit the amount of fat to 25 percent along with 15 percent protein. High carbohydrate diets produce more stored glycogen and have an effect on performance, particularly in endurance activities lasting more than one hour which effectively deplete these glycogen stores. In short-burst power activities, on- and off-ice, the glycogen stores are usually not fully depleted. Today's so-called junk foods (hamburgers, hot dogs, etc.) contain high fat levels, and it is important for the hockey player to limit intake of these foods and concentrate on those rich in carbohydrates.

The common prescription of three meals per day may be suitable for the average person, however, the hockey player, who may need twice as many calories, can eat five or six meals per day as well as indulge in planned nutritional snacks.

In addition to the daily meals, the hockey player must eat a well-planned pre- and post-competition meal, as well as some additional fluid and nutrition during the event.

CARBOHYDRATES

Carbohydrates, made up of carbon, hydrogen, and oxygen, commonly come in the form of starches and sugars. Carbohydrates, the main source of energy in intense exercise, supply the cells with glucose and glycogen, which are then converted to energy. Carbohydrates are found in three groups that vary in complexity and size of the molecules: simple sugars or monosaccharides; disaccharides (two linked monosaccharides); and polysaccharides or complex carbohydrates.

Monosaccharides, or simple sugars, are often found listed on food labels as glucose, fructose, or dextrose. The linking of two monosaccharides, such as fructose and glucose (common table sugar), creates a disaccharide. The joining of two monosaccharides also forms other simple sugars, such as maltose and lactose.

Polysaccharides can be of two types: starch and fiber. This complex carbohydrate is formed by the combination of a large number of simple sugar groups. Starches are found in grains and cereals, and in vegetables such as potatoes and corn.

Most food products contain a mixture of all three types of carbohydrates. It is important for both the hockey player and the coach to read and understand labels on food products in order to properly ascertain the carbohydrate value of the food.

In order for carbohydrates to be used as fuel for energy, the body must first break down the carbohydrates to simple sugars. This is accomplished by digestive enzymes in the stomach, after which the simple sugars enter the small intestine and are absorbed into the blood. Blood carries the remaining simple sugars to the liver, where they are then converted to glucose. Glucose can only be used directly by the body's cells. When glucose enters a cell, a portion is used directly, the rest is stored as glycogen for future use. Any excess glucose that remains after the glycogen stores are filled is stored as fat.

Glycogen stored in one muscle cell cannot be used by another cell. It is only the liver that contains cells that have the ability to convert glycogen back to glucose. Once converted back, the glucose can then be re-released into the blood stream and absorbed elsewhere in the body.

Insulin is also important for distributing glucose throughout the cells of the body. Insulin is released by the pancreas when there is an elevated amount of glucose in the blood.

Some specific foods that are rich in carbohydrates are:

- Pasta (spaghetti, macaroni, and even pizza)
- Cereals such as bran and oat bran. These cereals are provide a good supply of fiber.
- Vegetables such as potatoes, corn, and legumes
- Muffins, bagels, and whole-grain muffins (bran, oatmeal, corn) which are better than white flour muffins, donuts, etc.
- Whole grain and dark breads. Whole grain breads have more nutritional value than white grain breads.
- Fruit and fruit juice such as orange, banana, and apple

FATS

Fats, along with carbohydrates, supply the majority of energy to the body. Proteins, on the other hand, supply very small amounts of energy to the body. Fats are stored as triglycerides in specialized cells in the body. These cells are called "adipose tissue." Fats contain large amounts of carbon and hydrogen, and relatively small amounts of oxygen. Fats do no supply energy as quickly as carbohydrates do, but more energy can be stored as fat. Fats are an important fuel source, particularly during prolonged activity lasting more than an hour. Carbohydrates are used primarily during intense bouts of exercise of a shorter duration.

There are two types of fat sources: saturated and unsaturated. It is commonly believed that saturated fat from animals, as well as coconut and palm oil, are related to higher incidents of atherosclerosis and cardio-vascular disease, and thus excessive amounts of saturated fats should be avoided. Unsaturated fats from vegetable oils and plants, however, are considered better for hockey players. Since only 25 percent of the total diet should be made up of fats, hockey players in particular should take care not to exceed this limit.

Here are some examples of fats that should and should not be included in the hockey player's diet:

Good:

- Olive oil
- Canola oil
- Safflower oil
- Sunflower oil
- Low-fat cheese
- Margarine
- Yogurt
- Peanut Butter

Cut back or eliminate:

- Hamburgers
- Hot dogs
- Sausage
- Butter
- Cheese

The major problem with the fat content of a hockey player's diet is that it is difficult to maintain the desired limit of 25 percent. Most hockey players tend to have a higher proportion of fat in their diet, to the detriment of the larger (60 percent) proportion that should be carbohydrates.

PROTEIN

Protein, which should make up 15 percent of the hockey player's diet, is essential to the body in order to stimulate physical growth and also to facilitate the repair of damaged tissue. In addition, enzymes that control chemical reactions in the body are made up of proteins. These proteins are composed of chains of smaller substances called "amino acids," which are made up of carbon, hydrogen, oxygen, nitrogen, and in some cases, sulfur atoms. It is the nitrogen content of protein that makes it different from carbohydrates and fat.

There are 20 different amino acids, eight of which are "essential" because they cannot be obtained through the liver's conversion of carbohydrates, fats, and proteins. Three of these essential amino acids, namely valine, iolencine, and leucine, are essential in energy production.

The daily requirement of protein for the average person is one gram per kilogram (g/kg) of body weight. While training, an athlete requires 1.4 to 2.0 g/kg. The building blocks of proteins, amino acids, can be found in the protein of both animals and plants. Animal proteins, however, have a greater distribution of amino acids compared to plants, and are therefore considered a better source of protein. The average person's normal diet generally consumes more than 2.0 g/kg of protein per day.

Eating an excessive amount of protein, more than 15 percent of the total diet, is not recommended. With excessive amounts of protein the body removes the nitrogen and converts the remaining amino acid to fat or carbohydrates. Therefore, excessive amounts of protein cannot be stored. In fact, excessive amounts of protein have been known to cause dehydration and constipation because the kidneys use water to wash out the nitrogen (urea) and other waste products resulting from protein metabolism.

Since a well-balanced diet produces more than enough protein for the hockey player in training, and because the body cannot store excessive protein, the protein supplements on the market, many of which make unsubstantiated claims, are unnecessary. A diet with a normal amount of protein is quite adequate for all protein needs.

Some recommended sources of protein are the following:

- Lean beef
- Chicken and turkey
- Fish, in particular salmon, tuna, sardines, swordfish
- Peanut butter
- Beans, lentils, legumes, tofu, chili beans
- Milk, eggs, cottage cheese

VITAMINS

Vitamins are essential to the body. They are obtained through enzymes and coenzymes which are involved in the metabolism of carbohydrates and fats. They are not a direct source of energy themselves. Vitamins are also involved in the formation of red blood cells and bone. Vitamins are not manufactured in the body and must be ingested from through the diet. Some vitamins are water-soluble (C and B complex) and cannot be stored, so the excess is passed in the urine. Other vitamins are fat-soluble (A, D, E, and K) and are absorbed in the fat of the stomach and small intestines. Excessive amounts are stored in the liver and fat tissue.

Fat-soluble vitamins are required in small amounts and do not need to be supplied each day, though deficiencies can lead to serious illness or even death. Excessive amounts, on the other hand, can be toxic. As with all essential vitamins, additional supplementation is unnecessary. The well-balanced diet can supply an ample amount of the required vitamins for the healthy hockey player.

Water-soluble Vitamins

VITAMIN C (Ascorbic acid)

Sources of Vitamin C
- Oranges, tomatoes, apples, cranberry juice
- Broccoli
- Brussels sprouts
- Cantaloupes
- Green peppers

VITAMIN B (Thiamine B, Riboflavin B2, Niacin, plus others)

Sources of Vitamin B

Thiamine
- Lean beef
- Pork
- Poultry
- Fish
- Enriched bread

Riboflavin
- Green leafy vegetables
- Milk, eggs
- Peas, beans
- Lean beef
- Fish
- Whole grain cereals
- Enriched breads

Niacin
- Lean beef
- Pork
- Poultry
- Fish
- Enriched breads
- Whole grain cereals
- Peanut butter

Fat-Soluble Vitamins

Vitamin A
- Peaches, apricots
- Broccoli, spinach
- Cantaloupe
- Carrots
- Sweet potatoes

Vitamin D
- Sunlight
- Milk
- Eggs
- Fish
- Cod liver oil

Vitamin E
- Green leafy vegetables
- Wheat germ
- Vegetable oil
- Cereals
- Margarine, shortening

Vitamin K
- Milk
- Green leafy vegetables
- Cabbage
- Cereals
- Meats

MINERALS

Minerals are inorganic compounds that are found in small amounts throughout the body. They are essential to healthy body function.

Minerals include the so-called electrolytes, namely sodium, potassium, and chloride. They are also involved in bone metabolism, including calcium, phosphorous, and magnesium; and zinc and iron.

The Electrolytes—Sodium, Potassium, and Chloride

A great deal has been written about sport drinks as a means to replacing electrolytes during and after exercise. Electrolytes are charged molecules. Most molecules are neutral, with an equal number of positive protons and negative electrons. When electrolytes are consumed through food (mostly through fruits, vegetables, and grains), they combine with either the extracellular (outside) or the intercellular (inside) fluids (mostly water) in the body, though not in equal concentrations. Sodium ($Na+$) and potassium ($K+$) are found in the largest concentrations. Sodium is found in the extracellular fluids, and potassium is found in the intracellular fluid. The balance of the concentrations of sodium and potassium inside and outside the cell is critical to life functions, especially muscle contraction.

During exercise, water moves from the extracellular fluid through the membrane into the muscle cells. This fluid is replaced in the extracellular compartment by water from the blood plasma. The movement of water across the membrane causes a difference in the of concentrations of the electrolytes on the inside and outside of the cell. If excessive salt ($NaCl$) is taken into the body, the concentration of sodium becomes greater on the outside of the cell, and water is drawn across the membrane from the inside of the cell to equalize the concentrations. This movement of water out of the cell alters the chemical reaction that produces energy (water is important for this process) and impairs muscle contraction.

A similar situation occurs when water is lost through sweating, which also disturbs the electrolyte balance. When water is lost from extracellular space and the sodium concentration is allowed to increase, water again moves from inside the cell to the outside in order to balance the concentrations.

The electrolyte balance in the body can be kept at a normal level by the food we eat. An increase in the consumption of fruits and vegetables is the best method of replenishing the electrolytes, as well as drinking as much water as is comfortable. A regular, normal salting of food is also acceptable, but excessive amounts are not necessary. Salt tablets must be consumed with at lest one pint of water per tablet, and this method is not recommended. Electrolyte sport drinks are useful as they replace both electrolytes and water, though the cost may be a deterrent.

Potassium ($K+$) imbalance in the blood is also a problem with exercise. The rising concentration of potassium in the blood, called "hyperkalemia," is caused by potassium being released from the muscle cell and a subsequent loss of fluid from the plasma.

The best method of replacing potassium is through diet—fruits, vegetables, and lean meats being the main providers. Sport drinks also include potassium.

Some food sources of sodium and potassium are the following:

- Bananas, apples, apricots, oranges, tomatoes
- Broccoli, potatoes, squash, carrots, green beans
- Kidney beans
- Whole wheat bread
- Chicken
- Spaghetti with meat sauce
- Raisins

Calcium, Phosphorus, and Magnesium

Calcium, phosphorus, and magnesium are important in the make-up and formation of bones and teeth.

Of the three minerals, calcium is the most abundant in the body. As well as being found in bones and teeth (99 percent of the total amount), a small portion plays a role in muscle contraction, transmission of nerve impulses, and the breakdown of glycogen.

A calcium deficiency can lead to a decrease in bone density, a condition commonly known as "osteoporosis." Females with a smaller bone mass than men appear to be more susceptible to this condition. Stress fractures and muscle cramping are also possibly affected by calcium deficiency. It has also been suggested that a calcium deficiency may have a more severe effect than normal on females who are amenorrheic (a condition where the menstrual cycles have been suppressed). Calcium can be found in dairy products and various plant foods, although absorption through dairy products is superior to plant foods. Taking excess calcium is not recommended and may lead to kidney stone formation.

Some good sources of calcium are the following:

- Milk
- Cheese
- Green leafy vegetables
- Egg yolk

Deficiencies of calcium, phosphorus, and magnesium can be made up by adapting the diet to include more of the foods mentioned above. Supplements are not recommended.

Iron

Iron is one mineral to which hard-training athletes, particularly females, must pay attention. Iron is food to red blood cells and is responsible for the oxygen-carrying capacity of the blood.

Some good sources of iron are the following:

- Green leafy vegetables
- Egg yolk
- Liver, kidney, heart
- Nuts
- Dried beans
- Red meat
- Enriched bread and cereals

Water

Water is the most essential nutrient in the body. It is located in both the extracellular and intracellular parts of the body and makes up over half the body weight, over 70 percent of the muscle weight, and 80 percent of the blood.

Water replacement is essential before, during, and after exercise, as over 2 percent of the body weight can be lost through sweating. Also, water should be consumed regularly, with eight glasses or more being the minimum. During training or competition, hockey players should drink water frequently; three to six ounces at a time, every 10 to 15 minutes. Stomach cramps usually result from consuming too much water at one time rather than from drinking water that is too cold. A temperature range of 45°–55°F (7°–11°C) is ideal for drinking water as it has been shown that drinks at this temperature empty the stomach faster.

Lack of water in the body causes: reaction in muscular strength; lower plasma and blood volumes; lower oxygen consumption; decrease in work performance times; depletion of liver glycogen stores; and an increase in the amount of electrolytes lost from the body. Water can be taken alone, but it is also found in most foods, particularly:

- Watermelon
- Oranges
- Carrots
- Pineapple
- Apples
- Potatoes
- Lettuce
- Celery
- Pickles
- Broccoli

PRE-GAME NUTRITION

What and when the hockey player eats before a game is important. It should be mentioned that an ideal pre-event meal does not compensate and provide the fuel for energy if the player's diet has been lacking up to this time.

The main purpose of the pre-event meal is to help provide the fuel for energy by digesting foods that can be stored as glycogen. The meal also settles the stomach and removes the feeling of hunger, as well as preventing hypoglycemia (low blood sugar), which can interfere with performance.

The following guidelines should be followed for the pre-event meal:

1. The meal should be high in carbohydrates such as pasta, potatoes, and enriched bread, and low in fats. The meat can include small portions of protein such as lean meat, fish, or chicken. Avoid gas-forming greasy and spicy foods.
2. A normal-sized meal should be eaten at least three to four hours before the event. Smaller meals or snacks can be eaten two to three hours before. Liquid meals can be ingested one to two hours before. It is important that the stomach and small intestine be emptied before the competition begins. Some players now eat a large meal five to six hours before competition, and then have a small nutritious snack about one to two hours before. The time of the meal is more important before intense exercise than low-intensity endurance exercise. Meals should be eaten a longer time before intense exercise.
3. Avoid glucose and sugary food less than one hour before competition. Sugary foods stimulate secretion of insulin, and the amount of glucose in the blood is actually decreased. This in turn puts a greater dependence on glycogen in the muscle and therefore depletes the stores sooner, contributing to fatigue.
4. Drink plenty of fluids. Water and/or juices should be consumed regularly both before the game day and on the day of the event. Four to eight glasses, two to three hours before the game, and one or two glasses half an hour before the game is recommended.
5. Eat food with which you are familiar and enjoy. Do not experiment with new foods on game day, but rather try these foods on training days. Discomfort or a poor-tasting meal may upset the preparation for a game.

Some players may prefer liquid meals. There are several available now, including brand names such as *Nutriment, Ensure, Ensure Plus*, and *SustaCal*. These meals are easily digested and assist energy intake, as well as providing fluids. Do not use liquid meals for the first time on competition day. Many players prefer to have a full pre-event meal.

NUTRITION DURING THE GAME

Water should be consumed at regular intervals (10 to 15 minutes) throughout competition. Personal water bottles should be provided for all hockey players, and they should consume small quantities whenever possible.

When hockey training lasts longer than two hours, replacement of carbohydrates is necessary. Blood glucose levels with this type of activity may have dropped to a level where the deficiency affects performance.

The most popular methods of supplying the added fuel necessary seem to be sport drink or a combination of glucose and water. The liquid should have a pleasant taste and should contain 2.5 to 10 percent carbohydrates, and electrolytes such as sodium and potassium.

NUTRITION AFTER TRAINING AND GAMES

One of the areas most neglected by hockey players is when and what type of foods and liquids should be consumed after training and competition. The timing and what is ingested are very important to the recovery process.

Fluids

Fluids should be replaced as quickly as possible after competition. Water is the natural choice as up to, and sometimes more than, 2 percent of the body weight is lost due to sweating and must be replaced as quickly as possible. Fruit juices and sport drinks are ideal as they also replace carbohydrates, electrolytes, and vitamins. Watery-type foods such as grapes, watermelon, oranges, and soups are also effective.

Alcohol

Alcohol consumption is not recommended as a means of fluid replacement because it has a dehydrating effect on the body. If hockey players feel they would like alcohol (a couple of beers) after a competition, then advise them to drink a couple of glasses of water before or along with their alcoholic drinks. Alcohol is also low in carbohydrates, and there is no truth to the theory that alcoholic calories are stored as glycogen.

Carbohydrates

It is becoming increasingly clear that it is important not only to replace carbohydrates after training and games, but also to replace them within a certain time period following the activity.

The replacement of carbohydrates should start within one hour of a game and no longer than four hours afterward. The recommended amount is 10 grams per kilogram of body weight within the first two hours following a game, followed by the same amount two hours later. This amount should range between 75 to 100 grams of carbohydrates taken two times in the first four hours. Bananas and juices are an ideal immediate source after the competition. It is also generally recommended that hockey players eat a high-carbohydrate meal within two to four hours after the game. A typical pasta meal of spaghetti or macaroni is a good method of replacing the carbohydrates.

Electrolytes

Electrolytes such as sodium and potassium can be easily replaced by fruit juices and sport drinks. Bananas are also a convenient and easily eaten food after a game. The use of salt tablets and other pill-form replacements after games is unnecessary and not recommended.

Along with eating the proper foods after competition, it is equally important to rest in order to allow the body to restore the glycogen to its pre-event levels. Active players need between 8 and 10 hours of sleep per night.

Caffeine

Mention should be made of the effects of caffeine, found commonly in coffee and tea, before and after competition and training. Some players rely on coffee before competition as a "pick me up." Others avoid it because it makes them jittery and causes discomfort.

Caffeine appears to have a short-term stimulating effect on the nervous system. This may account for the fact that some players feel it makes physical effort easier. The effect does not last, however, and should not be a reason for a player to consume caffeine. Some research has shown that certain large amounts of caffeine allow fatty acids to be mobilized and can enhance an athlete's endurance.

It is interesting to note that the International Olympic Committee bans caffeine in large doses. Twelve milligrams of caffeine per milliliter of urine is enough for disqualification. This amount, however, would require the consumption of approximately 8 cups of coffee, 16 cola drinks, or 24 Anacin.

Smoking

Smoking affects athletic performance by reducing the oxygen-carrying capacity of the blood and increasing airway resistance during the in-take of oxygen into the lungs.

Oxygen combines with hemoglobin to be carried through the blood to the cells. When a person smokes, a by-product of the smoke is carbon monoxide (CO). Carbon monoxide has more than 200 times the affinity for combining with hemoglobin as oxygen does. If both oxygen and carbon monoxide are present, carbon monoxide will combine far more quickly with the hemoglobin. This results in a reduction by as much as 10 percent in the oxygen-carrying capacity of the blood with a heavy smoker.

The increased airway resistance caused by smoking can result in shortness of breath. The resistance causes the respiratory muscles to work harder to consume more oxygen. This added cost of ventilation could rob the working muscles of a percentage of their potential oxygen supply. During all-out exercise this could lead to reduced performance, and during submaximal exercise an increase in anaerobic metabolism may cause early fatigue.

For hockey players who choose to smoke, abstaining for 24 before a game can lower the oxygen cost of ventilation by as much as 25 percent, but is still 60 percent high than for non-smokers.

Besides the effect smoking has on athletic performance, it also causes a greater risk of coronary heart disease and lung cancer.

22. MENTAL TRAINING

There are many books devoted solely to psychological preparation that can be used by both athletes and coaches. Some of these books are listed in the bibliography. The purpose here is to provide an overview of the basic concepts, but coaches should do further reading in this area.

Psychology is an integral part of coaching in that how a coach schedules and organizes practices, instructs, communicates with athletes, and demonstrates how to behave, etc. are all derived from psychological principles (Vealey, 1994).

The mental-training skills discussed here are important for both the athlete and the coach. The mental skills presented include relaxation, positive self-talk, energizing, visualization, focusing (concentration), and the ideal performance state. These skills are used by athletes to develop a pre-competition and a competitive plan for mental preparation. Coaches should not only work with their athletes to develop these skills, but also use these skills themselves to better prepare for the job of coaching, which includes all the aspects of pre-event and event preparation; handling stress and pressure; decision making; relationships with athletes, friends, and loved ones; and developing the proper frame of mind to lead young men and women.

THE MENTAL-TRAINING SKILLS

The basic mental-training skills for athletes (in the order in which they are usually introduced) are relaxation, positive self-talk, energizing, visualization, and concentration. All of these psychological skills are used in developing the ideal performance state. These mental skills alone, however, will not lead to success. It is a combination of extensive physical and mental preparation which distinguishes outstanding athletes from the others.

Relaxation

Relaxation techniques are important for both the athlete and the coach. These techniques can assist in relieving the stress before competition and also allow both athletes and coaches to get a restful sleep before competitions.

The five common methods of relaxation training that are useful for athletes and coaches are:

1. Breath relaxation
2. Progressive muscular relaxation (PMR)
3. Autogenic training
4. Biofeedback
5. Visualization Imagery relaxation

Breath Relaxation

Orlick (1986) describes a very simple method of relaxation training which is used by many athletes before, during, and after competition. The procedure involves taking a deep breath with a long slow exhalation. At the same time, the athlete thinks about relaxing, and relaxes the muscles. This procedure is repeated several times and can be practiced before any stressful situation in and out of competition. It is the simplest and most often used method of relaxation.

Progressive Muscular Relaxation (PMR)

Progressive Muscular Relaxation (PMR) was developed by Edmund Jacobson in the 1930s. Its basic premise is that it is impossible to be nervous or tense when the muscles are completely relaxed. While this premise is not supported by research, PMR is effective in reducing muscle tension, which is essential for optimal sport performance. Its value, however, is in the recovery from, rather than the preparation for, competition. PMR is based on the principle of neuromuscular relaxation, where athletes are taught to tense the muscles and then relax them. Sixteen muscle groups are used initially, followed by seven, then four, and then the entire body is tensed and then relaxed. PMR is taught by a trained instructor and should be practiced three or four times per week, with effective results taking about six weeks of training. One hour per day is necessary at the beginning, but once the relaxation procedure is well learned, relaxation can be achieved in a few minutes (Nideffer, 1981).

Research supports that this method is effective in eliciting relaxation and, when used with other arousal and cognitive methods, can be associated with improved performance (Greenspan & Feltz, 1989; Onestak, 1991).

The PMR method involves the following steps:

1. Select a quiet environment with no distractions.
2. Make sure the athletes are dressed in warm, dry clothing.
3. The athletes should be well spaced from each other.
4. The athletes lie on their backs on a mat, with their arms at their sides and the palms of their hands facing slightly upwards. The calves of the legs are slightly touching, and the body is straight, with weight equally distributed. The eyes are lightly closed.
5. Muscles are contracted for five seconds and then relaxed.
6. Practice contracting and then relaxing one muscle group. Feel the muscles relax. The muscles may feel warm, tingle, or feel heavy. Concentrate on tensing and relaxing one muscle group only.
7. Practice breathing control. Do not breathe when you contract. Breathe out when you relax the muscle.
8. The exercises begin at the toes and progress to the head.
9. Use the following progression and, with the limbs, start with the left, then the right.
   – Toes curl backward (don't move ankles)
   – Toes curl under
   – Ankle bend-feet back to shins
   – Ankle stretch-point your feet
   – Knees pressed together
   – Thighs
   – Buttocks

Do eight even breaths between each exercise. Check to see if muscles are relaxed. If not, repeat the exercises.

Do 12 easy breaths.
The ankles, legs, and buttocks should be totally relaxed.

– Stomach
– Back. Pull shoulder blades together. Press shoulders into mat.
– Raise your shoulders. Pull shoulders toward the feet; reach fingers as far down the thighs as possible.

Check the body and legs to determine if they are relaxed. Count 12 small, even breaths.

– Pull the jaw down toward the neck.
– Press your head into the mat. Do not arch.
– Jut your jaw forward.
– Clench your teeth.

Eight even breaths.

– Spread lips as far apart as possible.
– Press your tongue against the roof of your mouth. Make your tongue as big as possible.
– Pull cheeks up and eyebrows down. Compress your eyes to the back of your head.
– Wrinkle your forehead. Eyes are closed.

Twelve small, even breaths.

Check whole body for heaviness.

Twelve slow breaths.

– Finish by moving each part of your body, starting from the toes up. Sit, kneel, stretch, and then stand (adapted from Coaching Association of Canada, 1992).

Autogenic Training

Autogenic (self-generated) training includes a system of standard exercises designed to return the mind and body to homeostasis. The basis of the exercises is passive concentration or self-hypnosis, and beneficial effects can occur without noticeable physical sensations. Athletes begin with three to five standard exercises repeated for 30 to 60 seconds. The athlete then activates and repeats another set of exercises. After about six months of daily practice, the athlete typically repeats commands for:

1. Heaviness: "My right arm is heavy. … My left arm is heavy. … Both arms are heavy. … My right leg is heavy. … My left leg is heavy. … Both legs are heavy."
2. Warmth: "My right arm is warm. … My left arm is warm. … Both arms are warm. … My right leg is warm. … My left leg is warm. … Both legs are warm."
3. Heartbeat: "My heartbeat is calm and regular."
4. Respiration: "My breathing is calm and regular."
5. Solar Plexus: "My solar plexus is warm."
6. Forehead: "My forehead is cool."

The athlete maintains a passive concentration and sees the statement as if it is written, says the command sub-vocal, and feels the area of the body where the statement is directed.

Autogenic training is used primarily in the recovery time between competitions.

Biofeedback

Biofeedback, short for biological feedback, training is the use of instruments to make usually unknown physiological processes, such as muscle tension or blood flow, available to the athlete so they can bring the system under voluntary control. The instruments transform the electrical signals, then amplify them and transmit them to a light or sound display. The goal of biofeedback is to eliminate the use of the equipment once the processes are learned. Commonly used biofeedback modalities include skin temperature, electromyography, heart rate, and electrodermyography (Wilson & Cummings, 1997).

Skin temperature is an indirect measure of blood flow. Some athletes express their increased tension by unknowingly vasoconstricting their arterioles, which reduces blood flow to the extremities and can easily be detected in cold hands or feet. Reduced blood flow impedes the transportation of oxygen to working muscles, as well as the removal of waste products.

Electromyography (EMG) measures the number of active muscle action potentials at a specific site. Although athletes are generally aware of major muscle tension, most underestimate or are unable to eliminate the smaller amounts of muscle tension that can interfere with flexibility or small motor skills or cause unnecessary fatigue.

Electrodermyography (EDR) measures the sweat response of the body, which is an indirect measure of emotional involvement. Under stress of any nature, most individuals record an almost instantaneous change in sweat, thus EDR is often used to teach athletes how to cope with thoughts or moods that may affect their performance.

Heart rate can be used to determine the total cardiovascular response of the athlete. Although the heart rate is most responsive to the physical load, some athletes have significant increases in heart rate merely from thoughts of competition or competitors.

Electroencephalography (EEG) is a measure of the amount of brain activity. Specific seeds and locations of brain waves are associated with specific actions of the brain. For example, fast brain waves, beta waves, usually indicate a very busy brain, while alpha waves are a more relaxed attention. Depression is associated with waves in one area of the brain, while happiness produces a different pattern in another area of the brain. Although EEG can be used with athletes, it takes considerable training and sophisticated equipment to obtain meaningful data, thus its use is currently limited in sport.

With some training, coaches and athletes can use biofeedback to learn to fine tune performance or decrease the amount of time necessary to learn relaxation or energizing skills.

Visualization/Imagery Relaxation

Imagery relaxation involves the athlete visualizing an environment or setting which is very pleasing and relaxing, such as waves on a beach or a picturesque mountain. The place must conjure up a good, relaxing feeling. The image must be vivid, and usually in color. The athletes must practice this visualization in a quiet place, and not only see the scene, but hear the sounds (e.g., waves lapping) and smell the air, for the image to be successful for relaxation.

Other methods for relaxation training include meditation, yoga, hypnosis, and physical means such as hot tubs, saunas, showers, and massage.

Positive Self-Talk

Talking to oneself in a positive manner is a confidence booster for athletes, and there is some evidence of its effectiveness. Rushall and colleagues (1988) did a study with elite cross-country skiers, using three types of self-talk. One method included task-like terms such as "uphill," "quick," and "grip"; another method included positive, self-assertive statements such as "feel strong" and "feel great"; and a third method included emotional mood words such as "drive" and "blast." All three methods used showed a 3 percent increase in performance, as opposed to a control group who used no self-talk and showed no increase in performance times.

Positive self-talk is an important way for the athletes to gain assurance that they can accomplish what they want to do. Athletes should be reminded of their strengths and their past successes.

As important as positive self-talk is, the opposite, that is, negative self-talk, can be very destructive to an athlete before and during competition. When athletes are stressed, they are more likely to engage in negative self-talk. Some types of negative thoughts for athletes include worrying about performance, self-criticism, self-blame, losing, being preoccupied with physical stress, dislike of teammates, and dislike of the coach.

The athlete must first recognize that he or she has negative thoughts that can affect performance.

Martens (1987) describes some steps the athlete can use to try to eliminate negative thoughts.

1. Discuss with the athlete whether the negative thoughts are disruptive for performance.
2. Try to identify the causes of negative thoughts.
3. Be able to stop or park the negative thoughts immediately.
4. Develop positive self-talk thoughts to replace the negative ones.
5. Practice these self-talk skills in training, and then in competition.

Ellis and Grieger (1977) described irrational beliefs that many athletes have, and suggested ways of counteracting these beliefs.

Belief

1. I must not make errors or do poorly.
2. You should blame people who act unfairly or are not kind to you.
3. A bad experience in my past has to keep determining my behavior and feelings today.
4. People and events should be the way I want them.
5. I must be loved and approved by every important person in my life.

Counteraction

1. Doing things well is satisfying, but I am going to make some errors.
2. Even though I feel I have been treated unfairly, I should not blame others for my performance.
3. A bad experience in my past should not affect my behavior today. I can change things by working hard.
4. People are going to act the way they want, not the way I want.
5. It is nice to have the approval of everyone, but I can still work and enjoy myself without it.

The old adage of controlling what you can control and not worrying about what you can't control definitely applies to self-talk. Self-talk should be confined to the positive and to the task. Athletes and coaches should identify both the positive and the negative self-talk they use, and work to eliminate the negative.

Energizing (Arousal)

"Energizing" (frequently called arousal) refers to the psychological feeling that an athlete has reserve energy to call upon. It is a positive feeling that leads to confidence and an ability to cope with and control the situation. Energizing is affected by things we do and things we think as the athlete prepares for competition.

Botterill (1986) lists a number of ways to energize:

1. *Energize by doing exercise.* A good-warm up or physical exercise on a game day can be energizing as long as it is not so demanding on the energy systems as to create fatigue. A short exercise session of about 15 to 20 minutes gets the body and the circulation moving and creates a positive feeling in the body.
2. *Stretching.* A good scientific stretching program stretching the major muscle groups, and holding the stretch for 15 to 20 seconds not only energizes the body, but also reduces tension.
3. *Read and react drills.* By working the skills of the game using simple read-and-react drills with hand eye and foot eye coordination, drills can energize the athlete.
4. *Tense and relax muscles.* Alternate tensing and relaxing different muscle groups.
5. *Showers and massage.* Temperature contrasts and physical massage can both energize and relax the athlete.
6. *Music.* Music can be relaxing or energizing. Energizing music is usually upbeat, rock-type music, but different types of music affect people differently. Some teams have a team theme song which has an energizing effect on the athletes.
7. *Videotapes.* Videotapes of positive highlights of team success accompanied by upbeat music can have an energizing effect on athletes. The videos should not be longer than 10 minutes to keep the athletes' attention.
8. *Pep talks.* The coach or a respected member of a team can give an inspirational talk to the athletes to energize them. The pep talk should be used selectively, in situations when it appears the athletes are not energized. This can be when the opponent is taken lightly or the athletes appear fatigued. The pep talk should be short and delivered with enthusiasm and meaning.
9. *Verbal interaction with the athletes and coaches.* Positive statements among athletes and coaches, such as "Here we go," "Let's get it done," "Show time," and "Let's do it," are examples of good interaction that helps athletes energize.
10. *Energize by thinking*
    – Visualizing and imagining. Develop a positive image in your mind about performing successfully and overcoming all obstacles.
    – Focus on positive cues and activities or rituals. Focus on cue words and phrases such as "Blast off," "Intensity," "Power to spare." Use positive mental rehearsal of the skills.
    – Park negative thoughts and concentrate on positive thoughts.
11. *Take energy from your environment.* Focus on energy from spectators, teammates, the sun and wind, and so on.
12. *Energy from faith.* Some athletes energize from their faith and beliefs in religion or related ways of life. Lectures in the areas of positive thinking and motivation have been known to energize athletes.
13. *Goal setting.* Positive goal setting by athletes and teams are methods of energizing if the goals are attainable and both short- and long-term.

Inverted U

The "inverted U" refers to the point where being overenergized can be detrimental to performance. Athletes must be energized to perform well, and this level must be reached by the athlete. Being overenergized can result in the athlete being psyched-out instead of psyched-up. The inverted U as illustrated in figure 4.1, is familiar to most coaches, but what is important to note is that the arousal level varies with the type of task being performed. Also, each athlete has a different arousal or energizing level. Martens (1987) notes that most athletes reach their peak performance when their psychic energy is high but their stress level is low. Therefore, coaches must try to teach athletes that psychic energy is important, but that the athletes must also keep their stress levels low by using various means of relaxation and focusing skills.

Task #1 Requiring direct simple expression of force, few accuracy requirements

Task #2 Requiring force, plus accuracy to a moderate degree

Task #3 Requiring extreme accuracy

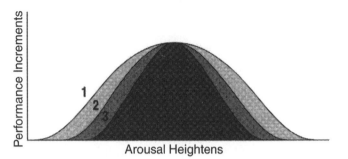

Figure 4.1: *The inverted-U principle of arousal with various types of tasks.*

It should be mentioned here that some experts in the 1990s have been critical of the inverted U theory, as they feel it is far too simplistic to account for the complex relationship between arousal and performance (Raglin, 1992; Weinberg, 1990).

Energizing is a skill that must be practiced regularly to be effective. The athletes should learn to be self energized, and psychologists and coaches can assist with this process.

Visualization/Imagery

A number of terms have been used to describe the process of visualizing a performance, including "imagery," "mental rehearsal," "visual motor behavior rehearsal (VMBR)," "cognitive behavior modification," and "success visualization."

"Visualization" refers to a process where an athlete sees himself or herself experiencing a movement or skill. This visualization can also involve any or all senses, including the kinesthetic sense of body position.

In a survey done with top athletes, 98 percent of them reported doing some type of visualization practice before competing (Nideffer, 1985). Visualization is used to help athletes learn motor skills, rehearse strategies and reactions in competition, see success (visualize best performance), familiarize with the competition site and possible distractions, and generally mentally prepare for competition.

Sport psychologists have identified two types of visualization: internal and external. "Internal visualization" refers to seeing the movement or skill performed through your own eyes. "External visualization" refers to seeing documentation of your performance done with a camera or video machine. The research done in this area has shown the internal method to be superior to the external, but both methods can and should be used.

Does visualization practice work in perfecting skills and planning strategy moves in a sport? A number of research studies support the premise that it does. Associated with these studies is the concept that visualization, coupled with relaxation training, is even more effective (Suedfeld & Bruno, 1990).

Kolonay (1977) and Lane (1980) studied the effectiveness of basketball free-throw success with visualization, relaxation, and a combination of visualization and relaxation. The combination method was the most successful. Davis (1990) noted that there was a significant relationship between performance in professional hockey and visualization.

Reviews of the literature by Richardson (1967a and 1967b), Corbin (1972), Martens (1982), and Williams, Rippon, Stone, & Annett (1995) support the position that visualization in a sport setting is effective.

It is important for both coaches and athletes to realize that visualization is a learned skill and must be practiced, as are physical skills, to get improvement. Cox (1994) suggests some steps to develop general visualization skills:

1. Find a quiet place where you will not be disturbed, assume a comfortable position, and relax completely.
2. Practice imagery by visualizing a circle that fills the visual field. Make the circle turn a deep blue. Repeat the process several times, imagining a different color each time. Allow the images to disappear. Relax and observe the spontaneous imagery that arises.

3. Create the image of simple three-dimensional glass. Fill it with a colorful liquid, add ice cubes, and a straw. Write a descriptive caption underneath.
4. Select a variety of scenes and develop them with rich detail. Include sport-related images such as a swimming pool, tennis courts, and a beautiful golf course. Practice visualizing people, including strangers, in each of these scenes.
5. Imagine yourself in a sport setting of keen interest to you. Visualize and feel yourself successfully participating in the scene. Relax and enjoy your success.
6. End the session by breathing deeply, opening your eyes, and adjusting to the external environment.

Martens (1987) uses three main steps in developing visualization skills specifically for sport:

1. Sensory Awareness
2. Vividness
3. Control Ability

"Sensory awareness" refers to the athlete becoming more aware of what he or she feels, sees, and hears when performing a sport skill alone or in a team situation. This past experience in being more aware of body position, timing, movement patterns, and so on in these situations helps the athlete to better visualize these movements in the future.

"Vividness" allows the athlete to develop distinct images, feeling all the senses, sound, smell, touch, as well as the visual. The vividness exercise allows the athlete to imagine the images more exactly in a setting mimicking the actual sport situation.

"Control ability" refers to the manipulation of the images to produce a successful sport movement or strategy. The athlete visualizes the movement done correctly with a successful outcome.

To practice visualization away from the sport setting, the athlete should be in a relaxed state in a pleasant environment. It is important that the athlete have a set routine for practicing the visualization skills and be motivated to train. Visualization can also be used when the athlete is injured or unable to practice because of weather, facility problems, and so on.

Visualization can be used to evoke concentration and, more commonly, to rehearse sport-specific situations such as a one-on-one in ice hockey, a penalty shot in soccer, or a pass-coverage situation in football. It also can be used to overcome anxiety related to a certain facility or venue.

When mentally rehearsing for the development of a skill, athletes can use visualization in three ways:

1. To practice the performance
2. To preplay the performance
3. To replay the performance

In practicing the performance, the athletes mentally practice the skill they have performed in the past. Preplay visualization occurs immediately before the skill is performed, as a diver would do immediately before the dive. Replay visualization is done immediately following a skill, when an athlete reviews mentally the motions performed. Golfers tend to mentally review the swing after the ball has been hit.

It is important for the coach to sell the idea of visualization training to the athlete. As mentioned earlier, most high-level athletes engage in some form of visualization training. Very few athletes, however, practice visualization skills in a systematic way throughout their training. In the discussion of periodization of the mental-training program that follows, a systematic program is suggested.

Coaches can use visualization as well as the athletes. Visualizing reactions to certain situations which occur in an athletic contest are commonly used by coaches. Visualization, coupled with relaxation, can also help the coach to alleviate stress during the competitive season.

Concentration (Focusing)
The ability to focus or concentrate during a competition with pressure and distractions often separates the top athletes from those with a similar level of physical skill. Certain cues become important, and the athlete must be able to discriminate between the relevant and the irrelevant ones.

"Centering" refers to focusing on one point or directing your thoughts internally for a moment to mentally check and to adjust your breathing and level of muscle tension. The concept comes from the martial arts and refers to a feeling of being calm, relaxed, receptive, and clear (Nideffer, 1992). The point that is consciously attended to is the center of gravity, which is located just below and behind the navel.

To be centered is to have the knees slightly bent, muscles loose, and breathing slower and slightly deeper than normal. The feet are apart, one slightly ahead of the other. The body is in a balanced position and able to move in any direction. Athletes and coaches are familiar with centering that involves lowering the center of gravity, frequently called "the ready position."

Centering is a combination of a physical positioning and a psychological feeling. Nideffer (1992) lists some cue words associated with centering, as illustrated in table 4.1. These cue words relate to both the positive and the negative physiological feelings that can affect the ability of the athlete to be centered.

Physical Feelings		Psychological Feelings	
Positive	Negative	Positive	Negative
Loose	Tight	Controlled	Beaten
Relaxed	Tense	Confident	Scared
Solid	Shaky	Powerful	Weak
Balanced	Unsteady	Commanding	Dominated
Strong	Weak	Calm	Upset
Light	Heavy	Tranquil	Panicked
Energetic	Tired	Peaceful	Worried
Effortless	Hard	Easy	Rushed
Fluid	Choppy	Clear	Confused
Smooth	Awkward	Focused	Overloaded

Table 4.1: *Positive and negative physical and psychological feelings associated with centering*

When an athlete is centered, he or she is ideally physically positioned for the particular performance setting. Becoming physically centered requires attention to breathing and refocusing. The athlete should feel confident and in control when in the centered position.

Dimensions of Attention

Nideffer (1976) described two types of attention to be applied to a sport situation, as shown in figure 4.2. The "width of attention" refers to whether we have a narrow focus or a broad focus of attention in a sport. A quarterback in football must have a broad focus of attention to spot the various pass receivers, whereas a baseball player must have a narrow focus when concentrating on hitting the ball.

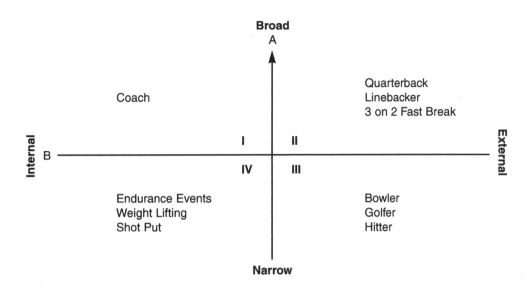

Figure 4.2: *Two-dimensional model for attention in sport*

The "direction of attention" refers to whether the focus is directed toward the external environment and things going on around us, or internally toward the thoughts and feelings.

In most sports, there is a time for both broad or narrow and internal or external focus. Martens (1987) expands on Nideffer's model, as shown in figure 4.3, to illustrate that the athletes must be capable of all the dimensions of focusing.

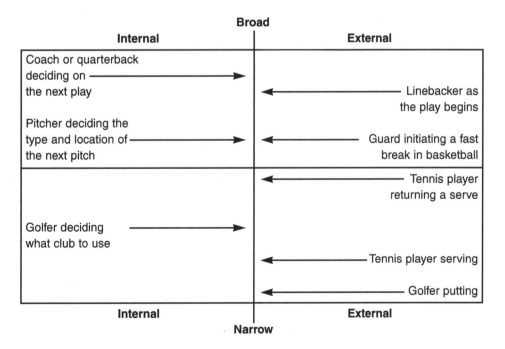

Figure 4.3: *Internal and external attention focuses shown as dichotomous rather than continuous. Reprinted by permission from R. Martens, 1987,* The Coaches' Guide to Sport Psychology. *(Champaign, IL: Human Kinetic Publishers), 141.*

The coach and athlete should analyze the attentional demands of the sport and determine the cues and their order. Keep the number of cues to a minimum.

Martens (1987) outlines some guidelines for improving concentration skills:

1. The sport should be analyzed to determine whether the attention should be broad or narrow and internal or external.
2. External attention should focus on a few discernible cues that an athlete can learn to respond to.
3. Internal attention should concentrate on positive and constructive thoughts.
4. Concentrate on the forms and execution of the skill, not the outcome.
5. Minimize distractions early when learning skills, but later add competition-like distractions.

Refocusing

Athletes should develop a plan to refocus when events do not go as planned and unexpected distractions occur. Develop a "what if" list so every type of distraction, and an appropriate response, is thought of beforehand. If a distraction occurs before the execution of a skill, shift focus, relax, then refocus. The athlete should always concentrate on only what can be controlled, and events that are out of the athlete's control, such as facility problems and late starts to events, should not be focused on. The athlete should be able to "park" any negative distraction and refocus.

THE IDEAL PERFORMANCE STATE

The psychological study of how athletes feel when they give their best performances has received attention from Maslow (1965), Ravizza (1977), Csikszentmihalyi (1979), and Loehr (1983).

Loehr asked athletes to describe their internal feelings and experiences when they performed well and when they performed poorly. Athletes described their psychological feelings when they had high energy and positive feelings as alert, lively, energetic, stimulated, vigorous, enthused, and high in team spirit. When their high energy was accompanied by negative feelings, they described themselves as fearful, nervous, anxious, angry, frustrated, upset, and vengeful. Low energy accompanied by pleasant feelings was described as tired, weary, exhausted, and low in desire. Low energy accompanied by negative thoughts produced feelings such as bored, disinterested, annoyed, irritated, and lacking motivation. Obviously the athlete wishes to have high energy and positive thoughts, and these characteristics are prevalent when athletes perform their best.

Loehr draws the following conclusions from his research:

1. An ideal performance exists for every athlete.
2. An athlete's performance is directly related to how he or she feels inside. When an athlete feels right he or she can perform right.
3. The components of the ideal performance state are the same for all athletes in all sports.

Loehr concludes from an analysis of hundreds of reports of top athletes that the following distinct feelings are present when an athlete performs optimally:

- Physically relaxed
  – looseness of muscles
- Mentally calm
  – feeling of inner calmness
- Low anxiety
  – feeling of lack of pressure
- Optimistic
  – feeling positive with no negative thoughts
- Effortless
  – mind and body working in harmony
- Automatic
  – performed without thought, played by instinct
- Focused
  – attending to the relevant aspects of play and blocking out the irrelevant
- Self-confident
  – calm, poised, inner belief in oneself
- In control
  – in total control of the situation
- Alert
  – heightened awareness, ability to read the situation
- Energized
  – most important: feelings of joy, challenge, determination, power, and intensity

BIBLIOGRAPHY

Almstead, J. (ed.) (1990), *On the Attack: A Drill Manual*. Ottawa, ON: Canadian Amateur Hockey Association.

Altar, M. (1990), *Sports Stretch*. Champaign, IL: Human Kinetics.

Argue, L. (1979, October), "A Father's Wish." *Reader's Digest*.

Arnheim, D.D. (1995), *Essentials of Athletic Training, Third Edition*. St. Louis: Mosby-Year Book, Inc.

Bacon, T. (1989), "The Planning and Integration of Mental Training Programs." *Scientific Periodical on Research and Technology in Sport*. Ottawa, ON: Coaching Association of Canada; 10, 1.

Baechle, T. (1994), *Essentials of Strength Training and Conditioning*. Champaign, IL; Human Kinetics.

Balch, F., and Balch, A. (1997), *Prescription for Nutritional Healing, 2nd Edition*. New York: Avery Publishing.

Blimkie, C., "Heat Stress and Athletic Performance: Survival of the Sweatiest." *Scientific Periodical on Research and Technology in Sport*. Ottawa, ON: Coaching Association of Canada.

Bompa, T. (1969), *Some Aspects of the Athlete's Psychological Recovery Following the Strain of Performance*. Conference on Research in Sports Psychology, Bucharest.

Bompa, T. (1993), *Power Training for Sport: Plyometrics for Maximum Power Development*. Gloucester, Coaching Association of Canada and Oakville, New York, London. Mosaic Press, PO Box 1032, Oakville, ON.

Bompa, T. (1999), *Periodization: Theory and Methodology of Training*. Champaign, IL: Human Kinetics.

Bompa, T. (1999), *Developing Champion Athletes*. Champaign, IL: Human Kinetics.

Bompa, T. (1999), *Periodization Training for Sports: Programs for Peak Strength for 35 Sports*. Champaign, IL: Human Kinetics.

Botterill, C., & Winston, G. (1984, August), "Psychological Skill Development." *Scientific Periodical on Research and Technology in Sport*. Ottawa, ON: Coaching Association of Canada.

Botterill, C. (1986, December), "Energizing." *Scientific Periodical on Research and Technology in Sport*. Ottawa, ON: Coaching Association of Canada.

Bowers, R., Ross, M., & Fox, E. (1988), *Physiological Basis of Physical Education and Athletics*. Dubuque, IA: Wm. C. Brown.

Bowers, R., & Fox, E. (1992), *Sports Physiology*. Dubuque, IA: Wm. C. Brown.

Boyle, M. (1994), *Elite Conditioning: Off Season Training for Ice Hockey*. Boston: Boston University.

Brook, G., & Fahey, T. (1987), *Fundamentals of Human Performance*. New York: Macmillan.

Canadian Hockey Association (1995), *Fun and Games*. Ottawa, ON: Canadian Hockey Association.

Chambers, D. (1994), *The Incredible Hockey Drill Book*. Toronto, ON: Key Porter Books.

Chambers, D. (1995), *Complete Hockey Instruction*. Toronto, ON: Key Porter Books.

Chambers, D. (1997), *Coaching, the Art and Science*. Toronto, ON: Key Porter Books.

Chevalier, N. (1983, October), "Understanding the Imagery and Mental Rehearsal Processes in Athletics." *Scientific Periodical on Research and Technology in Sport*. Ottawa, ON: Coaching Association of Canada.

Clark, N. (1990), *Sports Nutrition Guidebook*. Champaign, IL: Leisure Press.

Coaching Association of Canada (1992a), *Coaching Theory Level 1*. National Coaching Certification Program. Ottawa, ON: Coaching Association of Canada.

Coaching Association of Canada (1992b), *Coaching Theory Level 3*. National Coaching Certification Program. Ottawa, ON: Coaching Association of Canada.

Coaching Association of Canada (1994), *Coaching Assessment Workbook, Level 3 Theory*. Ottawa, ON: Coaching Association of Canada.

Coach Level Manual (1989), Ottawa, ON: Canadian Hockey Association.

Corbin, C. (1972), "Mental Practice." In W.P. Morgan (ed.), *Ergogenic Aids and Muscular Performance*. New York: Academic.

Cosentino, F. (1995), Lecture. Toronto, ON: York University.

Cox, R. (1994), *Sport Psychology: Concepts and Applications*. Dubuque, IA: Wm. C. Brown.

Coyle, E.F., Martin, W.H., Sinacor, D.R., Joyner, M.J., Hagber, J.M., & Holloszy, J.O. (1984), "Time Course of Loss of Adaptations after Stopping Prolonged Intense Endurance Training." *Journal of Applied Psychology*, 57, 1857–1864.

Csikszentmihalyi, M. (1979), "The Flow Experience." In D. Goleman & R. Davidson (eds.), *Consciousness: Brain, States of Awareness, and Mysticism*. New York: Harper & Row.

Davis, H. (1990), "Cognitive Style and Nonsport Imagery in Elite Hockey Performance." *Perceptual and Motor Skills*, 71, 795–801.

Dryden, K. (1983), *The Game*. Toronto, ON: HarperCollins.

Dubin, A. (1990), *Dubin Commission of Inquiry into the Use of Drugs and Banned Practices Intended to Increase Athletic Performance*. Ottawa, ON: Coaching Association of Canada.

Ellis, A., & Grieger, R. (1977), *Handbook of Rational–Emotive Therapy*. New York: Springer.

Fleck, J., & Kraemer, W. (1997), *Designing Resistance Training Programs*. Champaign, IL: Human Kinetics.

Gillet, W. (1972), "What is a Coach?" Lecture notes. Ohio State University.

Green, H. (1989), "Metabolic Aspects of Intermittent Work with Specific Regard to Ice Hockey." *Canadian Journal of Applied Sport Science*, 4(4):29–33.

Greenspan, M.J., & Feltz, D.L. (1989), "Psychological Interventions with Athletes in Competitive Situations: A Review." *The Sport Psychologist*, 3, 219–236.

Gwartney, D., and Stout, J. (1999), "Androstenedione: Physical and Ethical Considerations Relative to Its Use as an Ergogenic Aid." *Strength and Conditioning Journal*, 21, 1, 65–66.

Halliwell, W. (1994), "Mental Preparation for Coaches." In *Proceedings: International Coaching Symposium, Quebec City*. Ottawa, ON: Canadian Hockey Association.

Harre, D. (1982), "Principles of Sport Training." Berlin: *Sportverlag*.

Holt, L. (1989), *Scientific Stretching for Sport*. Ottawa, ON: Coaching Association of Canada.

Intermediate Level Manual (1989). Ottawa: Canadian Hockey Association.

Jackson, P. (1995), *Sacred Hoops*. New York: Hyperion.

Kolonay, B. (1977), "The Effects of Visual Motor Behavioral Rehearsal on Athletic Performance." In R. Martens, *Coaches' Guide to Sport Psychology*. Champaign, IL: Human Kinetics.

Kostka, V. (1979), *Czechoslovakian Youth Ice Hockey Training System*. Ottawa, ON: Canadian Hockey Association.

Kurtz, T. (1991), *Science of Sports Training*. Island Pond, VT: Stadion.

Lane, J.F. (1980), "Improving Athletic Performance through Visual–Motor Rehearsal." In R.M. Suinn (ed.), *Psychology in Sports: Methods and Applications*. Minneapolis, MN: Burgess.

Lariviere, G., Godbout, D., & Lamontague, M. (1997), *Physical Fitness and Technical Skill Appraisal of Ice Hockey Players*. Ottawa, ON: Canadian Hockey Association.

Liitsola, S., & Heikkila, L. (1997), *Finnish Dryland Training Manual*. Ottawa, ON: Canadian Hockey Association.

Loehr, J. (1983, January), "The Ideal Performance State." *Scientific Periodical on Research and Technology in Sport.* Ottawa, ON: Coaching Association of Canada.

MacAdam, D., & Reynolds, G. (1988), *Hockey Fitness.* Champaign, IL: Leisure Press.

MacDougall, J., Wenger, H., & Green, H. (1991), *Physiological Testing of the High Performance Athlete.* Champaign, IL: Human Kinetics.

Martens, R. (1982, September), Paper presented at the Medical and Scientific Aspects of Elitism in Sport Conference, Brisbane, Australia. In R. Martens, *Coaches' Guide to Sport Psychology.* Champaign, IL: Human Kinetics.

Martens, R. (1987), *Coaches' Guide to Sport Psychology.* Champaign, IL: Human Kinetics.

Maslow, A. (1965), "Humanistic Science and Transcendent Experiences." *Journal of Humanistic Psychology*, 5(2), 219–226.

Matveyev, L. (1981), *Fundamentals of Sport Training.* Moscow: Progress.

McKenzie, B. (1993), *Many Faces of Burns.* Toronto, ON: *Toronto Star*, May 9, G–1.

Neilson, R. (ed.) (1990–98), *Roger Neilson's Hockey Clinic.* Peterborough, ON.

Nideffer, R. (1976), *The Inner Athlete.* New York: Thomas Y. Crowell.

Nideffer, R. (1981), *The Ethics and Practice of Applied Sports Psychology.* Ithaca, NY: Mouvement.

Nideffer, R. (1985), *Athletes' Guide to Mental Training.* Champaign, IL: Human Kinetics.

Nideffer, R. (1992), *Psyched to Win.* Champaign, IL: Leisure.

Onestak, D.M. (1991), "The Effects of Progressive Relaxation, Mental Practice, and Hypnosis on Athletic Performance: A Review." *Journal of Sport Behavior*, 14, 247–282.

Orlick, T. (1986), *Psyching for Sport: Mental Training for Athletes.* Champaign, IL: Leisure.

Orlick, T. (1990), *In Pursuit of Excellence.* Champaign, IL: Human Kinetics.

Ozolin, N. (1971), *Athlete's Training System for Competition.* Moscow: Physkultura Sport.

Paterno, J. (1989), *Paterno by the Book.* New York: Random House.

Proceedings of NCCP Level V Seminar (1973, 1975, 1977, 1978, 1979, 1981, 1983, 1985). Ottawa, ON: Canadian Amateur Hockey Association.

Pechtl, V. (1982), "The Basis and Methods of Flexibility Training." In Harre, D. (ed.), *Trainingslehre.* Berlin: Sportverlag.

Plisk, S., and Kveider, R. (1999), "Creative Controversy?" *Strength and Conditioning Journal*, 21, 1, 14–21.

Poliquin, C. (1988, August), "Variety in Strength Training." *Scientific Periodical on Research and Technology in Sport.* Ottawa, ON: Coaching Association of Canada.

Poliquin, C., (1991), "Training for Improving Relative Strength in Sports." *Scientific Periodical on Research and Technology in Sport.* Ottawa, ON: Coaching Association of Canada.

Radcliffe, J., & Farentinos, R. (1988), *Plyometrics: Explosive Power Training.* Champaign, IL: Human Kinetics.

Ramsay, J.A., Blimkie, C.J.R., Smith, K., Gavner, S., MacDougall, J.D., & Sale, D.G. (1990), "Strength Training Effects in Prepubescent Boys." *Medicine and Science in Sports and Exercise*, 22, 605–614.

Ravizza, K. (1977), "Peak Experiences in Sport." *Journal of Humanistic Psychology*, 17, 35–41.

Rhodes, T., & Twist, P. *The Physiology of Ice Hockey.* Vancouver, BC: University of British Columbia.

Richardson, A. (1967a), "Mental Practice: A Review and Discussion (Part 1)." *Research Quarterly*, 38, 95–107.

Richardson, A. (1967b), "Mental Practice: A Review and Discussion (Part 2)." *Research Quarterly*, 38, 263–273.

Rowland, T. (1990), "Developmental Aspects of Physiological Function in Relation to Aerobic Exercise in Children." *Sports Medicine*, 10 (4), 253–266.

Rushall, B.S., Hall, M., & Rushall, A. (1988), "Effects of Three Types of Thought Content Instructions on Skiing Performance." *The Sport Psychologist*, 2, 283–297.

Sale, D. (1989), "Strength Training in Children." In C.V. Gisolfi & D.R. Lambs (eds.), *Perspective in Exercise and Sport Science*, pp 165–216. Camel, IN: Benchmark.

Sharkey, B. (1993), *Coaches' Guide to Sport Physiology*. Champaign, IL: Human Kinetics.

Sewall, L., & Micheli, L.J. (1986), "Strength Training for Children." *Journal of Pediatric Orthopedics*, 6, 143–6.

Suedfeld, P., & Bruno, T. (1990), "Flotation and Imagery in the Improvement of Athletic Performance." *Journal of Sport and Exercise Physiology*, 12, 308–310.

Twist, P. (1997), *Complete Conditioning for Ice Hockey*. Champaign, IL: Human Kinetics.

Vander, J.A., Sherman, J.H., and Luano, D.S. *Human Physiology: The Mechanisms of Body Function*. New York: McGraw-Hill Publishing Company.

Vealey, R.S. (1994), "Current Status and Prominent Issues in Sport Psychology Interventions." *Med. Sci. Sports Exercise*, 26, 495–502.

Vrijens, J. (1978), "Muscle Strength Development in the Pre and Post Pubescent Age." *Medicine and Sport*, 11, 152–8.

Walsh, B. (1993, January/February), "To Build a Winning Team." *Harvard Business Review*.

Walton, G. (1992), *Beyond Winning*. Champaign, IL: Human Kinetics.

Weinberg, R.S. (1990), "Anxiety and Motor Performance: Where to Go from Here?" *Anxiety Research*, 2, 227–242.

Weltman, A., et. al. (1986), "The Effects of Hydraulic-Resistance Strength Training in Prepubertal Males." *Medicine and Science in Sports and Exercise*, 18, 629–83.

Wenger, H. (1992), *Fitness: The Key to Success*. Vancouver, BC: British Columbia Amateur Hockey Association.

Wenger, H. (1997), *Fitness for High Performance Hockey*. Nanaimo, BC: Tafford Publishing.

Williams, J.D., Rippon, G., Stone, B.M., & Annett, J. (1995), "Psychophysiological Correlates of Dynamic Imagery." In *British Journal of Psychology*, 86, 283–300.

Williams, M.H. (1985), *Nutritional Aspects of Human Physical and Athletic Performance*. Springfield, IL: Charles C. Thomas.

Wise, G. (1998), *Off Season Training Program*. Toronto, ON: York University.